Sylvia Bowley gained the certificate of education at Salisbury Training College and is a graduate of the Open University. She has taught in senior and junior schools in Surrey, Tanzania, West Wales, and the West Midlands.

Since 1973, she and her husband have holidayed in Europe, mainly in France and Spain, in their camper van but on retirement in 1999 set about seeing the rest of the world on long-haul trips by plane.

For the past fifty years, Sylvia has lived in a small market town in Shropshire. She has a son and two step-daughters.

To Mike and our wonderful family. And to all my friends who wrote to me and kept in touch when I was abroad.

Sylvia Bowley

Butterflies in My Soup

Four Years in Tanzania

AUSTIN MACAULEY PUBLISHERS™

LONDON * CAMBRIDGE * NEW YORK * SHARJAH

A CIP catalogue record for this title is available from the British Library.

ISBN 9781398460867 (Paperback)
ISBN 9781398460874 (ePub e-book)

www.austinmacauley.com

First Published 2023
Austin Macauley Publishers Ltd ®
1 Canada Square
Canary Wharf
London
E14 5AA

My Thanks

To my late parents, for having saved all my letters and postcards without which I couldn't have recalled so many details or recaptured the mood of the times.

To Mike, for typing the first draft of the book from my rough, handwritten copy.

To Nicola, for typing and editing the second draft with detailed notes for me to work on before making her third draft in a form I could send to publishers.

To Louise, and her late husband, Jim, for being our companions when we revisited Tanzania.

To Jenny, for speaking sternly to me about publishing my work.

To Jill, whose P.S.s on her letters often exhorted me to write about my travels.

To the people at Austin Macauley Publishers, who read my manuscript and to my astonishment and delight, decided that it was worth publishing.

Chapter 1
Flight

"Cincinnati! Surely you don't want to go there, Sylvia." That was my mother's reaction to my exciting news. "Everyone knows American cities are full of gangsters and gambling dens. I saw 'The Cincinnati Kid'. That was enough for me," she finished.

It was June 1963. Unlike many of my contemporaries who had married their young boyfriends and started families, I was still living at home. Both my parents worked and had saved hard to pay the £300 a year mortgage on our terraced cottage at Heath End, near Farnham, Surrey. Determined to see more of the world before I too succumbed to the 'norm', I had answered an advertisement in the Times Educational Supplement (Times Ed) and was on the verge of accepting a teaching post in America.

In those days, few people could afford the unnecessary expense of a home telephone when there were public boxes within walking distance. So, after many telephone calls from our local kiosk to a London-based recruitment agency, I had, at last, received final papers describing the Cincinnati secondary school in which I was to teach for the next year.

My boyfriend, Tony, added even darker details to the overall picture painted by my mother. He suggested that the experiences of a 23-year-old woman, educated at a Girls' Grammar School and a Church Teacher Training College for Women, brought up in a quiet family, and accustomed to the relatively well-mannered children in our local Secondary Modern were totally inadequate to prepare her for the lurid life of Cincinnati. "A year in The States," he declared, "will ruin you."

He was right, of course, and so was my mother who, perhaps, had different motives from Tony for dissuading me from the projected trip—after all, she was used to me going off to meet pen friends in Europe—but hinted darkly that she knew about Americans from her encounters with them during the war. When I was a toddler, she and 'Aunty' Joan, our neighbour, had been to dances in Aldershot where servicemen of all nationalities had gathered to enjoy themselves. After all, both women were in their early 20s, their husbands were overseas and there were live-in grandfathers to baby-sit for them. So, it was back to the Times Ed, after a trip to the phone box to cancel my imminent departure. By this time, the summer holidays and the date for handing in my resignation from Weydon Secondary Modern School at which I had taught for three years were pretty close, and Tony had unexpectedly asked me to marry him.

That year, my parents had, for the first time in their lives, decided to drive to France for a family holiday in August, when Louise, my 16-year-old sister, and I would be on school holiday. A family hotel in Rotheneuf, in Brittany, was our destination; not a long trip from Calais by today's standards, but my mother insisted that my father should follow the detailed route which she had obtained from the AA. The ferry tickets and hotel were booked and we began the inevitably long, complicated preparations that preceded most family events. However, I was still determined to find that elusive foreign teaching post before we left England.

The Overseas Section of the Times Ed was my original travel book. The thrilling advertisements for staff to fill posts in oil rich academies in Saudi Arabia, colleges in mining towns in Northern Turkey or for privately owned factory schools in Rio de Janeiro always set me dreaming of exotic lifestyles. After all, with my meagre teacher's salary—all of ten pounds a week—I could hardly do worse than completing a fourth year in my current employment. Still consumed with a desire to teach 'overseas', I was scanning the columns one Friday when I saw an invitation to apply for the post of Assistant Teacher at Lushoto Preparatory School, Tanganyika. Instantly, I knew that was the one I'd been searching for. I clearly remember the single-mindedness with which I applied myself to securing that job, to the exclusion of everything—and everyone—else. I was glad I had not accepted the Cincinnati job. I was determined instead to go to Lushoto, in Tanganyika. Surely, Tony and my parents would be pleased that I wanted to go to Africa, a much safer place—I naïvely thought—than America! Missionaries, explorers and good people went to Africa.

In August, on the day we were to leave for France, my family departed by car for Dover and I, by train, to Waterloo for an interview in London with Mr and Mrs Scott, the owners of Lushoto Prep School. The middle-aged couple met me in the station buffet bar with a smile and a handshake. Mrs Scott was anxious for me to understand that the work would be 'very different from that in an English Secondary Modern'. How true that turned out to be!

Over lunch, they quizzed me about my qualifications, experience and family life. Then finally, Mr Scott, glancing at my engagement ring asked, "How will you feel about being away from home for three years?" That was the duration of the 'tour'.

I'd not considered such a long break from England, so I panicked and asked if the contract could be reduced to two years, a much shorter period, with only one summer holiday away from home. When I confessed that I'd only recently become engaged, the headmaster and his wife conceded and we parted, they to enjoy a summer vacation in Scotland, Mrs Scott's home, and me, to meet up with my parents and my sister for our two weeks' holiday in France.

Friday, 13 September 1963 was the date on my plane ticket to Nairobi. I can't remember much about the events, the making of lists or the conversations that followed the receipt of the job offer and my letter of acceptance. My father, a practical man, bought me a rust-proof, reinforced trunk for my books and clothes.

Anticipating the offer of a job abroad, I had, thanks to my fiancé's tuition and some eight lessons with a driving instructor, learnt to drive and passed my test first time, much to everyone's surprise. Tony wrote an article about my East African posting for the local newspaper.

As a journalist, he was interested in researching background information for his assignments but was unable to unearth much about Lushoto, other than that it was situated in North Tanganyika, in the Usambara Mountains, an area where African Violets grew wild.

Towards the end of August, Mr Scott sent me a checklist of injections that I needed to have before leaving England. The Yellow Fever vaccine proved to be the most difficult to locate unless one was prepared to travel to an establishment that dealt in Tropical Medicine. However, my doctor had a brilliant idea.

We lived not far from Aldershot, home of the British Army. He figured that soldiers needed to be vaccinated against tropical diseases, so why not ask the military hospital if they could provide me with some vaccine. It was quite an intimidating experience to present myself at the MO's office and wait outside until a squad of men was marched up behind me for their yellow fever jabs. Was I glad to be first in the queue!

Never having had a very extensive wardrobe, I chose to travel in my best outfit recently purchased for a christening. However, my fashionable winter suit, warm sweater, stockings and high heels were not the most suitable clothes for the flight to a tropical country in the southern hemisphere. It was a hot evening at Heathrow and I remember feeling eager to be off yet nervous about boarding the waiting airliner after the farewell kisses just before midnight.

It never once occurred to me that my departure might be of any significance to anyone other than myself. It is only with hindsight that I can appreciate how wounding it must have been for Tony especially, after all the problems we'd had convincing my parents that we were doing the right thing, getting engaged.

My mother had been so disappointed and angry that I could have done something, in her opinion, so stupid as getting engaged, that she left home to stay with a friend for several days. Undeterred, Tony had bought me the sapphire ring which already felt uncomfortable on my finger. What a romantic he was! Too good for me!

Looking back, I imagine it must have been difficult too for my mother to relinquish her hold on me, her quiet, biddable daughter. I had never done anything without reference to her set of values or to the rigid code of morals instilled in many girls who grew up in the 1950s. Then there was Louise, my sister, a lively, determined teenager of the '60s, whose individuality I loved and envied, although my parents didn't always appreciate these qualities, and there were fallings out.

At nearly 17, Louise was about to take her 'A levels', leave school and choose a career path—a crucial period. In retrospect, I don't think I ever considered that my leaving home for two years would have any bearing on that at all. Lastly, there was my quiet, patient father who always supported me in my desire to travel. It's difficult to imagine how they each felt. However, all the complications and complex emotions of being part of a family were soon to be left behind.

The Comet was the long haul airliner of the early 1960s. Of course, I'd never been inside an aeroplane before, having always travelled by rail or bus, so it was an almost brutal experience to be squeezed into the close confines of the seats, shoulder-to-shoulder with strangers, not knowing what to expect. I remember the heat, the smell and then the noises that rolled down the fuselage as the plane prepared for take-off.

The long hurl towards an unseen point at the end of the runway had us gripping our seats. Then finally, the cut-off point when the plane defies the pull of the tarmac to escape into another element and we were off to a new life that was to change me and several of my fellow passengers.

By the time we had touched down at Rome to trek what seemed like half a mile for a drink in the terminal, then again at Khartoum, where we were subjected to an hour on the runway without air conditioning, I was on speaking terms with David and Sally, the young married couple seated next to me.

Surprisingly, they too were going to the school at Lushoto. Arriving at Nairobi Airport, it was a relief to leave the confines of the Comet and embark on the next leg of our journey into Tanganyika. A smaller plane, an East African Airlines Friendship, took us to Mombasa and then down the coast and over the border into Tanganyika to the tiny airport at Tanga.

Later, sitting together in the bar of a hotel in Tanga with Sylvia, another recruit who had also been on the plane, we discovered that three of us, Sylvia, David and I, were teachers. We had all applied for the same job and hoped that there would be sufficient posts for us at Mr and Mrs Scott's school.

Before we could be sure, we had to endure the heat of Tanga until transport arrived to take us up to the school in the mountains. I felt disembodied, as if it were not me in that strange place but someone else surrounded by unfamiliar sounds and that hot, dry smell of red, African soil that was to seduce me in the years to come.

A rough, unmetalled road took us from the coast up to the plains some 110 miles upcountry from Tanga, through villages of mud huts and sisal plantations. Arriving at the foot of the mountains, we faced another 20 miles of steeply climbing, twisting dirt road which eventually brought us to the outskirts of the little township of Lushoto, 4,500 feet up the escarpment.

The only stretch of tarmac along the whole route started opposite Lushoto Prep School on the other side of a small river valley and continued for about a mile or so to the end of the township. From the 1880s, Tanganyika had been part of German East Africa. The little settlement near the school was still known locally as Deutchy Village and there were still descendants of original German settlers living in Lushoto.

After World War I, the League of Nations commissioned Great Britain to administer the defeated nation's colony and it was from the Custodian of Enemy Property that Mrs Fraser, Mrs Scott's mother, first rented the building, previously a German school, in which to establish her new Preparatory School in 1942.

According to the school prospectus of 1963, it was to be a school 'to provide an education in the Christian faith for pupils whose parents wish them to be prepared for entrance into Public Schools in the UK or schools of a similar standing'. It certainly wasn't a school for local village children whose parents, in 1963, could barely afford to feed or clothe them adequately.

In 1946, the redoubtable Scottish lady, Mrs Fraser, MA, had added a kitchen block and made the existing buildings into dormitories for the boarders. Then, as the intake of children and staff increased, she had extended the accommodation to include a staff room, a school hall, a split-level tuition block across a sunny courtyard behind the original building, and in the 1950s, three separate staff houses were added further up the hill.

The long, one-storeyed building with its neat lines, clear-cut windows and sturdy roof was a welcome sight that September afternoon in 1963. The Jacaranda trees along the front drive were in bloom, their amazing blue flowers on leafless branches shown to advantage against the whitewashed walls of the school.

During my stay, that 260-mile trip from Lushoto to Tanga and back was to become part of our way of life if we wanted a haircut, a day on the beach or some new clothes. In the rainy season, the mountain road became a dangerous, rutted trail of red mud where you might meet a bus coming up on the wrong side trying to avoid potholes or an old lorry without brakes desperate to steer clear of the sheer drop-offs on its way down to the plain.

In the dry season, the red dust followed you, keeping its distance until you stopped. It was wise to close the windows at that point. Conditions were worse on the 100-mile stretch between mountains and coast because corrugations, whether taken at manic speeds or cautiously negotiated, jarred every nut and bolt, every bone and blood cell in your body.

Journeying from the wearying heat of the coastal plains through the lush green of the lower slopes of the Usambaras, up to the sweet-smelling wooded areas around Lushoto for the first time, left no clear impression, but the first few nights in my new 'house' were unforgettably stark. My quarters were in the right-hand side of a bungalow overlooking the classrooms.

The other side of the bungalow, across a small entrance hall, was taken up by a living room, bedroom and bathroom for the young couple, Sally and David, whom I had met on the plane. My room with its red polished floor, dark bulky furniture made by the local 'fundi' and windows covered with a lattice of metal strips was, to say the least, unwelcoming.

An old print of a dejected woman carrying buckets hung from a yoke across her neck, the sole decoration, was soon replaced with family photos. The flat had clearly been a man's! The adjoining bathroom at the back of the room was similarly spartan, a wooden duckboard on the floor, the only extra. The separate lavatory next to the bathroom was entered through a tiny box room, a kind of safe haven for odds and ends.

Weary as I was on that first night, I must have fallen into a deep sleep only to be woken by the sound of distant drumming and voices making that, now familiar, high pitched African trilling. It was spine-chilling. Clearly, the natives were on the rampage.

They would soon be at my door and my offending white throat would be cut under the full moon. I had read about such situations in John Buchan's 'Prester John', and my English teacher had added her own lurid interpretations which had captured my over active imagination. Compared with such wild bloodletting, the streets of Cincinnati would have been pretty peaceful.

It wasn't until later that I learnt to sleep through these midnight rave-ups in the hills and to be prepared for rather tired-looking African staff after a full moon when much pombe, locally brewed beer, was drunk. What stamina to work all day, party all night and work again the next day, when for some, work and home were separated by a long steep walk up and down a mountain path.

Chapter 2
First Names

From the front door of the bungalow I shared with Sally and David, steep concrete steps led down to the school. The whole site occupied a hill rising from the river bordering the playing field below the main building to the second, staff bungalow that we called the Top House. Our accommodation was situated between that and the school.

Three upper classrooms of the split-level building looked up to our front windows and, across a corridor, another two classrooms, toilets and the headmaster's office looked down onto the courtyard. One of these first-floor classrooms was to be mine where I would teach the 8 to 9-year-olds English, Arithmetic, History, Nature Study and Handwork. Underneath, on either side of the stairway from the upper classrooms and the door onto the courtyard, were the two senior forms for the 11 to 13-year-olds.

The Board of Governors had been established and given a seal of approval by the Minister of Education in 1962, just a year before I and my colleagues had been recruited. The country had only recently, in 1961, gained its independence from the British Empire and hadn't started to crack down on such 'un-African' education systems, although Mr Scott's school was coeducational and open to all nationalities.

Indeed, the prospectus claimed that every term 14 or 15 different nationalities were represented. A few children, mostly from expat families in Lushoto, came as day pupils if the Board, which included the headmaster, gave approval. But most of our 120+ multinational pupils were boarders whose families lived hundreds of miles away in distant parts of Tanganyika.

Local children received a very basic education in the township. In those early years of independence, there were few teachers and no money for school buildings or equipment. I sometimes saw village children, barefooted and wearing ragged clothes, washing dishes in the river or heard them shouting as they ran along the road. I wonder what they thought of our school?

The courtyard often provided me with interesting glimpses of the matrons walking to and from their respective dormitories, on the right of the main building the boys' with their sunken, communal baths at the entrance and on the left the girls', which led through to the dining room and the kitchens beyond.

Strangely enough, during all the years that I was at Lushoto, I rarely went into either of these sleeping areas. They were the matrons' empires. Teachers had their classrooms.

Mrs Roberts, the boys' matron, was one of those wiry, no-nonsense women who, it was rumoured, kept discipline with a hairbrush applied bristle side up to recalcitrant backsides. No one cheeked her! A crisp uniform with nurse's buckle and fob watch complimented her sharp nose and grey perm. However, we the younger staff, nicknamed her Mrs Rubber Bones. We liked to think that her officious bearing hid a softer nature, possibly a secret past back in England.

Her companion, who matroned on both sides, was Mrs Morton. I can hear her South African drawl now as, between puffs of cigarette, she explained to me her love of zinnias and how much she missed her home. She had been married and had children but her world had shrunk to her room at Lushoto and her small patch of garden next to my bungalow.

An altogether more buoyant person was Maisie Hubble, the girls' matron. Although a large lady, an ample size 20, I should think, she was amazingly graceful and light on her feet. No cane rats, large rodents with yellow teeth that lived down by the river in front of the school, managed to get past Maisie's door on their way up the front steps into the courtyard.

She was a master craftsman at despatching them with a handily kept weapon—usually a sharp panga. Her lively laughter, bright smile and readiness to talk lured many an unwary victim to confide their all, and this went for the pupils too, I believe. Canasta was her favourite card game and she spent several evenings trying to teach me the rules, until she either realised I was a hopeless case or had satisfied her curiosity as to why I wore an engagement ring.

Nothing escaped Maisie. No teatime 'leftovers' destined for the kitchen but rerouted to the practise room and carefully stashed down the back of the piano remained in situ long enough to be collected by the purveyor. Maisie's controlling powers were acknowledged by domestic staff and children alike, yet she cared for her charges and spoke their languages.

Every Saturday evening, her girls turned up for the weekly film show in the school hall, looking for all the world as if they had been home, had their hair styled, sometimes quite outrageously for those days, and bought new clothes. How did she engender such enthusiasm in 50 girls aged six to thirteen for this event?

I suppose it was the 1960s with no television, pop music or discos in Lushoto. They were far from home and family, and the Saturday night film was the one time in the week when the older girls could, under Maisie's watchful eye of course, wear make-up, grow up a little, tease the boys and provide a focus of attention for the younger children.

During the week, the school hall was the domain of Miss Chloe Goodall who taught music. Everything about her was ancient. From my classroom window, I often saw her in the courtyard below, stroking the cats or talking to the school dog, whose siesta zone was outside the adjacent hall, office and staff room doors. Chloe loved animals, especially her old horse, Socks.

She sometimes rode up to my side door on a Sunday morning wearing antique riding gear, a tall raw-boned woman on a tall, white-haired horse, and in her exaggeratedly refined drawl called me out to look at Socks.

"Isn't he a sweetie!" she'd exclaim. We all thought that the poor animal should have been pensioned off years ago, but Chloe continued to transport bales of hay and straw for him in the back of her old American shooting brake round to the Lawns Hotel where her 'seis' stabled Socks along with all the other broken down nags.

Chloe lived in one room at the bottom of the entrance steps. Her door opened onto the front drive. I was surprised at her limited living space because we all knew that the uncle she visited in the Home Counties was a Sir something and she always effected an air of—albeit faded—gentility. Her effort to hang on to her long-past youth ran to excruciatingly awful make-up and red hair, which she wore plaited and pinned up round her head.

The matrons always complained behind her back about the long strands of hennaed hair blocking the bath in their shared bathroom. But then, I suppose Chloe never saw that because she was too vain to wear her glasses unless in teaching mode. She had obviously enjoyed a wild past in Kenya and had many friends in East Africa.

At a party, you could easily pick out Chloe's loud, slightly slurred tones telling stories of how she had been involved in a two-seater plane crash, when she'd hung upside down for an hour before being rescued, or of her exploits on Lamu Island. In school, one often heard her voice raised in song, out of tune more often than not. It was easy to make fun of her teaching methods but I'm sure the pupils enjoyed listening to classical music played on her wind-up gramophone. The crackly strains of a Beethoven Symphony sometimes floated up to my classroom from the school hall across the courtyard.

The unmusical sound of a Ford engine failing to start on the first turn of the ignition key, followed by the reluctant rasp as it responded to the second attempt, announced that Mrs Bajira was about to drive up the hill to the Top House in her Anglia. With her arthritic hands, she wielded the pen that kept the books and made sense out of the chaos in her little office next to the staff room.

Her gentle, old-fashioned air was deceptive. In an earlier life, she had been used to a position of power and was very short with the domestic staff and teachers alike. Woe betide any house boy who cut corners with the cleaning.

"Hi Fi," she screamed. "This won't do. Clean it again." She taught us to say "Lete chai," bring the tea.

Once, Sylvia and I had to fetch her 'house boy' Mohammed back from the village market place where he was enjoying a Saturday afternoon 'knees up', a ngoma with plenty of beer drinking on the side. Obviously, stupid with pombe and his red fez askew, he responded to our message that "Memsahib Bajira" was waiting for him and readily accepted our lift, knowing that he would receive a severe ticking off for being late, but it was preferable to losing his job.

Mrs Bajira was determined not to succumb to the disease that had made walking difficult. With the aid of two sticks, she would painfully descend the long flight of steps from the courtyard to the front drive where her car was parked. At the Top House, she kept her vehicle in a thatch-roofed, open-sided garage, just far enough away from the front steps to give her a short walk, further exercise each morning and afternoon.

Despite her rheumatoid arthritis, she still enjoyed playing her piano. It must have been a comfort to her to have Sylvia living literally next door. They both liked to talk and shared interests despite their age difference. Otherwise, Mrs Bajira maintained a ladylike distance from the other, older members of staff whilst keeping a quizzical eye on the younger set whose noisy parties held in the third flat in the Top House were restrained by the threat, "Sh! Mrs Bajira might hear."

19

It makes me cringe now to write of 'house boys' but in those days (the 1960s), and in those places, that was the correct title for our domestic staff, men from the surrounding villages who came into school to sweep floors, serve children and staff at meal times and to carry out all the domestic chores such as children's laundry, lighting fires for hot water and making beds. Some men acted as personal servants to individual members of staff.

Saidi was assigned to me and the other two in the bottom house. It was wonderful to have my breakfast and supper brought up from the kitchen on a tray, my curtains drawn and my bed turned down in the evenings, after years of having to shop, cook the family meal and wash up—all before I could start my homework, when I was at school, or my marking, when I was teaching.

A slow-moving, unobtrusive man, Saidi seemed to prefer his own company to that of his more exuberant workmates. He often sat on the bank below our bungalow or stood chatting to the old man with a panga who kept the grass short around the buildings. It was difficult to guess Saidi's age but I knew he had three wives in nearby Deutchy Village, so I assumed that he must have been in his thirties.

His sober dress of dark trousers, faded short-sleeved shirt and old black lace-up shoes added to his somewhat dignified appearance. I think he was a Moslem because he wore a little embroidered hat crammed onto his head. The only time I ever saw him move quickly was when his hat came off and, for once, he grinned as he retrieved it.

Communicating with Saidi was difficult at first but, with sign language and a few basic words of Swahili learnt from a 'Teach Yourself' book, I managed to make myself understood. Saidi, as most of the servants, could speak several languages: Kishamba, which was the tribal language of the local Washamba people, Kiswahili, the lingua franca and some German, a legacy from the days when Tanganyika had been in German hands.

I'm sure Saidi must have understood enough English to know what was going on in the school but perhaps, wisely, he never let on that he had a fourth language. He never spoke or responded to requests in English, in common with the band of barefooted men, some in Moslem fezzes and Kanzus, others in semi-western clothes, who moved unobtrusively about the school, fetching and carrying, gathering for a quiet laugh or a sour-faced grumble, and generally, making our lives out of the classroom more comfortable and free of chores.

My first autumn term at Lushoto Prep School was certainly different from autumn terms of my previous three years when I was teaching in the UK. My class of 8-year-olds was small (nine girls and six boys) and undemanding. They would sit in their old-fashioned desks with the sun streaming through the windows and shining on heads bent over a writing task. It was a fairy tale existence for a secondary school teacher used to quelling the mob from the safety of the front desk.

Sometimes, I stood at the back of the room and sketched those studious profiles. Sylvia, the other new arrival, taught the 9-year-olds in the class along the corridor next to Mr Scott's office. A primary school teacher, originally from Glasgow, she knew a thing or two about course books and curriculum matters and was appalled by the lack of text books, materials and equipment at Lushoto.

Our store cupboards contained a dusty jumble of old-fashioned bits and pieces, half-made wicker baskets, bundles of raffia and ragged books from the days when the school had been built. Sylvia was not impressed and, with Glaswegian directness, demanded that Mr Scott send off for new English and Maths books immediately. For my part, I relied upon my own texts and made work cards. Brown wrapping paper is amazingly versatile when used imaginatively in art lessons.

The 7-year-olds were taught by Rosamund, or Rosy as she was affectionately called, the young German wife of Ben who taught the 10-year-olds. David, the other new recruit, was appointed to teach the older children downstairs, whilst the top-class teacher was Mrs Harper.

She and another older member of staff, Mrs Stone, who eased the 6-year-olds into their first year at Lushoto, lived a short car journey away next door to the headmaster, in the third staff house. Mr Scott brought the two ladies to school each day. So, our staff consisted of seven full-time teachers plus Miss Goodall, Mr Scott (the headmaster) and Mrs Scott, whose speciality was fine sewing, as part timers.

The Staffroom, with its view down over the playing fields by the river and across to the road into Lushoto, was the perfect place to watch the comings and goings of the locals and to gather at morning break and teatime. There were delicate sandwiches of delicious freshly baked bread in the morning, then cakes, bread, butter and homemade jam at four o'clock on the round table in the centre.

The goodies were always attractively arranged on pretty sandwich plates. The smell of the polished furniture and floorboards, freshly made tea and scones, was to be relished. Often Chloe, in her customary window seat, would read her 'Yellow Peril', a collection of back numbers of one of the English tabloids bound in a yellow cover.

"Listen to this," she would boom when she came upon a particularly juicy piece of scandal, which she'd then read aloud; "Britain rocked by Profumo sex scandal revelations."

Her monthly Chinese magazine seemed an equally unlikely publication for her support. It was at the time of the *Little Red Book* in China, so there were always pictures of artists painting pictures of red flags or musicians, playing red music on red instruments for her to hold up. "How stupid they look," she would drawl.

Mrs Scott would sit in an armchair with little Evie, her hopelessly spoiled black and tan dachshund, on her lap. "Smile Evie," she would say offering the little dog a titbit and Evie always obliged with a quick show of teeth. The rest of us usually found a seat on one of the chairs or stools arranged against book cases filled with novels, outcasts from the genteel shelves of the Scott household.

The clang of the school bell rung by Solehe just outside the door summoned all back to class, or after school, to games for the seniors and playtime for the younger children. Solehe was a quiet, dignified African, whose duties were centred round the staff room and school office, and included caring for our school dog, an elderly Labrador. Our bare-footed bell ringer could always be relied upon for his time-keeping.

As soon as I had settled in, at least before a month had passed, Mrs Stone persuaded me that I needed a cat. Tonki was given to me as a tiny black kitten, the first pet that I'd ever had to myself. We'd always had cats at home, wartime tabbies like the oddly named Mick the Mugger, not to be trusted when food was on the table, as well as a whole series of black and white strays.

A photo of the latest one, named Sam, who found refuge on the doorstep after her brother had been squashed by the milk float, was one of the treasures I'd brought out from England in my wonderful tin trunk. However, Tonki was quite a different animal, hardly a pet in the English mode. But then, she was born in Tanganyika.

As she grew, Tonki looked more and more like a Siamese with a long lean body and pointed features. She was to develop a loud yowl which, embarrassingly, could be heard all over the school when she was tracking down a mate to satisfy her needs.

There was no way of having her 'doctored', there were no vets for miles, so Tommy Smith, the infamous local tom-cat was often pressed into service. How such a scabby, battered animal could father such beautiful babies was a mystery. Some years later, his services were terminated by a shot from a .22 rifle but by then, he had become pitiably decrepit.

Kittens were usually born outside in the safety of dense undergrowth, then brought back home. Tonki was a good mother, so if it was cold, she might head for the nearest or most accessible bed. Some years later, she actually produced one litter under the sheets and blankets of my new next-door neighbour, a young German girl who'd recently joined the kitchen staff. She was amazingly calm about the event when she returned from a late-night session of cooking to discover her bed already in use.

"What will you do with them all?" my friends asked. That was no problem. Such healthy animals made good ratters and found homes in the local village. Left to their own devices, cats are independent and can live off the country whilst sharing the occasional luxury of human food and shelter. At least, I trusted that that would be the way of things.

One kitten, a slim, grey creature, one of Tonki's earlier litters, wasn't keen on making the break. She returned one night, shortly after having been given away, landing dramatically on my bed, having launched herself through an open window. I was quite upset, thinking that she'd been treated badly but felt duty bound to return her as she looked unharmed and healthy. However, after the third midnight visit, I gave up and kept her myself. I called her Grey. She was a dainty, gentle cat who became Tonki's companion, even suckling her siblings when Tonki needed a night off.

Tim was the next addition to my household. I'd first seen him cowering under our friend Jackie's chair when Sylvia and I went to the Thompson's house in Lushoto for dinner. He was a perpetually sad-looking little dachshund, whose thin brown tail was always wrapped around his bottom and held firmly between his legs.

Jackie told me he was the runt of the litter, so she'd kept him. Tim was devoted to her and wouldn't respond to anyone else's advances. In complete contrast, his mother Penny was a vivacious, tail-wagging bouncy sausage of a dog, with huge flapping ears and a deep, throaty bark. Of course, we all loved her almost as much as Jackie's four children did.

"I'm having Penny. Would you have Tim?" Sylvia asked me one day in November, just before the Thompsons left Lushoto to return to England. They were heartbroken at having to say goodbye to their dogs but Sylvia had offered to take one of their beloved pets and that was some comfort.

They were even happier when both dogs were rehomed. So little Tim became my baby, to be loved and reassured through all those dark days when he was parted not only from his mother, Penny, but the only human being he could feel safe with. He couldn't hide under Jackie's chair anymore!

Dachshunds are remarkably intelligent dogs, so Tim made the transition from the comfort of a family home to a more basic form of accommodation with the minimum of fuss. The cats never bothered him; they were usually out chasing grasshoppers or stalking chameleons.

Later, dog and cats learnt to cuddle up and share the warmth of a fire on a cold evening. During the day, Tim liked to sit on the grassy driveway outside my door, head down gazing at his toes until he dropped off to sleep in the sun. He only came to life when Sylvia visited me with Penny on a lead, or when I took him for a walk.

"Would you like to come up to Magamba Golf Course with me?" Sylvia asked one wet, dismal Friday. She played golf back in Glasgow and had brought out her clubs. Golf Course was a bit of a misnomer for an area of scrubby bushes, puddles and assorted scrawny cattle which left messy hazards everywhere. "Here, try a swing," Sylvia said when she'd been round.

I was just taking a third swipe when Tim ran across the green and received the ball squarely on the nose. Poor little dog! How he yelped as blood poured from his nostrils into the puddle at his feet. I thought I'd killed him but a hanky soaked in water and laid across his nose stopped the bleeding. I didn't attempt any more golf and Tim stayed close to my heels whilst Sylvia was hitting the ball.

Ants were always a problem, especially when they were siafu, safari ants, on the march. An unwary animal sitting in their way could soon become a victim of the fierce jaws of soldier ants. I've known one pierce the rubber of a Wellington boot and leave a painful mark on a child's toe.

Horror stories of tethered goats overcome, and of chicken safely penned for the night only to be picked clean and reduced to skeletons by a river of shiny black ants, made me wary about letting Tim out at night. Sometimes, he stumbled onto a foraging party but he soon told me he was in trouble and it was relatively easy to pick off the dozen or so insects.

One evening, whilst sitting reading in my room with Tim and the cats beside me, I became aware of a slight movement on the carpet. A spider or maybe a cricket had scurried away. The next moment, I was altered to something else in the dim light, a moving black stream was spreading under one door, flowing across the red polished floor and out under the ill-fitting door on the other side. It was awesome in its purposefulness! Thousands of safari ants were on the move, decamping in search of better hunting grounds. Protected by large soldier ants, the mass was unstoppable. Outside, one could hear the sound of millions of tiny feet climbing the steep bank to continue on their journey through the undergrowth. No chance of escape for a snacking snail. Only its massive shell would be left the next day. There were other tiny sugar ants that invaded our food, but they were more of a nuisance than a threat. The only inconvenience was that food cupboards had to stand with their legs in tins of ant deterrent which needed topping up from time to time. Other more troublesome insects were found in the garden. If you dug in flip-flops exposing your bare feet to the soil, you would eventually get jiggers in your toes, and the resulting bumps would itch savagely until the offending eggs or mites hatched and dropped out or were removed. Mango worms also produced itchy bumps, but you had to wait until the grub was moving and you could see its head through the hole in the top of the eruption on whatever part of your anatomy the insect had chosen before you tweaked it out with a needle. I had several on my knees. After sitting under a shady tree at the Tanga swimming club, my neighbours, Sally and David, had Mango worms hatching on their eyelids, a gruesome experience.

Ticks were the most dangerous of the insects we encountered at Lushoto. They plagued the animals but could easily be missed when searching hair and fur for fleas. Having seen the school dog, an energetic, friendly Labrador reduced to a sad, anaemic bag of skin and bones by tick fever, I was always examining the convolutions under Tim's long floppy ears for the loathsome little red discs. They needed to be removed with the tip of a newly struck match. If you were tempted to pull off even the grossly inflated bodies, which sometimes hung off the animals' coats, the mouth parts were left gripping the skin and were certain to infect the area. Humans too could be affected. If you had been walking through the bundu in the tick season, you had to be vigilant about checking your midriff. Ticks loved to lodge themselves under your waistband and burrow into the folds of skin in that area, so I always inspected my belly button carefully before my evening bath.

Fleas just had to be harvested. Fortunately, dachshunds have little hair on their tummies so it was easy to roll Tim and Penny on their backs and pick off the fleas, one by one, from under the haven of their armpits. I always popped the shiny hoppers between my thumb nails exactly as my mother had done when de-fleaing our many cats. Naturally, Tonki and Grey saw to their own delousing.

Tim went everywhere with me and never strayed from the drive, so one day when he failed to respond to my call, I was surprised. Surprise turned to panic and soon I was searching and calling everywhere for him. He certainly wouldn't have gone courting because he wasn't a full male. As one of the helpers at the kennels where I boarded him in the holidays exclaimed, "Oh! His pennies haven't dropped."

My anguish lasted until Saidi came running with the news, "Tim's over in Deutchy Village. Come quick Mem Sahib." I didn't believe Saidi. It was inconceivable that my little stay-at-home dog would have found his way over there. However, I followed Saidi across the school grounds down through the bush and up the hill amongst the mud houses that I'd only ever seen from a distance.

It was my first encounter with the village people, the Washamba, the real natives of the Usambaras. There, inside a red mud thatched-roof rondavel, was my Tim. As I scooped him up, it dawned on me that this was someone's home, nothing but an earth floor, a few sticks of furniture and some cooking pots outside the door. Of course, I paid the ransom without asking questions. I didn't want to know what had happened, anyway. I was just relieved that Tim was safe.

The children loved having dogs and cats about the school, separated as they were from their own pets. Maisie the Matron had her peke, Tiggy, with her when she was on duty, and Mr Scott allowed Sylvia and me to have Penny and Tim in our classrooms during the day. After all, his wife was always accompanied everywhere by her 'little Evie'.

Sally, David's wife, made do with a series of mischievous kittens. Tonki had been bad enough when she was young, climbing up mosquito nets and into beds, often having to be chased out of the dormitories by the matrons, but Sally's kittens gave themselves major injuries or just didn't make it to adulthood.

I remember her caring for a little Siamese which spent most of its short life with its back leg in a plaster cast. Later, she developed a passion for tiny, hopeless chicks she'd rescued from goodness knows where. She tried so hard to coax life into each little yellow ball, but inevitably they died.

Flies we had in plenty, their numbers waxed and waned according to the season; not the four seasons of temperate zones but instead a period of short rains around the turn of the year to allay the high temperatures of the December sun, and a period of long rains in April followed by the relative chill of June.

The little green tree frogs revelled in the warm rains that sometimes shrouded the mountains in cloud. It is amazing that such beautiful, jewel-like creatures with wondrous sucker-like feet can make such an unlovely noise. Their sharp metallic calls cut through the mist as it swirled round the trees below my house.

In the same trees during dryer weather, we found chameleons, creatures which came with a variety of facial adornments. I had never really believed the story about them being able to change their colour according to their surroundings, but it was true; from a bright green they could switch to a dull black.

The Africans would not touch them, not because they were afraid that they would bite or sting but because they were convinced that contact with the slow-moving reptile would result in impotence. For my part, I enjoyed watching the animal's tiny but all-seeing, swivelling eyes, the prehensile tail and the deliberate forward movement of the outthrust foot, each foot as if in slow motion steadying the body with its clever clasping toes.

If there were flies about, a chameleon was an ideal companion. Sitting on the doorstep, I could smoke a cigar in comfort with a chameleon on one arm to blot up any incoming insects on its deadly tongue.

Snakes also enjoyed the warmth of the red polished steps. It's a wonder I didn't tread on them but the house boys were always there before me. The metre long, blue snake made a wonderful specimen for nature study when it was pickled in a big screw top jar but the smaller red snake was another matter.

Saidi wasn't satisfied that such a deadly reptile was dead until it was unrecognisable. At its demise, there was much shouting and smiling. There were green snakes too but they stretched themselves languidly along the branches of trees in the plantation at the edge of the playground and didn't worry us.

Surprisingly, no child or adult ever suffered a snake bite, perhaps because the sensible reptiles always took to the bushes when they heard us coming. Horror stories of a great goat-gorging python came from 'the town' as we called

Lushoto, but one goat satisfies a big snake for a long time. It would not show itself again until it was hungry.

Chapter 3
A Hot Christmas

Tanga had seemed hot when we arrived in September but 4500 feet up in Lushoto, the temperature was much lower, a mere 60 °F as opposed to over 80. It was the ideal climate to refresh and stimulate children from the humid coast or baking up-country.

Girls and boys would arrive looking tired after hot, sleepless nights at home but the mountain air and cool evenings restored their vitality and soon put colour back into their cheeks. However, as the year progressed, the days grew hotter even in Lushoto. The southern hemisphere was preparing for its 'upside-down' summer, round about Christmas time.

With the approach of the short rains of early December that first term drew to a steamy close. It was a novelty to feel so hot when normally, I would be shivering in the depths of winter. It's surprising how quickly you can forget how uncomfortable real cold weather is and how easily your body can adapt itself to a new climate. I think that it takes much longer to achieve the reverse and reacclimatise to the ice and snow of the northern hemisphere.

Early in December, presents arrived from my parents before I had even thought about buying gifts to send home to them. Throughout my time in Lushoto, I always found it difficult to think ahead and post early for birthdays and Christmas.

My tin trunk was still somewhere on the high seas, but whilst in Tanga making enquiries about my errant luggage, I had been able to collect a Tanganyika driving licence. Sylvia had already bought a car but I didn't think for one moment she'd let me drive it when she realised how inexperienced a driver I was. I envied her independence and longed for my own vehicle. Still, a driving licence was a start.

The term ended and the children went home in the rain. When the roads were no longer under water, Sylvia proposed that we should drive up the coast to Mombasa, in her newly purchased VW Beetle, stop the night in a hotel, then drive north and spend Christmas on the beach at Malindi. It was a thrilling prospect.

She had brought a tent and other camping gear out with her from Scotland, so all I had to do was buy a Lilo to sleep on and some beach clothes. Sylvia had worked in Africa before, so she knew the ropes. Her trunk was filled with useful items such as rugs and lamps to make her flat look like a home from home, whereas my trunk contained only books and more books.

The dirt coast road from Tanga to Mombasa was like an oven. I could hardly breathe trapped inside the Beetle which Sylvia drove at speed over the corrugations and potholes. "Are you all right?" she asked peering into my red face. But I couldn't speak. I couldn't even think. I'd never been so hot.

Sylvia later confided that she'd thought I was going to die, but we booked into the Shelley Beach Hotel in Mombasa and I recovered. I don't think I knew about the dangers of dehydration in those days or I might have paid more attention to my fluid intake.

That night, I was awoken by sounds of drumming and singing. A party was in progress celebrating Kenya's Independence Jamhuri. As I listened, confident this time that I wasn't going to be killed, I became aware of a closer noise, a scraping sound. In the dark, someone was trying to enter our room. A drink-crazed reveller, perhaps? Sylvia slept on as I slipped out of the bed and tiptoed to the door, my senses on red-alert. The scrabbling stopped abruptly.

Beside the door stood a large chest of drawers and it was from within that the noise came again after a few seconds. My heart still thumping, I opened the top drawer and bravely looked inside where a small white shell was the only clue to the disturbance. Then, a tell-tale leg emerged. A hermit crab had been scratching its tiny feet over the bare wood in a frantic effort to locate sustenance for a midnight feast.

Breakfast, next morning, was delicious. Cornflakes and cold milk were a special treat after school breakfasts of cold toast and a plate of greasy fried food. The hotel proprietors provided us with an ample packed lunch and a thermos of coffee for our journey when we set out at nine. After all that people had said about travelling on Kenya's Independence Day—they'd warned us against it for a variety of reasons—we met with no difficulties whatsoever.

On the contrary, everything was easier and cheaper, with no tolls on bridges or fares on ferries. Everyone we met looked happy and not in the least likely to throw stones at us; they were too busy enjoying themselves.

Most of the shops in Mombasa were open and decorated and the market was very busy, cashing in on the holiday mood of people revelling in their country's independence or at least allowing themselves to view the future with more optimism than usual. The temptation to stop and buy was irresistible.

Animal earrings, Indian sandals, palm leaf mats and baskets and wooden dishes were examined but in the end our purchases were very mundane; Sylvia bought underwear and a plastic tablecloth and I bought some postcards. We were on a tight budget.

There was no shortage of eager young boys willing to see us out onto the crowded highway once the car had been filled with petrol. Then, we were on our way on a fine tarmac road, with me at the wheel for the first time. It took considerable concentration to speed along the single strip of tarmac knowing that in the distance, there might be another vehicle hurtling towards you along that same narrow track and that to avoid a collision you would have to flick your two onside wheels into the sandy verge at the last minute in order to pass safely.

You trusted that the other driver would have made a similar manoeuvre, thus allowing you to keep at least two wheels in contact with the hard surface. It was almost a relief to hit the dirt road where you could choose which bit to drive on.

Sylvia sat quietly, gripping her seat, as I began to enjoy accelerating over the ruts, but just before the first pontoon bridge, she said she'd had enough of my driving and would I like to move over so that she could take the wheel again.

As we neared Malindi, the harsh red landscape softened into green bush. Now, there were ebony-skinned women making their way along the road carrying calabashes on their heads. They wore only bracelets and skirts. It was the first time I'd seen women in public with their breasts uncovered, a custom I found quite disturbing. Like a voyeur, I wanted to gawp but I was constrained by an upbringing that had taught me that bare bosoms were rude. Rain started to fall giving some relief from the humidity but we hurried on, aware that it wouldn't take long for the road to degenerate into an undriveable skid pan.

Malindi was a small resort in 1963. There were, perhaps, three or four large hotels and some shops but towards the edge of town, the beach was 'undeveloped' save for a small palm-thatched restaurant, the Driftwood Club. We sited Sylvia's tent on the rough camping area close to the sand and facing the reef-ringed lagoon, not a time-consuming job because it was one of those old-fashioned tents with a 4-foot pole at each end, and a canvas roof and walls held down with guy ropes and pegs. Inside, there was just enough room for two inflated beds and a walkway between.

Our belongings had to be stowed in the boot of the car which, in a Beetle is of course, at the front. Sylvia engaged John, a local lad of about 18 who could speak English, to stand guard over the property whilst we were away and to keep the area inside and around the tent tidy. I have a photograph of a dutiful-looking John, lurking behind our modest canvas shelter.

There were other people, mostly holidaying families with bigger tents than ours, on the campground but I don't remember them having needed guardians. However, Sylvia insisted that she'd always employed someone like John when she'd camped in Northern Rhodesia, now Zambia, where she'd worked some years before.

After a very hot night, it was blissful to wake up, put on a swimsuit and run into the warm shallow water inside the reef. As I didn't like venturing out of my depth, it was a perfect place to swim without having to check the bottom all the time.

One couldn't be so incautious when it came to using the rudimentary toilet facilities back on the beach. The thatched hut which housed a wooden seat over a long drop toilet should have had a sign outside—'Beware the wee beasties lurking where bum touches seat'.

"Like to come into town?" Sylvia asked when she, at last, emerged from the tent. "We need to buy some food and I'd like the fundi to make me some shorts. We ought to look at snorkels and flippers too. I fancy going out to the reef tomorrow, perhaps."

So we spent several hours trying on snorkelling equipment after we'd been to the Goan tailors. It was all a bit of a laugh, horsing about in full face masks but secretly I dreaded the moment when I'd have to clamp the rubber gum shield between my teeth and breath through the plastic tube.

Writing postcards, relaxing on the beach and drinking tea with the people from the neighbouring tent was as much as we could aspire to for the rest of the day. Tired out with even that much exertion, we settled down for an early night only to be awoken by the sounds of a vehicle circling our tent.

"You awake in there?" hailed a masculine voice.

"Like to come to a party?"

"Come on!" yelled a second voice. "You'll love it." This was a challenging proposition but we hesitated before committing ourselves to a late night.

"Are you coming out or shall we come in?" we heard above the revving engine.

"Give us 15 minutes," shouted Sylvia. The 'party' turned out to be a quiet drink at the Driftwood Club with Stewart, a tea planter, Hue, who was in sugar, and a young couple who spent the evening in conversation with the unfriendly proprietor. He had a notion to build rondavels along the beach in order to attract fishermen and water skiers to the bay, big money spenders rather than mere campers. The tone was raised momentarily by the arrival of two tough looking young men but they soon left with the unlikely excuse, "We're going fishing tomorrow. We need an early night."

Next morning, Sylvia had a thick head but revived after breakfast and we were on the road to Casuarina Point by eight o'clock. We were going snorkelling with our neighbours from a nearby tent.

The boat lay a considerable walk out from the beach, at almost low tide. It was a long way to carry our baskets and equipment, through the warm, ankle-deep water, silky sand beneath our feet. Everything on the craft was handmade. The hull, long and narrow, was a hollowed tree trunk reinforced with a layer of wood. This effectively raised the sides above the inner core and meant that we sat high up out of the water on seats built atop the wooden skirts. The mast was a bamboo pole, the triangular sail coarsely woven, sun-bleached pieces of material, held together with large stitches.

The young boy at the prow skilfully furled it up as if he were wringing out wet washing, until the fabric was at one with the mast. Grasses had been plaited to make the supporting ropes whilst the wooden pulley blocks and outriggers were also fashioned by hand.

Seated in the stern was the mzee, the boat's owner. The old man wore very old clothes, just a wrap for his lower half, a ragged vest and a straw hat with rags bound round the crown to keep it firmly on his head, I suppose. With his white, prickly whiskers and his refined features, he displayed a dignity which transcended his simple outfit.

The sail was hoisted after the boy and the man had poled us out of the shallow water. Then, we were crossing the first reef and sailing in the deep blue-green waters of the channel outside. Sylvia and the others were soon out of the boat and away in their goggles and flippers exploring the reef, but I was frightened and couldn't leave the safety of the outriggers. Looking up at the silhouette of the slender hull, I marvelled at the grace of the vessel and its occupants. They seemed an integral part of the scene, sharing a natural beauty with the coral and amazing fish that we saw that day.

At sundown, I suffered for my time spent collecting shells on the sandbank and poking around in pools looking for sea urchins. My new daringly cut bathing costume had exposed areas of white flesh previously covered by the old-fashioned garment I'd worn in England. I went to bed at eight o'clock feeling sick and very sore, only to be rudely awoken at ten by voices trying to coax me out of the tent. Oh no! It was Stewart and Hue again. Their entreaties were augmented by Sylvia who emerged from next door's tent where she had been having a night cap with the Rastrick family, an English couple camping with their children.

"Come on, everyone's waiting for you." I groaned but got up and spent a slightly more entertaining evening down at the Driftwood Club drinking orange juice and watching the rest of the revellers becoming increasingly inebriated on Coast beer and many gin and tonics. It was 2.30 a.m. before the tooting of car horns and goodnight shouts ceased and I could resume my sleep back in the tent.

Later next day, talk was of fishing as we sat having sundowners with the Rastricks and our other new acquaintances at the Blue Marlin, a bar in town. I'd been persuaded to join Mr Rastrick, Hue and Stewart on a game fishing trip next day. Other than catching mackerel off Beachy Head from one of those little seaside boats, I'd never fished before, so it was to be a novel experience for me. Several other parties had arranged a similar expedition for the following day so a note of rivalry soon entered the conversation. The upshot was that Mr Rastrick and I bet that we'd win the proposed competition by bringing home the heaviest catch.

At 6 a.m., the three men and I arrived at the quay and were transported by motor boat to the surprisingly big fishing boat. Soon, we were speeding out in the cool morning breeze to the cobalt waters of the Indian Ocean. During the next eight hours, I was to have plenty of time to feast my eyes on the beauty of the sea, the changing blues and greens shot with purple lights. Deep sea fishing isn't the most active of sports—that is, until the fish arrive. The men each donned a heavy-duty belt with a central holster to support their massive rods. I started with the jig for smaller fish.

The boat toiled up and down the coast, some 10 miles North of Malindi. Soon I felt frazzled and thirsty. In my rush to be ready, I'd snatched up only a packet of biscuits instead of making sandwiches and had brought nothing to drink but fortunately I had remembered my hat and a towel to put over my legs.

After about two hours, the dejected air of fishermen who hadn't caught any fish suddenly changed. "Hell! What's that?" someone shouted. Simultaneously came the cry "Something on my line!" then "Oh damn! It's gone."

"It's on my line now!" came another shout.

"Hang on," we all bawled. The water frothed and a huge 62-pound sailfish leapt out of the depths, a beautiful, fierce-looking creature with a long sword-like beak. I was the next to feel its tug on my jig but, in a panic, I couldn't remember which way to turn the reel and it was off again. We all wrestled and lost until Mr Rastrick shouted, "It's mine!"

The ensuing battle between fish and man had us gasping at the strength of the creature as it exploded from the water, first on one side of the boat and then the other before escaping out to sea on the end of the steel line. Gradually, the fisherman began to prevail, there was a frenzied flapping of the animal's great sail-like fin as it leapt and plunged round the boat on Mr Rastrick ever shortened line. Then the prize was landed, gaffed and laid across the width of the boat. Sadly, the shining steel blues of its scales soon turned to dull brown once it was out of its element.

Today, I don't think I could have stood by and watched such slaughter or gone on to contribute another fish, a bright yellow, nine-pound falusi, to the catch. This came about an hour later when a sudden violent jerk on my rod made me shout, "I've caught one!" But I hadn't.

The fish was away with the bait and a line rapidly unwinding out of control as I screamed "What do I do? Help!" It was a hard struggle but with instructions and encouragement from the others, the muscular creature was finally brought alongside the stationary boat and landed.

The experience was exhilarating. I felt proud and excited at having achieved something uniquely different from anything I had ever attempted before. We won our private competition beating a disgruntled Hue and Stewart who deemed it unfair that a mere woman should have out fished them, and also notched up the best catch of the day back on the quay where both fish were hung up and sold.

Chloe Goodall arrived at Lawford's, one of the best hotels in Malindi, for Christmas. When the temperature on the beach became unbearable, Sylvia and I went there to sit on the cool veranda, sip iced lemon and think of nothing but palm trees blowing in the breeze.

Chloe wasn't impressed with her room, so she too spent her time on the veranda where she delighted in reading the news to us and recounting horrific stories about Mau Mau murders. "I want some shorts," she announced one afternoon, so we took her on a tour of all the hotel boutiques and sports shops in town. Poor Chloe was unlucky. No one stocked her size. "32 waist," she confided out of the corner of her mouth.

A gregarious person, she soon had us meeting her friends. We were included in invitations to dinner, as Chloe relied on Sylvia to be her chauffeur. On one such occasion, we drove out to a holiday home, a barn-like house complete with bats in the roof. The owner, a man with a scarred, bulbous, red face gave us a scornful look, but his Irish wife was more welcoming.

Before the meal, we sat grumbling about the 'situation' in Kenya and the inefficiency which they believed inevitably followed independence, to the accompaniment of geckos scuttling about on the walls and bats squeaking in the rafters. It was a relief to leave the wind tunnel of a veranda, which faced straight onto the sea, and proceed to the dining room, although the orange table linen decorated with frangipani flowers was the most imaginative part of the meal.

Never at a loss for words, Chloe kept us entertained with her recollections of travelling in a dhow. "Unhygienic, smelly vessels," she warned. "Dangerous too. This year eleven of the oldest fleet have been lost on their voyage to India. Some run down by ships at night." She went on to tell more stories of her adventurous life in Kenya. Old as she was, she still liked to be the centre of attention in her low-cut dress and white court shoes.

Christmas decorations were appearing in many of the hotels but Sylvia was having to hassle the Goan tailor to complete her dress and shorts before the 25th. He had a strange habit of changing his mind about the day of collection. His 'tomorrow' invariably meant the day after that—in the afternoon of course, when we turned up in the morning.

Musing on the pace of life as we took an evening stroll, it struck us that the setting—sandy roads, heat, poverty and the emphasis on survival rather than the amassing of material possessions—was perhaps closer to that of the original Christmas than we'd experienced at home. The locals seemed contented living off their home-grown fruit and vegetables, working on their shambas to produce the local cash crop, cotton, to be sold at the nearby ginnery—for a good price we vainly imagined—and staying healthy on the abundance of fish caught daily and sold cheaply.

The picture of carefree innocence that we conjured up that evening sounded alluring, although we did acknowledge that the scene might lose something of its rosy glow without the African sunshine. The following afternoon, we were made to revise our shallow conclusions.

John, our tent-minder, had invited us to his house in town. "Come and meet my wife, Mary" he'd said. So, at about four o'clock, we were on our way through the back streets of Malindi. John directed Sylvia to stop the car beside a gate in an earth-coloured wall.

Sylvia and I had been curious to know why such a well-spoken and presumably intelligent young man was guarding tents on the beach for a few shillings when he might have been earning a proper wage in a shop or one of the hotels.

When we'd asked him where he'd learnt his English, he told us, "I went to a Christian School. I was baptised John. My African name is Kenga. I had to leave because my father couldn't pay for me to complete my education. So I married Mary. Her father has money." It sounded a weak solution. "What else could I do?" he appealed. Yes, he'd worked part-time for a while at the Eden Roc Hotel, but his education had stopped short of qualifying him for a clerical job and he was loath to tackle the rough manual work on offer.

The gate opened into a dusty courtyard. John's one-roomed house stood in the far corner. Mary came out to greet us, a surprisingly young girl of about 14 or 15, dressed in a skirt, white blouse and a string of pink beads. The usual female covering of a colourful kanga would have hidden the fact that she was heavily pregnant. John said, "I want to call our first baby Uhuru, if it's a boy and Kenya, if it's a girl." Such optimism was beyond our comprehension. Undoubtedly, more babies would follow.

Our feeling of hopelessness for the young family was compounded on entering the house which was little more than a mud-brick hovel with a beaten earth floor and tin roof. It appeared that the only significant piece of furniture that John and Mary owned was the bed, discretely hidden behind a length of sheeting.

Little chairs had to be brought from a neighbour's house for us to sit on whilst John took up his position on a stool with his back to the flimsy partition. Thus settled, Mary handed us glasses of African coffee, a refreshing drink made by boiling a weak mixture of ground coffee beans in a kettle. Such hospitality was touching, humbling too, yet profoundly disturbing. I felt out of my depth with people who could make a life out of so little, whose lifestyle was quite different from anything I'd ever encountered, even in fiction.

Of course, Sylvia and I were the oddities that afternoon, two white women in shorts and flip-flops to be stared at and assessed. Through the open doorway, I could see and hear women washing clothes in the sink at the end of the yard. Other bibis stood about talking and smoking.

When they had finished eyeing us, they disappeared inside the neighbour's house but no sooner had they pushed the door to than there was a sudden conversation-stopping screech of laughter from within. A little boy popped out, as if to check on the veracity of what had been said by the grownups, but he quickly ran back into the gloom when he realised that I was observing him.

As usual, Sylvia did most of the talking but when she'd finished her teacher-like questioning of our two young hosts and our coffee glasses were empty, it was time to escape. We left carrying a gift of bananas, a heavy bunch that would ripen off over the next few days. It was a generous present.

All I had to give Mary was one of my silver bangles which I slipped onto her wrist as we said our goodbyes and made for the car. Instead of backing out and retracing our route, we drove down into the African port of Malindi, along narrow tracks between tightly packed houses of yellow concrete and mud brick. There were a few people about and the usual totos to shout "Jambo".

Ending up in someone's courtyard, we decided to retreat, then another wrong turning brought us outside a house where there was an old woman wrapped in rags asleep on a bench. The rumble of the VW engine must have awoken her because she grimaced at us—or was it a toothless smile? Then, she stretched out her hand in an all too familiar gesture. She wanted money.

With a mixture of fear, shame, pity and unease at being outsiders from a different world almost, we hurried back to the safety of our tent where we resolved to buy John and his wife some crockery and other useful presents for Christmas.

The Rastricks left just before Christmas to be replaced by a family of four: Tom Arches, his petite wife, Iris, and two daughters, Lucy and Marina. Tom was always shouting to his fair-haired girls. His cries were usually couched in loving terms, the trouble was, he started at about six in the morning. Their blue tent, with mosquito gauze over the air vents, a sewn-in ground sheet and aluminium, instead of wooden, ridge pole and uprights, was pitched with military precision. A vast fly sheet sheltered the tent and extended to the veranda of an empty building nearby, thus giving shade for the girls to play in. The whole rig packed neatly into the trailer that was drawn up alongside. "I renovated that," Tom boomed, after we had been given the grand tour, and went on to point out the unique square mudguards that provided shelf space. Secretly, Sylvia and I thought he was a bit of a bore. He also had a tendency to chip in with the most unhelpful comments when one was having difficulties with, say, the car or the tent. We admired sweet-tempered Iris's gentle treatment of such a great bear of a man. The bluster was bravado, though in reality, his three little blondes had him round their little fingers!

I awoke on Christmas Eve morning feeling terrible. The extreme heat, odd meals, late nights and perhaps the dubious hygiene of life camping on a beach had conspired against me. However, after a swim at 7.15, a shower and breakfast, I felt more in tune with the festive season by ten o'clock. Sylvia took me to the hairdressers first then we shopped for presents; a copper bracelet and a cuddly dog for herself and gifts for Lucy and Marina. Tom and Iris had invited us to a Christmas Day picnic at Turtle Bay, stopping off at the lost city of Gedi en route, so we also spent some of our diminishing assets on food.

"Are you going to the Carol Service?" I asked when we had given them our contribution to the meal. "Good gracious, no! We have all our carols on tape. Come over and listen to them. Far better singing, and by world famous choirs. Don't bother with the communion service, either. It'll be very short. It's very low church in Kenya," Tom scoffed.

A light alfresco meal instead of the traditional roast and heavy pudding was exactly right for that steamy, hot Christmas Day on the beach, the first Christmas I'd ever celebrated away from my family. In the morning, we'd explored the ruins in Gedi National Park about four miles from Watamu, just off the main Malindi to Mombasa Road. Modern guide books give detailed descriptions of the excavated buildings and suggest that the town forms one of the principal historical monuments on the East African coast. When Sylvia and I came upon the ruins in 1963, they were still relatively unknown to tourists, so we had the site to ourselves. It was exciting to wander in the shade of tall tropical trees surrounded by butterflies and noisy insects and pick out the shapes of walls and arched doorways of the Arab houses. According to archaeologists, the House of Cowries had been built at the end of the fourteenth century. The tomb of the Fluted Pillar, the Great Mosque and the Palace, with its impressive main entrance still standing set my imagination flying on that sultry day. Where had all Gedi's inhabitants fled to and why had they deserted their comfortable, white, coral homes at the end of the sixteenth century? Life in the old city must have been heavenly compared with the crude existence in twentieth century Malindi.

Later that afternoon, Sylvia and I returned to our camp site at Silver Sands feeling slightly more 'Christmassy' than we had done the previous day. We sat outside our tent until sundown brought a cooling breeze off the sea and a star display in the sky. Three months of independence and of meeting such a mixed bag of people had sent my, somewhat restricted, view of how one should behave right out of the window. Having been brought up on the command, "Do as you're told!" the possibility that you could do as you pleased took some getting used to. More importantly, my ignorant self-righteous attitude to poverty—I'd always felt good about being able to make do and mend—had been shot down when I saw what real poverty meant.

Chapter 4
Fifi and A Floating Beetle

What should have been a pleasant, relaxed trip to Tanga one Sunday in February 1964 turned out to be a series of mishaps that, at the time, left Sally, David and me wondering why we hadn't stayed in Lushoto. In retrospect, the sequence of events reads like a badly written comedy.

Our day started before six, with me scuttling about in the cool, having staved off the worst of a Saturday night hangover with several aspirin tablets. Sally and David, also out of sorts, delayed the intended early departure by having an argument, so we all climbed into their car later than scheduled, only to find that the battery was flat.

Their little Renault Dauphine, Fifi, was a most unreliable machine but today it was David's fault. The first twist of the ignition lit the panels, a second started the engine. David had not switched off properly the previous night and consequently, the battery needed recharging.

So, out we jumped and tried pushing but we hadn't the strength to move the vehicle up the steep rise beside our house. "I'll go down to the kitchen and see if I can get some help," Sally shouted. She'd soon recruited several beefy men and between us, we pushed Fifi up the hill so that David could run it down the end of our very steep drive to the road. We were away by seven.

We congratulated ourselves on having remembered to pack our cameras; mine, an ancient much-loved Brownie box camera that had belonged to my parents, and David's, an expensive new Pentax. We also had on board, two baskets containing everything we'd need for an afternoon on the beach after Sally and I had been to the hairdresser's in the morning.

Once out of the mountains and onto the tarmac road, the car was well away, its engine purring along in the heat. There'd been a frightening moment when we'd skidded in the thick dust on the mountain road, but we knew that Fifi's tyres hadn't much tread left on them and needed renewing. Some 70 miles from Tanga, they were to let us down again. Loose chippings caused the problem this time and we developed a flat in the offside rear wheel. That was soon changed though and we were in Tanga by 10.15.

We parked the car on the main street in front of the Tanga Pharmacy, the town's largest chemist. Delighted to find the store open, when we thought it would be closed, Sally and I went inside. Reluctant to leave the air-conditioned shop, we dallied aimlessly around the shelves until I decided to buy a bottle of Tweed Cologne and Sally some peroxide, a great find which would enable her to bleach her own hair back in Lushoto, instead of bemoaning dark roots until she could get to a hairdresser in Tanga.

Next, we crossed the road to Dekays, a fairly large Indian store where I bought some Denby Ware plates for Sally's 21st birthday, the following day, and a pair of irresistible sandals with leather thongs and toe loops decorated in blue and gold.

Well pleased with our purchases, we decided to delay going out in the heat a little longer by joining David in the Twiga Café above Dekays for an iced drink. Feeling slightly less hot, we considered ourselves ready for our appointments at Nina's, the hairdressers so out we trooped to get back into the car. After standing in the sun for an hour, the seats were red hot and almost unbearable to touch let alone sit on.

"Oh, you've left your basket somewhere, Sally," David said looking round at the back seat. "No I haven't. I didn't take it out of the car," she responded. Someone else had though. My basket was still there but it had been selectively rifled. Gone was my probably worthless camera, as well as a large torch and a sweater needed for the cool journey back to Lushoto.

Sally and David's loss was far more costly; expensive new swimwear, towels, sweaters and shoes, all Sally's makeup, recently sent out by her mother to replace another lot that had been stolen, as well as David's camera. We couldn't believe it. We'd locked the doors.

Then we noticed that the catch was not quite down on the front window nearest the pavement and realised how foolish we'd been to leave anything visible on the seats. Someone had neatly spirited away some £60 worth of our possessions—several months' salary in real terms.

Dazed and angry, we drove around until we found a police station where we reported the theft. The car was checked and dusted and photographed for prints, whilst Sally and I were at the hairdressers. Afterwards, we returned to have our prints taken, a novel experience which, after some careful work by a most patient policeman, resulted in a collection of thirty black blobs.

We laughed when we realised that the officer had assumed that David had two wives. However, despite such thoroughness on the part of the police, not one of our stolen items was ever recovered or a thief apprehended.

In a better humour, we returned to the Twiga, the only place open for a meal at five o'clock, for prawn curry before treating ourselves to an evening at the cinema. The film was 'Walk on the Wild Side', a rather gruesome movie with a sad ending but we paid for first class tickets which entitled us to rather battered seats at the back of the air-conditioned auditorium.

Goodness knows where fourth-class ticket holders sat. Everyone partook of snacks and drinks bought in the foyer and sat outside between performances. It was altogether a more laid-back experience than going to my local Rex or Regal in Surrey.

The homeward journey began uneventfully. At least, we were confident that nothing else could have been stolen this time. Tired and parched, we stopped off at the Mheza Hotel to drink a cool Fanta before settling down for the rest of the journey, leaving the driving to David.

Two miles up the escarpment on the final 20 miles to Lushoto, we came to a sudden halt—we had another puncture. The bad news was that our spare tyre also had a flat, having lain in the boot all day, unrepaired. Hot and tired, we decided that there was nothing to do but continue. Now on a tarmac road this would be considered foolhardy but on a mountain road consisting of rocks and sand it was just plain stupid.

Nevertheless, David, in a black mood, continued the ascent heedless of the damage he might do to suspension and steering. We limped another eight miles shaking and jumping like an old wheelbarrow before fate dealt us another blow. We ran out of petrol.

At this point, we were too exhausted to form any sane plan of action. Our only torch had been stolen and we couldn't risk walking anywhere in the pitch black. On that stretch of the mountain road, there were no houses for miles and anyway, at nearly midnight, all garages, tin shacks with one hand-worked petrol pump, were closed. So we resigned ourselves to a night in the car.

"Someone's bound to come along," said the ever-optimistic Sally.

"You'll be lucky," scoffed David.

But we were lucky. After half an hour, a man in a Volkswagen stopped when he saw us in his headlights. He was on his way up to Lushoto and offered us a lift. Leaving Fifi looking out across the mountain, we hoped nothing would run into her during the night and send her crashing down into the valley several hundred feet below. I was too tired to consider the consequences as I thankfully rolled into bed.

Next morning, David mended the puncture in the spare wheel which he'd brought back the previous night, although with a final backlash of bad luck he managed to smash his watch whilst replacing the tyre. Sylvia then drove him down to where the Renault was parked. Fifi was still in good shape but new tyres would have to be bought—when finances permitted.

April 1964 was to bring me face-to-face with the evil spirit of African weather which lies in wait for the unwary and inexperienced. Envious of Sylvia's Volkswagen, I had been looking out for a Beetle for myself. I'm not sure where I first saw the car advertised, but on Friday April 2, at the end of term, I went to Tanga to inspect a Beetle owned by an Indian bank clerk.

He was the third owner and had sprayed the body dark blue which had faded under the hot sun and salty wind of the coast. Mr Ramada wanted £275 for the vehicle, so I paid him £200 and gave him five post-dated cheques for £15 to be cashed on the first day of each month until September.

I was lucky that he accepted such an arrangement without asking for interest. In fact, I could have paid for the car outright but that would have left me with no money for the Easter holiday.

The larger of the two 1959 models, my car needed a decoke and new plugs but without these, it still zoomed along reaching 70 with no effort at all. Inside, it suffered from rough treatment by its first two owners, tea estate men, but Mr Ramada had fitted new front tyres and the rear wheels had re-treads. Ironically, as it turned out, the car was licensed up to February the following year.

Mr Ramada ruefully confided that he wouldn't have spent out on the full licence fee if he had known he was going to sell it so soon. Poor man! He would have been even more regretful if he could have seen into the future. So, all I had to pay was £29.50 comprehensive insurance, £10 for the transfer of names on the registration book, and £1.25 for a check by the garage, before the beautiful blue Beetle was mine.

Perhaps it was an ill omen but the first thing I did to the car was to dent one of the bulbous chrome hubcaps when I parked too close to the kerb in Tanga.

The pavements were quite a step up from the road to allow for the deep storm gutters. "Still," as I confided that night in a letter to my father, "it can soon be put right. If it were a £500 car, then I would be scared about scratching it or taking it over bumpy roads." My car was destined to endure more than a few scratches or dents.

It was all very well buying a car in Tanga but one had to drive it the 120 miles back up to Lushoto after a tiring day in the heat of the coast. With five gallons of Esso Extra in the tank, costing £1, I set off. Sylvia had driven me down in Mrs Bajira's Ford Anglia, so we took it in turns to lead the way on the homeward run. The first 50 miles of straight tarmac road allowed me to get the feel of the vehicle, then came 50 miles of twists and turns to test my gear-changing skills, before the 20 miles of dirt road up the mountain, with its hairpin bends and sheer drop-offs to test my nerve. We met only two lorries coming down and after a while, other hazards such as blind corners, rocks on the road and the cloud of choking dust thrown up by the other car became less terrifying. However, I was glad when we finally arrived at the house.

With a car parked outside, holiday planning could begin. Sylvia opted to stay in Lushoto, but Sally, David and I set out on our first safari to Tsavo National Park in Kenya on the following Monday, 6 April. We were to share the driving and stay overnight with a friend in Moshi, then make a day trip over the border into Kenya. We were looking forward to our first sight of Africa's wonderful wildlife in the biggest game park in East Africa. First, though, we had to endure the notoriously bad stretch of dirt road from Mombo to Same on the way to Moshi. In Moshi, I bought an Olympus Pen, one of the first half frame cameras, to replace the stolen Brownie and that, together with the cine camera my mother had given me, a heavy wind up Kodak machine in a brown leather case, would record the events.

Following the map, we checked out the suggested points of interest in Tsavo West, but all I can remember is a visit to Mzima Springs with its snorting hippos and huge fish, which we viewed from a sunken, glass-panelled room. It was an overcast day and we spent rather longer than we had intended following the park roads, so the daylight was fading when we left Tsavo and set off in the rain to return to our friend's house.

Darkness falls quickly in the tropics. Soon, we were relying on our headlights to show us the stony dirt road which led us through the bush, up and down the low hills. Thunder rumbled and distant flashes of lightning made us speed for home. No one likes to be caught out in a storm.

Tired after a long day, we peered anxiously ahead, a wall of black on either side. Three newcomers to the vagaries of African weather, we motored on, heedless of the rain. David was driving with Sally beside him when we began a steep descent down to a little bridge. I was in the back seat looking out between their heads.

As we neared the crossing, I could see what looked like water, black in our headlights, across the road ahead at the bottom of the dip. Ignorant of the danger awaiting us, we sped onto the bridge. Immediately and horrifyingly, we realised that the water was deep.

The Beetle was lifted off its wheels as soon as we were halfway across. Retreat was impossible. In an instant, amid the roar of frothing brown water, we were at one minute thrown against the concrete balustrade and the next we were carried over the top and into the flood. The headlights shone out on the chaotic, unbelievable scene as we were tossed downstream in a mad dash to a savage death.

Trying to recapture those moments, I can still see, hear and smell the water— heavy with red dust that had lain sweltering in the sun for months. My memory shows a series of shots in slow motion. In reality, everything happened so swiftly that we had no time to react, even to call out, until our little car, out of its element, failed to negotiate a bend, some 100 yards from the bridge, and we were thrown into the branches of a tree growing out of the bank.

All around, the deafening roar of frenzied water continued, but the Beetle's big chrome bumper—strengthened by a log that had jammed underneath— latched onto a small but sturdy tree trunk.

Sally shrieked, "I'm getting out," trying to open her passenger door, but that gave into the deepest part of the flood. She would have been drowned.

"No!" I yelled as I leant forward to stop her, my arm over her shoulder and round her neck. By now, water was coursing through the car via the open windows, in at the driver's side and out of the other. Our only escape was through the windscreen and onto the tree, guided by the submerged headlights. It's very difficult to break glass with your bare knuckles even when you're desperate.

The heaviest thing to hand was my cine-camera, by now part of the sodden luggage behind my seat. "Use this!" I screamed. First Sally, then David, climbed out of the jagged hole, cutting hands and knees as they crunched over the broken glass. Then it was my turn to make my way fearfully from the back seat, across the steering wheel, and out onto the slippery, sloping boot cover at the front of the car, to the relative safety of the tree's branches.

Shock makes you shiver. We shivered as we stood on our separate perches in the cold rain, wondering how long the tree would withstand the force of the water swirling around its base and the violence of the thunder storm overhead.

Shock was soon replaced by anger which made us shout and swear above the noise of the elements.

We sang hymns at the tops of our voices 'Onward Christian soldiers' and 'Abide with me'. We made up outrageous jokes about what we would tell people about the incident. We willed each other to hold on, to believe that we would survive, somehow. In such circumstances, time takes on a different dimension. I have no idea how long we clung to our tree but it seemed like a lifetime.

The darkness of night in the bush is total, so there could be no mistaking the far-off lights of an approaching vehicle. We allowed ourselves to hope that it might be our means of salvation. It was another age before we heard voices shouting across the water to us from the road.

A bus battling through the storm on its way down to Mombasa from Nairobi had come upon the swollen stream and wisely stopped. The driver knew all about flash floods. A long time later, when the waters had subsided, some brave passengers carrying torches ventured across the soggy ground separating us from the road, drawn by a mysterious light.

When we had plunged over the railings into the water, David had for some unknown reason put out the right trafficator, a device like a small pointer which could be flicked out on the side of a vehicle to indicate which way the driver was turning. It was the orange light from that practical gadget and the kindness of the bus passengers that secured for us a much happier ending to our safari than it might otherwise have been.

Encouraged by our rescuers, we left the security of our branches, climbed down to where the tree overhung the top of the bank, and waded behind them across the field away from the engorged stream and down to the welcoming lights of the bus.

We must have been a sorry sight, soaked to the skin, dirty and completely dazed, unable to speak for shivering. The bus dropped us off at the next village, Voi, where the policeman, the only person awake on that stormy night, invited us to spend the rest of the night, soaked as we were, in his little sitting room. He gave us glasses of beer but could do no more to help because the accident had occurred outside his jurisdiction on the other side of the border.

After a few hours of drifting in and out of sleep sitting upright in our armchairs, we awoke, sore and parched. I felt as if I had a hangover—that drained, dehydrated state which makes thinking difficult. To add to our discomfort, the temperature in the little room was rising and, in the warmth, flies were already busily searching out the raw cuts on our hands, arms and bare legs.

Before the policeman arrived to check us out, we'd finished off the remainder of our beer, a few flat dregs of Tusker left in the bottom of the bottles, and decided we needed help. David had discovered some coins in his pocket, so we phoned our friends in Moshi, explained what had happened and asked them if they could pick us up. Nothing could be done about salvaging the VW from its tree or recovering our possessions in the boot until we were back in Tanganyika.

When I first saw my battered car after it had been recovered and taken to a garage, I naively thought that the dents and sagging bumper could be repaired. Photographs of it don't look as dramatic as one might imagine. However, river bed rocks had smashed the suspension and TAA 164 was deemed a write-off. It had been mine for only seven days.

The insurers in Tanga were most put-out when I made my claim the following week and, as for Mr Ramada, he almost broke down and wept when in answer to his question, "How is the car going?" I told him it wasn't and never would be. It was wrecked. People do get attached to Beetles! Still, if it had been any other car, it would surely have sunk. Only Beetles float.

On our return to Lushoto, we were somewhat underwhelmed with sympathy. The general feeling seemed to be that we'd paid for our folly in venturing out in a rain storm in East Africa in April. We learnt the hard way that April is the month of the Big Rains, when roads are invariably washed away and safaris are to be avoided.

Still, we'd survived and, apart from the car, lost only a few items like cameras and, inexplicably, Sally's ring which must have been washed off her finger as she put her hand out of the window when we'd come to rest against the tree. It was months before the reddish tinge from the muddy water washed out of the clothes that had been in my suitcase in the back of the car. Sally and David had left theirs back at our friend's house.

Amongst my luggage was a letter explaining to Tony why I was returning the engagement ring. (I'd not worn it for months because it cut my finger when my hand was hot.) The paper was only a little muddy and the ring securely packed so, as it had been such a difficult letter to write, I sent it off together with a note about the accident.

Of course, I felt badly about ending our romance, but if I'd been more experienced at the outset of our relationship, I might have recognised that sisterly friendship isn't a strong enough basis for marriage. I wanted a brother, he a lover. I would have made a most disappointing wife for such an acknowledged 'good' person. His habit of sending me air letters containing biros if I didn't write every week was beginning to make me feel guilty but at the same time inexplicably irritated.

To be honest, I had fallen under the spell of the headmaster's son, Sandy, although I could never have put my feelings into so many words until later when I wrote a dutiful letter to my parents explaining why I'd broken off the engagement with Tony.

Actually, before the accident, he'd sent me a sarcastic note—it was the first time he'd ever written me such a bruising letter—about wanting the ring back to sell, so that he could buy a new football for his youth club. Still, I didn't tell my parents about that and destroy his image. I just hoped that Tony would feel a little remorse for having made such a crass request when he saw the muddied epistle and read my note.

Sandy was the manager of a tea estate in the Usambaras. He visited his parents at weekends when work wasn't pressing, and it was at a drinks party that Mr Scott introduced his son to me and the other new recruits on the teaching staff. Sandy's blond hair, blue eyes and tall, tanned body didn't go without notice.

It wasn't until a return visit that he invited Sally, David and me to his estate to watch tea being harvested and processed, and I actually spoke to him. It's amazing how romantic it is to stand in a shed, dusty with the sweepings after the best leaves have been boxed, listening to someone you secretly love. By then, Tony hadn't a chance in my affections.

Chapter 5
Heading Out

Lushoto had been a German hill station in a past era and it still retained some of its public buildings, but most of the life went on around the green, a flat area on either side of the main road in the centre. Here, there were two very good 'dukas', general stores run by Indian families.

At one owned by Mr and Mrs Hagee, you could buy freshly made samosas; I remember how surprisingly addictive I found them, so different from anything I had ever cooked or tasted at home. When you stepped into Hagee's, the sharp, sweet smell of wood smoke which always hung in the air gave way to an exotic blend of curry spices. Other buildings clustered round the green included several churches, a rudimentary doctor's surgery used by visiting medics, and a dentist's where a nun once patched up my teeth with the latest fillings from Germany.

For presents and items of clothing, we often visited a small shop, owned by an elderly German lady, cunningly situated between school and town starved of the joys of High Street shopping. We were often lured inside Mrs Barkli's by her window display of goods 'just received from Germany' then found ourselves shelling out unwittingly for, or even paying a deposit on some grossly overpriced item. Most of the women on the staff had something from Mrs B's on tick.

Every day the school car, an ancient Peugeot which was eventually replaced by a VW Combi, drove the short distance to Lushoto Post Office to collect the mail. Our strange address, Lushoto Prep School, Private Bag, Tanganyika, was accurate because the Private Bag was exactly that, a lockable leather bag. Salim brought the post back to the office, together with all the boxes of groceries we had ordered from the dukas, to be sorted in time for tea. At four o'clock, the first port of call in the staffroom was the letter rack to check the mail for those longed for letters from home.

The school staff weren't the only expats in the area. Several forestry and ministry of agriculture officers from overseas lived in town with their families and, as their children were day pupils, we were often invited out to parties at their houses. There was always wonderful food at these gatherings—avocado starters and other luxuries that I'd never tasted before, and plenty of alcohol. Having had little experience with drink, except for the obligatory glass of cherry brandy at Christmas and some wine in France, I soon fell foul of gin and tonic. I quickly learnt to enjoy the G&T habit shared by many of our group until one Monday morning, after a particularly heavy weekend, Mr Scott called me into his office. He told me how worried Mrs Scott and he were by rumours they'd heard about me climbing out of a window, passing out beside the road and later, having to be brought home somewhat the worse for wear. I assured him it was all nonsense. Actually, the truth was worse, and I amended my grocery order by crossing off the bottle of Gilbeys, at least for that week.

After school on weekdays, Sylvia and I sometimes played tennis on the court outside the Boma, the old German government house. There were also several ancient, very bony horses that could be ridden at the Lawns Hotel. On my first and only excursion into the hills, I was dumped in a bush by my unwilling steed and had to wait there until the others realised I was missing.

Parties and outings were the highlight of each weekend. We often gathered in Ben and Rosie's flat in the top bungalow to dance to music – early Beatles and Buddy Holly LPs were favourites – played on a battery-powered record player. The clip-on cover doubled as a loud speaker. We drank Tusker beer, Cinzano or Fanta Orange, crunched our way through pounds of peanuts fried in butter, and sometimes smoked long, king-sized Rex and Sportsman cigarettes. All very innocent fun which couldn't emulate the wild ngomas enjoyed by the locals across the hill in Deutchy Village.

The cost of living a European lifestyle in such a poor African country was very high. Taxes were levied on everything. There was both personal tax and local tax to be paid. Rent was deducted from our salaries, as was the cost of our meals, breakfast, lunch and dinner, which were cooked in the school kitchen. Some people found the fare barely edible and were even more disinclined to partake of the oily Indian curries, stuffed cabbage leaves and other treats prepared by the German cook after they had visited the kitchen where flies were legion and chickens perched on open windows. But I had been brought up to finish everything on my plate so 'gannet-like' I never went hungry and consequently stayed fit and well without having to spend out on extra food.

My bank balance always seemed to be teetering on the edge of disaster, but with only £50 a month of disposable income, it was difficult to save. Letters home are full of promises to send the £26 owed to my parents who'd been paying for my insurance, something that working class people did in those days, only to apologise for non-payment in the next letter.

Mr Ramada still wanted his £15 for the car and, although a full payment for the wrecked vehicle had been made, it was some time before the insurance cheque for £275 was actually in my hand. At that point, I had only £29 to my name. However, I still hankered after a second car.

Ben and Rosy intended to leave at the end of the summer term, 1964. They were going to Ben's home in Yorkshire first, before flying out to Tasmania to start a new life. I had considered buying Ben's old but lovingly preserved Beetle. (On a test drive, he initiated me into the secrets of double declutching in a 1955 car without synchromesh gears.) Nine years old with only 33,000 miles on the clock, it was still a beautiful machine, cream outside with red leather seats and details that every Beetle fancier would rave about today.

However, I didn't feel that I had Ben's expertise and I wouldn't have been able to minister to it when it needed attention. So, after a 15-minute shouting match on the telephone with the British India Insurance Company who said they didn't issue comprehensive policies on such old vehicles, I decided not to buy it. The VW's deep throaty engine continued to roar up the hill past my bungalow and my bank balance stayed in the black—just.

May's weather did little to raise our spirits. Sylvia, Sally, David and I were not used to so much rain, day in, day out. The children had to stay indoors because there was nowhere for their clothes to be dried. The dhobis found it difficult enough to cope with the usual weekly wash of sheets, towels and children's clothes.

These they scrubbed down by the river and dried on the grass and bushes. However, with the temperature in the 50s, and the surrounding hills and valleys shrouded in low clouds even when the rain stopped, all drying had to go indoors. By June, at 4,500 feet it was cold enough to wear the duffel coat I'd thrown into my trunk as an afterthought. The only way to get warm was to take a trip down to the coast.

Sometimes, we went to the European Swimming Club in Tanga where we could sun ourselves on a well-manicured beach or sit in the shade of a massive baobab tree, drinking a cool beer. Next door was the Indian Swimming Club but I didn't go there until a few years later. On one memorable occasion, we drove to the sea at Pangani, south of Tanga, where we spent a blisteringly hot day lying in the shade of the palm trees at the back of the beach.

If we wanted to cool off in the water, we had to steel ourselves to cross a strip of white, hot sand that left bare soles red and sore. Another favourite destination further down on the coast was an old slave port, Bagamoyo, meaning 'lay down your heart'—a fitting name for a place from which hundreds of Africans must have looked their last at their native shores before being shipped off to a life of slavery.

As the summer term came to an end, we began to plan safaris. Sylvia had put her name down for a tennis tournament in Dar es Salaam and suggested that I might like to go along too for a change of scene. The tennis event lasted a whole week, somewhat boring for a non-player, so I had planned a trip down to the border with North Rhodesia, a country I'd heard Sylvia talk about.

She'd taught at a school on the 'copper belt' where life amongst the expats was stimulating and there were always lively parties and safaris to enjoy. Inspired by such glowing reports, I wanted to take a look at the country for myself. The railway link with Rhodesia—or Zambia as it's known now—hadn't been built in 1964, so the journey had to be made by bus; one from Dar to Iringa then another from Iringa to Mbeya, a distance of some 500 miles, along dirt roads.

A study of the East African bus timetable convinced me that the safari could be completed within the week, so the day after we arrived in Dar es Salaam, I set out on the first leg. Imagine an ancient bus crammed with hot, sweaty bodies three to a seat, the top and any available space inside taken up with boxes, bundles wrapped in material and passively hanging upside down the odd chicken. I was the only white face in the noisy, gesticulating crowd.

The driver was soon into his stride, handling the bus like a grand prix competitor, although it wasn't other vehicles he had to avoid—pot holes were the hazards. When he misjudged a stretch of road, things really became rough for the passengers on the back seat.

"Pole, pole—slow down," they shrieked as they became airborne and in danger of having their skulls crushed against the roof. Their pleas were effective

53

for five minutes or so, then the driver, mindful of the long journey ahead, would put his foot down again, the best way to ride corrugations, some say.

Stops along the route were for us to relieve ourselves, women to the right, men to the left. The driver always, thoughtfully, chose a boulder strewn area so that those ladies of a modest disposition could go behind a rock instead of ducking down in full view of the bus.

After 300 miles of this, I was able to enjoy the earthiness of the experience and the closeness of so many fellow travellers. The sweat and heat of an African bus is quite different from the garlicky crush of the Paris Metro, but both forms of public transport bring people together—metaphysically and physically.

Accommodation was at a Railway Hotel, a single storey building where the bathroom was somewhere in the grounds, a walk away from my room. After I'd booked in, I dashed for a hot cleansing tub but found that the previous occupant, a man whom I'd passed, steaming out, had left something behind, a thick layer of scum all around the bath. After nearly a year of being cosseted, it came as a shock to have to clean up after someone else.

The second day, the bus took me down to Mbeya, to a second Railway Hotel. From there, I'd hoped to travel further to the tea plantations near the border but there was no public transport and I didn't know anyone at that time who could take me there or with whom I could stay.

The countryside was too inhospitable for me to venture into without support so, somewhat disappointed, I had to admit defeat and wait for the next bus back to Iringa. On my return to Dar es Salaam, I found that Sylvia had been knocked out of the tournament in the first round and had spent a miserable week with nothing to do except watch tennis with people she didn't know. I think she was glad to see me again and return to Lushoto.

As the months passed, Sylvia became less enamoured with the set-up at school, both from an academic and a social point of view. At her teaching post in a big copper belt town in Rhodesia, there had been adequate equipment and plenty of things to do in her leisure time. Clearly, she was not going to complete her contract and had started applying for other jobs.

So, Tuesday, 28 July 1964 saw us setting out in Sylvia's car, this time headed north for an interview at Arusha School. We left Lushoto at 8.30 a.m. driving carefully down the escarpment to the plains, to turn right at Mombo and head for Arusha. The dirt road from Mombo to Same, to the East of the Pare Mountains in those days, was much better than it had been at the start of our disastrous April trip when we had followed the same route.

This time, the corrugations were softened by sand, but the PWD—Public Works Department—had obviously been busy because there were no drifts on either side to trap unwary motorists. We left great clouds of dust in our wake and had to bake with windows shut when another vehicle passed. Nevertheless, Penny and Tim, our dachshunds, settled down very well in the back and we didn't stop until we reached the tarmac.

At 1.30 p.m. we arrived in Moshi and drove round to the Otterman Bank where we'd arranged to meet Mrs McKenzie. She had invited us to lunch when she'd collected her daughter Melanie from school at the end of term. Such invitations were one of the delights of teaching at Lushoto. Parents were generous and always included us in their house parties.

In that way, we met a succession of interesting people, mostly European expats in managerial or administrative posts, or teachers like us. From having had no social life at home, such experiences were to be relished after I'd overcome my ingrained reserve and fear of grown-up society.

Of course, there were always plenty of staff—cooks, servants and cleaners—to look after us whilst the Bwana and Memsahib entertained their guests, so the McKenzie's cook soon fixed us a late lunch of omelette and soup.

The kennels where we were to leave Penny and Tim were difficult to find and Sylvia nearly came to grief in a concrete drift hidden in a dip in the road before we located them. Despite being full, the owners took our two—by then, irritable—little dogs who received a scaring reception when the other dogs started barking. Afterwards, we booked into the Safari Hotel in town where it was much warmer at night than in Lushoto.

Sylvia's interview at Arusha School was the following morning. While she was seeing the headmaster, I put my newly bought camera to use, snapping exotic flowers and an enormous tortoise, a queer, grey, wrinkled old thing, in the school ground. The interview over, we went to have re-entry permits put into our passports to legalise another year's stay in Tanganyika. Then, on to the hairdresser's next door to the Safari Hotel.

The luxury of having a cut and set was spoilt when I was bluntly informed that my hair was falling out and that I must take vitamin A and B tablets to prevent me from going bald. We had lunch and set out for Namanga, just north of Arusha, across the border, in Kenya.

To begin with, the scenery was very barren, a series of mountains rising from the plains like enormous deposits of waste rock. As the landscape became greener, we passed groups of Masai tending their cattle before the road descended to the lowlands. From the bushes, three ostriches, some gazelle, then—to Sylvia's great delight—a giraffe, made their way across the road as we sped over its blissfully smooth surface.

The Namanga River Hotel with its mekuti roofs, exposed beams and whitewashed walls looked a good place to stop off. Our room was in a thatched cottage. It was July and cold enough by African standards to appreciate the log fire—whole tree trunks were burnt—in the dining room. The garden in front was one blast of colour, so my camera was out again recording bougainvillaea, green and red poinsettias, cannas, geraniums, frangipani, budgerigars in an aviary—everything.

Outside the gate, I bought a bracelet, a strip of leather decorated with beadwork, beads as tiny as grains of sugar, from a Masai girl. She took it off her wrist when I'd paid her, then allowed me to photograph her for an extra shilling.

Masai are fine-looking people. There's something eccentric about the men's reddened limbs and clothes, and the women's wide, bead collars. One man wore an ice-cream carton in his ear, a lobe having been stretched to accommodate the novel earring. Others had bits of metal stamped with the "Shell" logo in their jewellery. Added to their many skills, like being able to live in such hostile surroundings, they could also speak English.

Over tea with a Berlin Classics Master, one of a party of Germans at the hotel, Sylvia and I talked over our plans for the rest of the holiday, which was to begin with a visit to Amboselli Game Park in Kenya. There, we had been assured, we would be able to photograph plenty of animals.

Next day, with the help of a guide whom we'd picked up at Ol Tukai Lodge, Amboselli, we were able to see a silver-backed jackal, antelope and hundreds of bright birds, but as so often happens, the big game eluded us. Our guide directed Sylvia to drive off the tracks and across country to a place where he knew there was a cheetah and her young. But we couldn't find them in the long grass.

Instead we saw two foxes and their hole and later, an old earless rhino lying down in a swampy place. Ox-peckers were making red holes in its hide picking off ticks. When we returned, we saw it again and it was rolling around in the mud, this time attended by white cattle egrets. But although we scoured all the nearby bushes, we couldn't see any lions.

We did see signs of a big herd of elephants but despite the encouraging trail of destruction and dung only one pachyderm appeared. However, before we left Amboselli, we were able to add Grants gazelle, buffalo, lots of giraffe, zebra and wildebeest, a few impala and a group of indignant warthogs to our list.

Nairobi, with the noise of so much traffic and so many people, was quite a shock after the quiet of the bush but the next day its shops, and even the alarmingly expensive Woolworth's kept us busy from 9 a.m. until closing time. We were staying with the Archer family—Tom and Iris and their young daughters, Lucy and Marina, whom we'd met at Malindi on our Christmas holidays. They'd only just moved to a whitewashed wood and tin house, 8 miles out of the capital. We spent a happy Saturday with them, sharing the excitement of a visit to the bazaar and huge market in Nairobi to buy food for a picnic, a tour round the snake park and—after tea—a film at the Belle Vue Drive-In. Iris had made hamburgers for supper, a treat after school food.

After lengthy preparations on Sunday we finally set out north for Thika with our picnic. En route, we stopped off to feed the Archers' dog, Bucklane and a cat that lived at the factory Tom owned, where he manufactured a general cleaner with the amazing name, Tiger Polish. Somehow, he also made face-cream and disinfectant amongst the muddle of tins and vats of cream and polish. After fixing a puncture, we were on our way to Thika, a place I'd been looking forward to seeing since reading a book about its famous Flame Trees. It wasn't really picnic weather. The countryside looked very messy with wet, red soil, but the Blue Post Hotel was attractive and the two nearby waterfalls spectacular, hurling down thousands of gallons of brown, frothy water. The noise and smell brought back uncomfortable memories. It rained heavily but Tom stood outside, boasting that he enjoyed getting wet, whilst we females sensibly picnicked under cover. Before we left, we did get to see the Flame Trees in Thika township but they weren't as spectacular as I'd imagined.

Back in Nairobi, Sylvia and I saw our first wild lions in the city's National Park, where we had taken Lucy and Marina whilst Tom and Iris went home to heat water and cook supper. Excitedly, we drove off the road into the bush where we'd spotted the great cats and were amazed to be able to observe the lion and his wife from such close quarters. Soon, occupants of other cars sped to join us and crowd round the totally laid back couple. Much to everyone's amusement, the animals, undeterred by spectators, began a vigorous session of love-making.

When we realised what was happening, Sylvia put the car into reverse and sped off before the girls started asking awkward questions.

The evening finished with a concert in Nairobi Cathedral given by the Kericho Ensemble. It was a wonderful mixed bag; a Bach flute concerto, a Benjamin Britten choral piece, a Handel concerto and Vivaldi's 'Gloria'.

Our 'summer' holiday finished with a trip to Nakuru, northwest of Nairobi, and the lake to view the flamingos. It's one of those sights that feature in wildlife programmes nowadays, but even brilliant camera work can never recreate the illusion that the millions of birds have been transformed into a great swathe of pink candy floss. We didn't have binoculars to zoom in on movement and shape for the details, so I had to be content with a picture postcard.

Equally as stunning was my first glimpse of the Rift Valley. Sylvia stopped the car so we could look down from our highland road and take in the enormity of the miles-wide, green corridor stretching away to the horizon. Nowadays, pictures of it on television bring back that feeling of jaw-dropping disbelief that such a place could open up before us.

We would have stood there longer, marvelling at the vastness of the slice of countryside that we had come upon, but it was cold and we were soon back in the VW and on our way to the Equator. Crossing the line at 9,000 feet in Kenya was something of an anti-climax.

There was nothing to do but take photographs of each other horsing about underneath the sign marking the geographical division between the North and South Hemispheres beside the deserted road before the long drive back to Lushoto.

A letter awaited Sylvia on our return, informing her that she had not been selected for the teaching post at Arusha. She would have to continue working for Mr Scott, at least, for another term.

Chapter 6
Something About Islands

"Let's have sports day," suggested Mr Scott one morning. The sun was shining, but it wasn't too hot. The grass on the games field had been cut and it was a perfect day for races. All we needed to do was set up the high jump, rake the long jump pit and assemble the children dressed in shorts, shirts and floppy, grey sun hats. It was as simple as that. The younger staff were used to organising games: athletics, football and cricket for the boys and athletics, hockey and rounders for the girls. (I'd tried to introduce netball on the old tennis courts but the red earth was usually so dry that, after ten minutes, the dust that was kicked up made it impossible to see the goal posts.) So, it was a stress-free afternoon of races, javelin throwing, high jumping and long jumping, enjoyed by the whole school divided into three teams. No complicated scoring system was needed. The headmaster added up the points gained for each event and awarded the cup to the winning team.

Parents weren't invited to sports day. In any case, most lived too far away and made the long journey only at half-term weekend. East African Airways had discontinued their flights to the nearest airstrip at Mombo at the foot of the Usambaras, so some parents came hundreds of miles by road. We always enjoyed watching out for the expensive cars to roll up on Friday afternoon. Anne-Marie's father was one of the few European ministers in President Nyerere's government, so his vehicle always sported an official flag.

While some families left immediately to be the leaders in the convoy down the 20 miles of twisting mountain road, others took their offsprings round to the Lawns Hotel for the weekend. Inevitably, there were always some pupils left in the school but the matrons did their best to make the weekend different for these children, and, whenever we could, we helped by taking them out.

A favourite trip was to the Viewpoint, an awe-inspiring look-out where the Usambaras dropped 3,000 feet down to the Masai Steppe. Nearby, the forestry commission had built a wooden fire look-out platform that just begged to be climbed on and jumped from many times, until enough energy had been expended to justify the eating of a slap-up tea at the Lawns Hotel.

During that first year at Lushoto, we experienced several earth tremors. One occurred on a warm morning shortly after the children had gone out to play. I was alone in my classroom with all the windows open to catch the breeze that curled up from the cool courtyard below when I was suddenly aware of a deep rumbling sound, rather like an underground train.

As the noise grew louder, the windows began to swing on their hinges and the wooden furniture came to life. It was frightening. On another occasion, I was in the dark, listening to the radio as I tried to sleep off the evil side effects of a painful typhoid injection. It was November 1963 and I'd just heard the startling news that President Kennedy had been shot, when my bed grew wheels and responded to the shock waves that rolled under the floor. "The end of the world has come," I groaned.

The following January 1964, there was another event to worry us—a revolution in Zanzibar. In December of the previous year, Zanzibar had become a constitutional monarchy with the Sultan at its head, when the UK terminated its protectorate of the island. However, just a month later, the Sultan was deposed during the revolution. In the fighting, some 20,000 people were killed, whilst others escaped to the mainland of Tanganyika.

Although 'up-country' and over 100 miles from any of the trouble, we felt threatened by twisted tales of rape and murder brought across to Tanga by fleeing Europeans. There were further troubles in Dar es Salaam. Shots were fired, a bridge blown up and people killed before an aircraft carrier, one of Her Majesty's ships, arrived.

Parents phoned, not knowing what to do, but Mr Scott took things calmly. He figured that the hatred was directed by Zanzibar Africans against the island's Arab population. Colonists from Oman had settled on Zanzibar and nearby Pemba Island in the early nineteenth century, assumed possession of the best arable land, and eventually occupied most of the higher positions in the civil service.

The plight of the socially impoverished African community was not improved when Indian immigrants arrived to fill posts in the commercial and retail sectors. Britain tried to introduce a parliamentary electoral system but, according to some writers, the speed to change from 'protected Arab Sultanate' to democratic independent state was mis-calculated. The time scale should have been measured in months not years.

There were many complex reasons behind the 1964 revolution. There had been election day riots in June 1961, when 68 people died, but an inquiry discredited the suggestion that the motive was racial. The Afro-Shirazi Party (ASP) polled the most votes in the 1963 election but was prevented from forming a government because it had gained insufficient seats over all.

Many Africans on Pemba and Zanzibar supported the coalition of the other two parties. Believing themselves to have been cheated out of power by the way that constituency boundaries had been drawn up, ASP members began to grow bitter. It is fascinating to follow the subsequent build-up to the overthrow of the government in Clyde Sangers' introduction to 'Revolution in Zanzibar' written by John Okello, the self-styled Field Marshall who claimed to have affected the nine-hour coup.

It is ironic that, soon after the event, Okello found himself a penniless exile, having been given the cold shoulder by politicians in Kenya, Tanganyika and even Uganda, his country of origin.

That January, a rifle leaning up against a bookcase gave us a feeling of security as we speculated on the possible knock-on effects of the unrest. But the Washamba were a peaceful, fun-loving people. They dutifully listened to the TANU (Tanganyika African National Union) party speakers who took over the community hall in Lushoto—at such times, I had to take my Advanced English lessons for local adults in the bar, seated on a high stool—but then went back to digging their shambas and brewing pombe. We were safe.

Zanzibar gained its independence without the long period of confrontation predicted by some pessimists. In April 1964, the new republic merged with mainland Tanganyika to form the United Republic of Tanganyika and Zanzibar.

After some thought—I heard a rumour that it was the result of a national competition—this was shortened to become the United Republic of Tanzania within which Zanzibar was to remain a semi-autonomous region with a socialist government led by the ASP. The only change we experienced was to the address on our headed airmail letters and note paper—no longer Tanganyika but instead Tanzania.

With Ben and Rosy having left, there was a shuffle of staff in September 1964. To cut costs, the headmaster took on a full timetable himself instead of employing another teacher, and Mrs Harper's daughter, Daisy, was drafted in, initially on a temporary basis.

Daisy had no teaching certificate but what she lacked in academic qualifications she more than made up for in vivacity. It was her job to cover classes that couldn't be squeezed into a revised teaching schedule with new timetables, which meant more work for all of us.

After only three terms, Sylvia was fed up with Lushoto. Whereas my social life had improved a thousand-fold, Sylvia's had, by her standards, dwindled to nothing. She decided to pay her own fare back to the UK at Christmas rather than be miserable for two more terms and complete her 2-year contract. "You'll have Penny won't you, Sylv," she said one day.

How could I say 'No'? So that would be two dogs as well as two cats to feed, flea and find homes for when I went off on safari. Then Sally pronounced that she'd also be off in December too. She'd discovered that she was expecting her first baby and after several bouts of ill health, mainly I think due to poor nourishment because she hated the school food, wanted to get back to home comforts and a healthier life style.

I was to miss Sylvia's confident, knowledgeable way of doing things and her long accounts of her life teaching in Rhodesia and Scotland. I can see her now, puffing a king-size cigarette, slumped in a chair with flip-flops hung off her feet, as in her slow Glaswegian accent, she conjured up for me manic goings-on in the suicide season before the rains in a Copper Belt town. She also described how refugees from the war-torn Congo on their way to South Africa passed through, selling off their possessions, which included African grey parrots.

Sally called Sylvia 'Cup Cake' to identify her from me as we were both Sylvias. Our surnames sounded similar, both ending in 'son', and to our amazement, we discovered we were both born on November 27, although not in the same year.

There were no other similarities. She was a strict teacher, used to having a belt or strap tucked away in her drawer with which to inflict the ultimate punishment, whereas I was much more satisfied with my class's conduct. In the 1960s, caning was a legal means of chastisement as was smacking. I know how it felt because my mother had smacked me. Only once was I tempted to threaten a miscreant with 'the ruler' but never again.

Sylvia and Sally began to look forward to their flights back home but I realised that without a car, I would be stuck in Lushoto with no friends. It would be a lonely Christmas. "What are you going to do?" asked Sylvia, but it was Sally who showed me the advertisement in a newspaper for a cruise around the Indian Ocean. "You'll love it," she enthused.

These days, some cruise ships are like floating resorts which stop in chosen ports only to decant the passengers for a little light relief from the frenetic round of eating, drinking and partying on board. There are also genteel, expensive cruises where one dresses for dinner, takes notes at advanced level lectures and relaxes with a gin and tonic after returning from a practical history lesson among the ruins. My cruise was to be quite different from either of these.

Saturday, 19 December 1964 saw me sitting in Mombasa Port's Baggage Room waiting for the SS 'State of Bombay' to move out of number one berth so that my ship, the 'Jean Laborde', could come alongside. I had made my way to Tanga by bus, a tiring, steamy trip with my devoted daxies, Penny and Tim.

Friends were looking after them whilst I was away. After another bus journey to Mombasa and an uncomfortably humid night at the Rex Hotel, I was looking forward to getting away from the coast before the arrival of the rains.

A French ship, owned by the grand-sounding Compagnie des Messageries Maritimes, the Jean Laborde made the round trip from Marseilles to Mauritius via the coast of East Africa, Madagascar and Réunion. En route through the Indian Ocean, it picked up and dropped off passengers, mainly French expatriates working on those islands, as well as a few tourists.

The ship also had a refrigerated hold for its cargo of 'viandes, salsaisons, et charcuterie'. 150 metres long and nearly 20 wide, it had cabins for 88 first class passengers and 112 tourist class, and space below for 280 'rationnaires'. I was to see some of them later.

Paintings had been specially commissioned and colour schemes carefully chosen to decorate the vessel, whose elegant, old-fashioned rooms are described in flowing phrases on a leaflet I still have. The black and white photographs show a smoking room, hairdresser's, bar, children's games room filled with exquisite wooden toys and furniture, deluxe bedroom, music room and the slightly less opulent 'salon-bar de la classe touriste'.

There were no slot machines on which to while away the hours, certainly no television. 'Des séances de cinématographe' provided the only entertainment to be looked forward to after dinner. The first film of the trip was an English one, but old even in 1964—starring Spencer Tracey. I don't think many people could have enjoyed it apart from myself and the two Englishmen in first class.

My cabin, down in tourist class, was perfect; two bunks, double wardrobe, folding chair, wash basin, and best of all, air-conditioning. At the outset of the trip, there were only a few first-class passengers on board, so I spent much of the day in and around the swimming pool, really a small deep hole in the fore deck where the pale blue tiles designed by a certain 'Michaelis' were supposed to 'evoke the pleasures of the water'. My pleasures of the water were cut short when more first-class passengers poured on-board and I was politely told to keep in my place, aft with the tourist class.

It must have been difficult to find a suitable spot in the dining room for a single 25-year-old woman and I was put on a table with a French family: a mother, father, 16-year-old girl and two young boys. At first, they were rather shy and I felt like an intruder but after a while, I was able to spread my limited small talk and enter into conversation with them. They were all suffering from the heat of course, as they'd left France in the grip of winter to head straight into the humidity of a tropical December. In fact, they were, the smiling blond mother told me, from the Pyrenees and were on their way to a three-year tour in Réunion. The father's view that 'it was fine for French people to be in Africa as they were no longer colonialist' was as typically Gallic as his little black moustache. He condemned the American and Belgian activities in the Congo and pointed out that no French people had been taken prisoner during the uprising there. "Good for them," I thought, remembering all the horror stories that Sylvia had told me about people fleeing from that troubled Central African country during her time in Rhodesia.

Whilst at sea, after an initial spell of seasickness, time passed slowly. Reading isn't the most physically demanding of occupations and I found myself having to take a stroll round the deck at regular intervals. With no one to speak to, I felt bored and lonely, so it was an interesting diversion to be given a tour of the engines fore and aft—two ten cylinder diesels, capable of reaching 17 knots.

The two engineers must have talked about me because I was often teased, flirted with and generally harassed by other crew members until I gave in and enjoyed the unlooked-for attention. Loneliness and boredom can lead to disastrous relationships, especially if you're surrounded by French sailors far from home, so I had to tread a fine line between encouragement and English coolness. It wasn't easy with my sense of humour.

For me, one of the highlights of the trip was stopping at the Comoro Islands. I had read about the coelacanth, that fish relic from the dinosaur era, once thought extinct that had been landed from the sea around the islands in the 1930s, and was thrilled by the notion that there might be more prehistoric creatures swimming about under our feet.

We couldn't go ashore as there was no harbour big enough for our ship. Instead, we hove to whilst the Comorians, the most scantily dressed, blackest skinned people I'd ever seen, sold exotic vanilla pods and cinnamon sticks to passengers high up on decks far above their flimsy floating shops.

On its outward journey, the Jean Laborde had damaged one of its propellers when it passed through the Suez Canal. Repairs were carried out when the ship docked at Majunga, which meant some discomfort for us when the air conditioning had to be turned off.

On the other hand, we were treated to the rare sight of the fitting of a large copper screw far down on the hull of our stranded ship. I spent an hour trying to photograph the scene with sparks from the welders' torches illuminating the cool, green depths of a Madagascan dry dock.

Going ashore anywhere was quite a challenge for me, not only because it was too hot to walk far, but also because if I got lost and ran into trouble, there would be no one to register my absence. I'd be left behind. On one occasion, a middle-aged French gentleman, a passenger from First Class, escorted me round the market when we docked at Réunion.

According to my diary, he instructed me on the difference between real and water melons, the origin of hydrangeas, and about using green peppers in sauce. All the Chinese merchandise on the stalls was closely inspected before he left to catch the bus to Saint Denis and I returned to the ship.

Our approach to the Isle de la Réunion had been through a mysterious, grey mist but, once the rain cleared, the island's impressive mountains revealed their jagged peaks. In dock, there was a beautiful French cargo boat with its quarters aft, and several British vessels, rather ramshackle-looking things.

My French family, the Chomels, had reached their new home. Mr Chomel had donned his gendarme uniform for the occasion. I think he was quite a high ranking official. However, that didn't stop him from springing from his chair, eager to see if we had docked. Little Phillipe was so excited, he couldn't eat his steak so Madame Chomel smacked him and threatened "No ice cream!" But seeing the child's sad face, the steward gave him some.

It was interesting to watch the people I had grown to recognise over the eight days since leaving Mombasa, meeting their relatives. There was the funny old couple—Dad always in braces and shirt sleeves, mum trying to be regal but nodding off to sleep, another middle-aged pair—mother at breakfast in her dressing gown and father in pyjamas sucking away at bread dipped in coffee, and the two 'love birds'—she always in white shorts or a bikini, he with a moustache making him look older. They all went down the gangplank.

Josie Furet was amongst the new passengers to embark. She was to share a cabin with me. The first I knew of it was when I came upon a large, leafy pile of lychees that she'd brought on board and stowed under the bunk. It was good to have someone to talk to and help to dispatch the big brown cockroaches that had started to come up out of the sink at night.

By that time, I was beginning to wish that I'd stayed at home. There was just nothing to do on board ship! However, Josie was to liven up the evenings with her stories. She'd been sent away to Réunion by her family on Mauritius to stop her marrying the wrong man, but Josie had served her sentence and was returning home, the danger having passed.

It was difficult to put my finger on it but there was a strange similarity between the patterns of our lives over the past year, different in backgrounds as we were. When we docked in Port Louis, Mauritius, on 30 December, her family were all there. They came on board and after much hugging and kissing, took off for home in several cars. I found myself in a taxi squashed between Josie's mum and three sisters. It was the start of a hectic, very-exciting dash across the island.

We stopped at the market in St Louis. I had never seen such stacks of fruits and vegetables. There were also piles of shoots and leaves which looked like young bean plants, millions of everything.

"Try this!" Josie said, handing me a strange pink drink which contained pips and yellow shreds. "Do you like it?" Before I could make up my mind, we were off again through Rose Vale, Curepipe, and out to the Furets' home, the taxi driver roaring along. I could see myself ending up in a Mauritian hospital.

The Furets lived in the country amongst fields of sugar cane, five miles from the sea. Their house of corrugated iron and wood came as quite a shock. I had imagined something grander. What a snob! But what the house lacked in sophistication, it more than made up for in homeliness. The front room was furnished with several tables, a sideboard and radio and large photographs chronicling each addition to the family hung everywhere.

As soon as I stepped through the door, the youngest boy came straight up to me and gave me a heart-stopping, sweet kiss. He must have been about eight, the next boy eleven, and the eldest eighteen or more. The three sisters all looked about the same age but younger than Josie. Gertie was shy and quiet whilst the others laughed and exclaimed over me. It was quite overwhelming.

The rough-looking cousin who had several front teeth missing turned out to be the most comprehensible and informative. He told me that every patch of sugarcane was used up by the industry and that, although tea had been introduced as an extra cash crop, there still wasn't enough work for everyone. He complained of living expenses being high, whilst salaries were inadequate. I could believe that, having heard from some South Africans I'd met on the boat that the standard of living was even lower in Mauritius than it was in Réunion. Apparently, the government was trying to build up a tourist industry but it was a slow process. Today, Mauritius has many fine hotels round the coast and has developed into a 'high end' holiday resort. I tried some sugarcane. It was gorgeous. The sweetness that could be extracted from such a dry splintery stick was amazing. There was a moral there somewhere.

The return journey to the Jean Laborde was a rush, even though we started lunch at twenty to eleven! Spicy chicken curry and lots of sweets, including iced sponge, all washed down with wine, followed a starter of ham sandwiches, and brandy and soda, quite a mixture on a hot morning. By dint of driving at what seemed like 80 mph along the narrow roads, we arrived back at the Jean Laborde at five to twelve. The ship was due to leave at noon. We screeched to a halt on the quayside, aware that passengers on-board were crowding the rails trying to see who was keeping them waiting, but I shook hands with Josie's wonderfully warm-hearted family and rushed up the gang plank. It was a moment to be savoured as we steamed away through the deep blue waters of the Indian Ocean leaving behind the ragged peaks of Mauritius.

New Year's Eve was spent at Tamatave on the East coast of Madagascar. Three of the dining room stewards took me to a dance at the local night club. The crowd inside was dense and steamy. People were sitting at tables around the illuminated dance area, which was separated off by big under-floor lights shining through transparent blocks. We found a table, already occupied by one of the lesser species of officer busy with his local lady friend, and ordered drinks.

Jean-Pierre, my particular favourite of the three stewards, did his best to cheer me up. He was concerned that I had such a sad face. "December 31 is a time for looking to the future and making new resolutions," he chided, but all I could think about was my past disastrous love life.

I had ditched a doting fiancé who had been prepared to wait two years for me and had fallen in love with someone else but lacked the confidence to encourage his friendship. So much for a strict moral upbringing!

However, in retrospect, I think that it was just such an upbringing endorsed by my mother, my teachers at school, the sort of literature I read as a young girl, and my involvement with a very high-minded local church, that gave me direction during my African experience.

Midnight came and went amid a round of Happy New Year hugs and moist kisses. Shortly afterwards, Jean-Pierre made his exit and left me with his friends. The rather conceited 23-year-old steward from near the Swiss border spoke little English.

"I can't make up my mind," he said loftily. "Should I marry my girlfriend in France or the one in Singapore?" as if trying to decide which flavour of ice cream to choose. Personally, I thought that he didn't deserve even one girlfriend. The third steward was an older man with a good voice. He stood up and sang "Arrivederci Roma" several times, then very courteously took me by the hand and danced with me. I was well looked after.

In time, Jean-Pierre reappeared and made his excuses for his absence explaining that he'd bumped into an old friend but I had a nasty suspicion about what he'd really been up to and where he'd really been for the past half an hour! At 3.30 a.m., we started to think about returning to the ship. Jean-Pierre had again disappeared, so I was obliged to go in a taxi with his burly friend.

Taxis couldn't drive right into the port, so we had a trek through the wet, back to the Jean Laborde. I thought that I could trust my cavalier but my confidence was misplaced. A passionate embrace by a Frenchman in the pouring rain of Madagascar was a never-to-be-repeated start to a New Year.

Foreign Legion troops crowded onto the boat on the following Sunday morning. They arrived with their bibis and babies, leaving a trail of mud and noise everywhere, before the hatches were battened down on them in fourth class. I had watched three lorry loads of them shriek down the streets when I had been in town that morning.

I wasn't surprised that the soldiers were cheering their own departure. With its dirt and broken streets, Tamatave was a miserable place. From time to time, the legionaries came up from the depths for an airing and, herded as we were into our Tourist Class deck space, we almost felt sorry for them with even less space below in which to move around.

The departure of the Chomel family meant that I had to be found new dining companions. I think that the steward in charge of the dining room must have had a wicked sense of humour because he singled me out to sit next to the most taciturn man I had ever met. He was an adjutant who had arrived with the legionaries and was clearly used to dining alone.

He was never moved to say much even when I resorted to asking him all sorts of stupid or unnecessary questions. Every so often, I would look up and catch the stewards sniggering behind their hands. Probably, they were amused by my efforts to communicate with the stiff army officer who was probably more accustomed to issuing orders and to the company of rugged men than to having his ear bent in halting French by a single and, therefore, dangerous young woman. It must have made supper a hoot for the dining room staff, but for me, it was just another frustration on a trip that was becoming increasingly boring.

At the outset, a cruise round the Indian Ocean sounded the perfect way to spend a Christmas holiday. In the end, I was glad to be back in East Africa. I had looked forward to seeing something of Madagascar but realise now that it is a huge island and, even with several weeks at one's disposal, one couldn't see a fraction of it.

The bright raffia work, a big, lidded work basket and a woven handbag, bought from the offshore islands of Nosi Bay and Majunga on the west coast, and a carved wooden spoon with a simple paddy field scene painted on the scoop, remind me of my solitary walks around the port areas.

Grilling sunshine, Asian traders and white-washed mud buildings set along baked mud roads come to mind too, with a dim recollection of enormous webs draped across shaded corners with frighteningly large spiders waiting in the wings to trap tropical insects.

Chapter 7
African Magic

Somewhere along the line, Africa must have got under my skin. There was so much freedom to do as I pleased, so many people of my own age, if not near at hand, then prepared to come to Lushoto for a weekend party. Above all, there were endless opportunities to travel and indulge my increasingly restless spirit, to go and see places for myself.

Discussions, exchanges of ideas, a heightened awareness of political issues gleaned from letters from home, visitors from other parts of the country and sometimes from Radio Kenya, all contributed to the change that was to turn a self-conscious, diffident daughter of rural Surrey into a slightly more worldly wise woman.

I'm not sure that the drugs, sex and rock 'n' roll of England at that time would have had the same impact on me. I was just a bit too old and much too narrow-minded to have been caught up in the culture of the swinging sixties. I needed to go abroad to sow my wild oats, make mistakes and cope with the consequences, without my mother coming behind me to wave an accusing finger. Yet, I looked forward to going home, to seeing my family again, but not on the same terms that I had left them.

Teaching at Lushoto Prep School was, of course, just as demanding of one's free time as it is anywhere. Lessons to plan, books to mark, exams to write and reports to compose, eat into after-school hours wherever you are on earth. However, my class, such a mixture of nationalities, 13 at one count, boys and girls from a wide range of lifestyles, made me realise that I was much more sympathetic to the needs of small children than I had ever been to the vagaries of older secondary school students.

To share the openness of young children, their need to know about things and their ability to enjoy a wide range of activities, however simple or complex, filled me with a deep satisfaction. This, I suppose, formed the ground bass of my life at Lushoto, a steady theme played out against all the twiddles and squeaks of my own erratic development.

Daisy was the chief inventor of the fun we had for the first part of 1965, by which time, she had become a full-time member of staff. A free spirit, always ready to engage in mischief, she enlivened many rainy afternoons with her hastily scribbled notes.

When her class, next door to mine, was being difficult and she was just as fed up as the children, a note which began "Dear Gin Sling"—proposing in earthy phrases that we go out to lunch at the Lawns Hotel—would arrive, carried by an emissary who would wait while I tried to compose an answer in like vein.

On good days, Daisy broke into verse, usually full of double entendre and rude rhymes. She was at her best after a night on the tiles. References to Morgan's organ made me laugh, but it wasn't until some years later that I realised that I hadn't quite appreciated my friend's wit.

In the dry season, Daisy and I were sometimes invited over to the nearest tea estate for the weekend. There were always huge Sunday curries served with dozens of different sambals, accompaniments, carried in on trays by servants in white kanzus and red fezzes.

The Schmidts, a Swiss family whose daughter was a weekly boarder with us, liked to invite a big crowd of people to their estate, so you could always be sure of meeting someone new or interesting, like Norman and Angus, two young tea planters, Angus the Scot, with a wicked sense of humour, and Norman the Englishman. As well as being great fun, they were also gentlemen in the old-fashioned sense.

Then, there was the wife of another tea grower. She had a penchant for collecting and cooking fungi and would tell us about growing up in Central Europe where she had learnt to differentiate between poisonous and non-poisonous mushrooms. The ultimate test was to try them out on herself first before serving them up for the family breakfast.

Kifungilo, a boarding school for African girls in the Usambaras, was another venue for parties. The three American Peace Corps girls working there, invited European expats from Lushoto, as well as teachers from missionary schools miles out in the wilds and from down on the plains.

At 9 p.m., the nuns who ran Kifungilo would put out the lights, leaving us with kerosene lamps and candles for the rest of the evening. There was always dancing, usually the twist and rock and roll, and plenty of lively talk punctuated by rugby songs, somewhat refined and adapted to the company. I had already heard the original versions on boozy evenings at our own private parties. Dinner parties were more formal affairs. They usually started with a traditional sherry or beer but sometimes ended with guests eating the flowers.

Once when my bank balance was in the black, I treated Daisy and some friends to a meal at Oaklands, a tiny hotel at Magamba, north of Lushoto. The menu, which included hors d'oeuvres of olives, little salad things and stuffed eggs, a choice of oxtail soup or fish soufflé, a main course of pork or mutton with sauerkraut, green beans, potatoes and appropriate sauces, then coffee and lemon mousse decorated with fresh cream, was amazingly ambitious.

French white wine was served with the meal, which was laid out on exquisite napery with good silver cutlery and china dishes. To decorate the table, there were two vases of red carnations (it was some of these that were eaten) and a silver basket of grapes grown, as was everything else, by proprietors.

It was hard to believe that such a fine meal produced by Mrs Abbot, the German wife of the owner, came from her kitchen 5,000 feet up in the wilds of the Usambara Mountains and hundreds of miles from any comparable establishment.

At eleven o'clock, we left to drive down the red dirt road through the forest, our headlights picking out huge ferns and the massive trunks of tropical trees. There had been sightings of mountain 'lions' in the area and at least one late night motorist reported a wild cat actually leaping from a high bank over his car as he passed, but the combination of mountain air and Tusker beer was known to sharpen the imagination.

Drivers in the East African Safari Rally had to contend with the worst of Tanzanian roads. It was a feature of our Easter break during the long rains to watch the likes of Stirling Moss, Eric Carlson and Pat Moss Carlson negotiating hairpin bends on treacherously sticky mountain roads. Sometimes, they roared through town, the Saabs, old 2-stroke models, making a terrible noise, especially after they'd had their silencers knocked off on a rocky section of the course.

Then the matrons would allow the older children to stay up late, look out of their dormitory windows and enjoy the exciting spectacle as the cars sped along the welcome stretch of tarmac opposite the school. Next day, all would be re-enacted on the muddy playground at break-time.

Despite the steep climbs and the axle deep mud, the drivers had to keep up an average of 30 mph or they'd incur penalties for arriving late at the next check point. It was always exciting to drive down the back roads to the plains during daylight hours and see the support crews and hear the latest gossip about race leaders or smashed cars. Even today, the rally—re-named the Safari Rally—is considered one of the toughest and is held in high esteem by rally drivers.

Easter provided me with another chance to be off exploring. I badly wanted to see Uganda before I left East Africa. So, having no car, it was out with the bus timetable again. I was never very good about spending money on food and drink when travelling, so I often ended up with a stomach ache and a headache. The latter was probably brought on by worrying about buying tickets and catching buses and trains.

Nothing was ever straightforward or simple at that time but the challenge of getting from A to B always spurred me on. I loved maps and timetables. It never occurred to me that anything could go wrong or that I might be in any danger. In fact, the worst inconvenience was having to wait so long for transport.

Kampala, Uganda, was my destination. There, I visited the Anglican Cathedral on Namirembe Hill with its view of greenness and trees and the whiteness of Kampala's modern buildings grouped down below. Near the cathedral, a group of big drums under their thatched roof struck me as unusual; used instead of bells, I supposed.

Monster cactus plants growing against the red-brown walls added to the overwhelming impact of the building. Inside, the cathedral had the air of a place newly finished with dusty concrete and unfilled corners awaiting the final touches.

It was a strange mixture of foreign and familiar; the familiar pews, pillars and altar one expects in a church but surrounded by the smells and sounds of Africa. With the doors wide open, it looked as if you could fall out and roll down the hill.

At the back of the church, there was a display of some of the possessions of Alexander Mackay, a Scottish Presbyterian Missionary to Uganda in the nineteenth century. A practical man, his missionary work included teaching skills such as farming and carpentry. For this, he was known as 'Muzunguwa Kazi', white man of work. He died of malaria when he was 40.

It was exciting to be looking at artefacts belonging to someone I'd read about. I remembered the chapter headed 'Mackay and the Ugandan martyrs' in the blue religious instruction books we'd used in religious education lessons at the school where I'd begun my career. The man and the subject had seemed, like many things you read about, insignificant details that would never feature in my life.

Yet, there I was in Uganda, thrilled to find in the meagre collection of a dead man's property, a link between my past and my present. Although such a tiny incident, it was a comforting experience.

The town was crowded. The women's dresses were quite different from the ubiquitous kangas worn by most females in Tanzanian villages. Instead, the Ugandan ladies wore buttoned tops with big puffed sleeves and long, flowing skirts. Colours were brilliant. It seemed that many women had had their hair straightened and most of them wore silk scarves. They looked so graceful.

It took almost an hour to get south to Entebbe, another town on my list of places to be visited. By that time, it was really hot and I spent a frustrating hour searching for the travel agency where I hoped to pick up information about the area. But despite tantalising glimpses, I failed to find even the shores of Lake Victoria, let alone the famous Botanical Gardens. After a milkshake and a wash at the Lake Victoria Hotel, I trailed back to the bus, taking with me an impression of trees and the rolling greens of a golf course. Details were to be added at a later date.

The next day, Sunday, I was in Nairobi and, after a long walk from the bus station, I was enjoying the coolness of the Coryndon Museum. On this second visit (my first was when Sylvia and I had stayed with the Archer family), I found it easier to recognise many of the smaller African cats, serval, civet and caracal, but longed to have enough time to learn the names of some of the birds so that I could identify the ones round school and those I'd seen on my travels. Having read a book on snakes by Ionedes, the Snake-Man who described how to pick up deadly puff adders and live, I was attracted to the snake park. Watching the mambas uncoil themselves from a potted cactus, like a miniature tree weighed down with its burden of green bodies, was an absorbing experience. From the grace of restless reptiles pouring themselves about their quarters, I moved on to inspect a heap of baby crocodiles, all beady eyes and heads sticking out at stiff angles. The big crocs were just squashy lumps cooking in the sun, elbows bent, their projecting teeth giving them a satisfied air. It was sometime later that I was to see such creatures in the wild. At two o'clock, I telephoned the Archers, whom I'd not seen since the previous summer. It was a lovely surprise to find them in.

"Haven't you got a car?" Iris enquired.

"No, that was the other Sylvia."

"Well, we'll come down and pick you up. Perhaps, we can go out somewhere. See you soon."

Iris, Tom and their two little girls arrived in a VW Kombi. They were converting it in preparation for their journey home, a trip across Africa and Europe.

"Now, I think the hotel is a bit pricey. So we can either go to the airport or to the animal orphanage for tea," boomed Tom. The choice was obvious. We spent a unique afternoon stroking a baby rhino and being introduced to some of the other young wild animals which the orphanage had rescued.

Back at school after the Easter holidays, there was my journey home at the end of term in July to plan. There was the possibility of sailing from Dar es Salaam to Durban on the Kenya Castle, a train journey from Durban to Johannesburg, then a flight home for £135. I wasn't sure how much Mr Scott would contribute to the cost, although at the end of my two-year contract, he was obliged to finance my return to the UK.

Daisy had developed an interest in Tarot cards and suggested in mock seriousness that she should try to look into my future. So, we sat down one gloomy afternoon and Daisy set about interpreting the message on the cards.

"I don't want to upset you, Sylve. But I can see some bad news for you. A journey, but not on the sea. A change of plan, perhaps?"

Several weeks later, a letter came from my mother. She described the accident that my father had had. He'd fallen off the top of a load of wood on his lorry. The fastenings that he was securing had snapped and he'd landed on the road 14 feet below, breaking his pelvis and damaging his shoulder. He was in hospital. My carefully planned leisurely return was now out of the question. I wanted to see my father as soon as possible at the end of term, so I cancelled the boat trip and Mr Scott bought me a plane ticket. There would be no time to pack and ship my possessions and no time to rehome my two dogs and two cats.

I'm not sure when I made the decision, but it must have been around that time that I surrendered to my addiction to East Africa and decided to renew my contract for a further two years. I couldn't bear to think about leaving what had become such a fulfilling and exciting life with possibilities and challenges such as I'd never had at home. I had no qualms about spending another two years at Lushoto Prep School teaching 8 to 10-year-olds.

As for Daisy, she finished with her Tarot cards. We were both too shaken by what they had revealed.

Chapter 8
Life at The Top

Arriving home after two years absence, one can't help noticing details that have been part of the pattern of life before and, therefore, unremarkable. I remember being amazed by my mother's strong country accent—West Surrey bordering on Hampshire.

Both she and my father seemed quiet and deferential at first whereas I was confident, with a deep tan and an alien twang to my words; 'Africa' had become 'Efrica'. It took me a while to tone down and fit in with family life again.

My father had made a good recovery and, with his usual grit and determination, was getting about, even driving again. We enjoyed some wonderful days out with my mother and my sister, Louise, visiting Salisbury, the coast, friends with new babies. Louise had received her 'A' Level results and was set to go off to college, so it would be all change again at home within a few weeks.

Mr Scott wrote early in September, anxious that I had booked my return flight. "The planes seem to be well filled at this time of year," he warned. He concluded by asking me to buy him two sets of the 'Battle of Britain' stamps which the post office had recently issued.

In September 1965, I flew to Dar es Salaam via Paris where I would have missed the connection if a kindly Air France steward hadn't driven me out to the plane, a Trident with its back door just about to close. As we came in to land at Dar es Salaam and I saw the red tracks and scrub of the plains, I knew I had done the right thing in returning.

It was the first time that just looking at the sun-baked countryside, so different from the green of Surrey, brought a lump to my throat. For many years to come, a long time after I'd left Tanzania, pictures of and films about East Africa never failed to move me to tears. The sounds of the bush, the smell of wood smoke and the distant noises of people living close to the earth were not easy to forget.

After such a rush at Paris, it was small wonder that my luggage went missing when we landed at Dar es Salaam. As a last resort, I was allowed to climb up into the baggage hold to make a final search but it was impossible to find my bag in the scrum of cases.

The plane flew on to Madagascar and returned to London before the missing item was found and returned to my parents. They had to write a detailed list of its contents in French for Air France before it could start the journey all over again.

In headmasterly fashion, Mr Scott had included a list of the children I was to escort up to school from Dar es Salaam the day after my flight. They included two ginger-haired American brothers, several Italians, the sons of a West African diplomat, some Greek children with long names, the clever daughter of a politician in Zimbabwe, and the two Weiss boys whose father was stateless at that time. There were seven new pupils amongst the 14 boys and 21 girls to look after on the eight-hour coach journey, on a dirt road with no restaurants or toilets en route.

Parents arrived with their children at 7.30 a.m. and settled them into their seats in the bus, a big, built-to-last machine with no refinements like air conditioning, seat belts or interior trim such as one would expect these days for a far less strenuous expedition. Everyone brought an ample supply of carefully wrapped sandwiches, cake, fruit and bottles of drink.

There were no handy snacks in plastic bags to dip into or cans of Coke to keep cold in an ice box, even if we'd had one. Some children had already travelled very long distances off sisal estates up-country or from tea-growing areas in the South and must have been tired before we started.

However, there was never any fuss. They were mostly self-contained children used to amusing themselves with the minimum of equipment on such long journeys. This ability was to stand them in good stead on another journey that didn't go quite as smoothly as that one on Thursday, 16 September 1965.

The bus always received a noisy welcome when it pulled up outside school. Whilst matron and men whisked children and trunks to dormitories and awaiting friends, I went up to the Top House to sort out my new accommodation, a much roomier flat vacated by Sylvia when she left earlier in the year.

I was to occupy one corner of the bungalow, with bedroom windows looking down the steep drive and a view out to the Vuga Mountains at the front. I had two rooms separated by hand-built wooden cupboards and bookshelves.

The backs of the wardrobes in the bedroom faced into the sitting room, giving it a panelled look. There was a big fireplace with a wide mantelpiece that encircled the chimney breast where log fires were to cheer many cold evenings.

A side door, one of two in the sitting room, opened onto the veranda, which had steps down to the front garden. The other door led into a small hallway off which opened the bathroom, a wide communal dining room, and the flat next door, which had been Mrs Bajira's home until she returned to England. Fiona, a new recruit to take the place of David, who'd also returned to the UK, was to be my neighbour.

Fiona was another Scot, a tall, refined young woman from Argyllshire. Her dark hair made her pale skin look too delicate for the African sun and her cultured accent was without a trace of her northern origins. At first, she seemed rather aloof and serious but that was until you noticed the hint of mischief in her large, grey eyes.

Although she remained a rather private person and never discussed intimate details, as some women do, Fiona was to become a wonderful friend who would teach me some of the niceties of life. She was an accomplished horsewoman and certainly no weakling, having been educated at Gordonstoun, so she told me, when her mother was a teacher there. Fiona brought a certain 'class' to a household that had a year earlier rocked to the sound of the Beatles and rude rugby songs.

The married couple's flat where Ben and Rosia had lived, on the opposite side of the bungalow, also had new inmates, Mr and Mrs Peterson. In his letter to me, Mr Scott had written that the couple had had 'an interesting journey' travelling overland in their decrepit van.

After radiator trouble in Algiers and no-entry visa for Libya, they had managed to get on a Danish boat from Port Sfarx to Egypt in time to embark on a Scandinavian boat to Mombasa. Then, after some string pulling in Dar es Salaam, Mr Scott had got them Tanzanian permits on September 2 and, with these, the Kenyan authorities allowed them to come from Mombasa to Tanga by road!

As they were on a cargo boat, there was no guarantee when they might tie up at Mombasa and make the road journey, so Mr Scott had to make several trips to

Tanga before he could be sure of meeting his new teachers. The pattern of problems was to continue. Mr Scott had no idea what he'd let himself in for when he took on the Petersons, but it soon became clear as we got to know them.

The trouble was that Mr Peterson had a mission. It seemed as if he wanted to liberate the Africans from their white masters and make them stand up for their rights. First, he went into Lushoto and tried to alert the local people to their oppression, as he perceived it, then later he went in for rallying speeches. I'm not sure how the TANU representative responded to all this but Peterson, a tall, blond Dane, cut quite a dash in the marketplace, although he was soon to earn the name of Apollo for his posturing and preaching. He had a weakness for health regimes and open-toed sandals. The Europeans in the township regarded him as an eccentric curiosity but the local Washamba laughed at him behind his back, so I was told. They were much too sensible and stable to waste their time listening to such an upstart.

At school, Peterson taught geography on a few occasions but goodness knows how he was allowed to get away with his Marxist slant on the subject. He certainly stirred up his class with his rousing ideas and they responded with equal vigour. His ideals stretched to the sports field where he introduced pole vaulting, javelin and cross country running, but he had as little success with that as he had with football coaching. The match that he refereed between our boys and some boys from the village, not surprisingly, ended in a 10-0 victory for the barefooted African children.

Mrs Peterson was quite the opposite. Quiet and gentle, she never seemed to enjoy good health and found the walk from school to the Top House exhausting. Although only a little older than Fiona and me, she rarely opened up or confided in us, even when she discovered she was pregnant shortly after her arrival in Lushoto. We felt sorry for her having to work full time whilst her husband occupied himself with semi-political matters. When their twins were born, Peterson, in his usual high-handed manner, insisted that they should be laid naked on a blanket in the sun. When challenged by everyone, he explained "Sunbathing is healthy, especially in the nude." The two little red bodies survived and, before they were much older, about a year later when the Petersons left Lushoto, were subjected to the rigours of an overland journey back to Europe in the same van that had given problems to their parents on their outward safari.

Fiona and I ate breakfast with the Petersons in our shared dining room. The view out over the veranda across our wild, sloping front lawn and away to the distant hills was very beautiful. The table was laid every morning by the 'boys': slices of pawpaw with a wedge of lemon or lime, something cooked such as bacon and tomatoes or scrambled eggs and plenty of toast and marmalade.

Tea was made in our little kitchen but the rest had to be carried from school on a covered tray because, to begin with, we didn't have a fridge, only an old-fashioned safe, a cupboard with metal gauze instead of wood on the sides and door to let in the air and keep out the flies.

Whereas my two dogs kept out of the dining room, my cats—Tonki in particular—fancied that the breakfast table had been laid for her. If the doors were left open, she considered it her right to have the first pickings. "Bloody cats! They've been on the table again," Mr Peterson's voice would echo round the room.

I could hear him through the walls as I was getting myself together next door. The morning greeting of, "Your blotty cats should be—!" uttered by the tall Dane was quite bracing really. Of course, I tut-tutted and spoke sternly to Tonki but, well, cats will be cats and her bush craft benefited from the challenge of an occasional theft of butter.

There wasn't always time to exchange views at breakfast but, on one memorable occasion, Fiona became embroiled in a political argument with Apollo. It must have been entertaining for Saidi and Mohammed, listening from the safety of the kitchen as the Marxist and the Capitalist battled for the moral high ground.

Voices rose, the contenders rose and a cup of tea that Fiona was holding rose, its contents preparing to be dashed against the Dane's jutting jaw, but the storm ended there. School awaited and the walk down the steep path, through trees and heavy undergrowth where snakes lurked and sometimes rustled across the track at the sound of our footsteps, usually put Fiona and me in a good mood.

The path continued on up past our house and into a plantation of wattle trees. Beyond that was the forest. Women passed each afternoon on their way home carrying cloth-covered bundles or sometimes, a single heavy pole of wood on their heads. It was weird to be sitting in my room and see a small tree travelling horizontally past the window.

Often, there was a baby asleep on the mother's back supported by mum's bright kanga. With total disregard for safety, she might be balancing a panga on her head, the blade inches above the infant's skull. If the side door onto the veranda was open, Penny and Tim would leap up from their slumbers and race down the front steps as fast as their short, dachshund legs would carry them and give chase. I didn't like them doing that and called them back, but no one was ever hurt. Word got around that it was not good to linger along the path in front of Top House.

Some time after moving to my new accommodation, I noticed that every evening at sunset, a flock of bats flew over the garden and disappeared into the valley. They were a spectacular sight silhouetted against two palm trees at the end of the lawn. A crescent moon sometimes completed the picture. As they were such big creatures, I thought they might be fruit bats and decided I should be able to track them down. So, one hot afternoon, I took the dogs for a walk up the trail past our house, through the wattle plantation and into the forest. It was a place of tall slender trees, trailing lianas and butterflies floating between shafts of sunlight. With a sense of déja vu, I realised here was the scene I had painted in an Art lesson at school some ten years before, but this time I was the girl standing in the clearing. A strange experience! The discovery of the fruit bat tree was just as extraordinary. The noise made by dozens of agitated flapping wings, as the bats hung their brown furry bodies from every available branch, made it impossible to miss the roost. I stood and watched the creatures jostle for position and decided to go no nearer.

Trees in the school grounds and surrounding hills always provided a green canopy; leaf fall was imperceptible. There was no autumn. I was surprised to feel a nostalgia for those misty English mornings in mid-September which burn off into golden afternoons with a final burst of warmth, colour and a decadent smell of late blooms and decaying leaves. In Lushoto, seasons were marked by different flowers, brilliant tropical blossoms which always amazed me with their vigour and colour; the orange and shocking pink of the bougainvillaea, white trumpeted moonflowers by the river and, at the end of the year, the azure blooms of the jacaranda trees. Migrating butterflies, resting on a ten feet tall poinsettia bush in our garden, turned the scarlet bracts to white with their wings.

There were wild flowers too which flourished after the rains; balsam and flame lilies were spotted on nature walks when we went to check on the weaver bird colony. But it was difficult to identify many plants, or come to that, birds, because there were so few reference books available.

When there was fruit on the trees behind the Top House, black and white hornbills came and with their great clumsy looking beaks daintily selected the juiciest berries, until disturbed by troops of visiting monkeys.

I agree with the words of a certain former senior Rural Education Officer in Western Region Nigeria, G F Thistleton, in an introduction to his book on African birds, that natural history is 'not a subject that can be taught satisfactorily merely using a text book; numerous specimens, pictures and cuttings are all needed to make this part of the curriculum a living thing'.

There were no relevant text books at Lushoto Prep School, but there were plenty of specimens to observe and classify. The nature table in Class 3 might have received a very black mark from OFSTED officials, if any had been around then, but the dozens of matchboxes and empty king-size cigarette packets contained an exciting hoard of natural treasures collected by children as they moved about the school and its environs.

Most of the specimens were dead, but there was one indignant long-horned beetle that resented having its red and black body cramped up inside a cardboard cell. The noise of its crunching was difficult to locate at first, until a child noticed the Rex box moving as the beetle freed one of its long antennae.

Ink and Oink, my two guinea pigs, given to me by Anita, the daughter of a local tea estate owner, lived in a hutch at the back of the classroom, whilst Penny and Tim occupied the two lower shelves of a bookcase at the front. So there was no shortage of pets to handle and write about.

The local carpenter had made me a wooden cage that gave easy access to the guinea pigs and made cleaning out as straightforward as possible, but keeping the rodents quiet was altogether more difficult. They would trundle through their bedding, sending out stalks and seeds, or set up a high-pitched squeaking that would end in an angry duet if not checked in time. Of course, they were adored, and of course, they produced babies.

It was fortunate that Fiona liked animals and didn't mind sharing the bathroom with the cats. Tonki and Grey had discovered a unique 'safe house' for their kittens, the walled-in space beneath the bath. As the only entrance was through a small hole in the wall next to the lavatory pan, one might find oneself being scrutinised by feline eyes whilst sitting on the toilet.

We worried about the kittens drowning if they climbed onto the seat, but it was a waste of time trying to get them out from under the bath because they were always shoved back by mum. We just had to wait until they were weaned.

Another hidey hole turned out to be less of a creche than a death trap. I had heard a scratching noise coming from beside the fireplace. It seemed to be low down behind the skirting board. I thought it might be insects or vermin but couldn't understand how anything could have penetrated the space between the partition walls separating my flat and Fiona's.

To add to my consternation, Tonki had been acting strangely, yowling and roaming round the house, quite unlike her normal independent self. The mystery began to unfold when Saidi told me he had just seen Tonki going into the roof space and to 'come quick'.

She'd jumped off the brick boiler house at the back and entered under the roof's corrugated iron overhang. When I climbed up through the trap door above the hall, I found the anguished cat pacing the roof timbers. She could hear her offspring but couldn't find them.

Next to the flue and forming part of the wall was a hollow brick pillar, like a deep well shaft, which started at ground level and finished just above the ceiling of Fiona's flat. By the light of a torch, I could see what had been making the scrabbling noise, three kittens trying their hardest to climb the unclimbable walls of the shaft.

Tonki must have air lifted her babies into the roof, where they had gone exploring and tumbled down into the chasm. What was I to do? Nobody could get down there to rescue them; the shaft was too narrow and too deep. It was terrible to hear their desperate cries and to see their appealing upturned little faces.

It was their tiny claws, sharp from scratching the wall, that gave me an idea. "Bring me a kikapu and some string," I yelled. A soft basket made of palm leaves and a ball of wool were passed up. Having tied one end of the wool to the handles, I unwound the ball and gently lowered the basket down into the hole. It was like fishing.

Just as I'd hoped, one kitten stretched up its paws to investigate the object and clung on, its needle-like claws finding a purchase on the woven leaves. That was the moment to pull up the basket and, praying that the kitten wouldn't fall off, I lifted the kikapu over the wall at the top of the pillar and handed the baby to Fiona. All three kittens were thus rescued.

The strange aftermath was that, for several weeks, the kittens had to be kept in a deep box where they could adjust to their surroundings. They had developed long muscular back legs and, until their front legs had grown, they found it difficult to move about on all four limbs.

Chapter 9
A Blue Beetle

"We must have a car," Fiona concluded after we'd planned an exciting safari for the Christmas 1965 holidays. The trouble was, neither of us had enough money to purchase even a modest vehicle. So, to keep our minds off the problem, we busied ourselves in the kitchen, baking cakes for polite tea parties and I developed an interest in the garden, at least I planted some seeds.

Teachers from Magamba called in occasionally at weekends and the Forester family from Lushoto were marvellous about inviting us to their house for lunch. One Sunday, they treated us to wild duck, shot by Paul, and one of Sheila's delicious mulberry pies. Afterwards, we went out in the Land Rover with their three little girls, up through the forest to the end of the track, then a walk of several miles to the viewpoint on top of the world.

Day-to-day life in such a close community could be less than stimulating at times, especially when cold weather, rain and heavy mountain mists made the great outdoors so inhospitable. Then, we felt cut off and dispirited with only Radio Kenya to keep us in touch with the rest of the world. At such times, letters from home played a major role in keeping our spirits up.

Sometimes, when it was wet and cold, sickness and mysterious flu-like symptoms kept children and staff in bed, but only for a day or two. There was no malaria locally but we were supposed to take prophylactics, since we often went down to the plains. However, as I was never troubled by mosquito bites, I was foolhardy enough to allow the medication to lapse.

Two years previously, Sally and I had spent a night in an area notorious for black water fever, the dreaded mosquito borne missionary killer. We had been sitting in a car with windows wound down at a railway station on the plains, expecting to pick up Sally's husband, David, on his return from escort duty in Dar es Salaam. The train had broken down, so we'd had a long wait. Matrons at school were horrified at our stupidity and dosed us with the strongest and biggest tablets they could find in their medicine cabinets when we returned, but we were lucky. Anyway, I'm convinced that mosquitoes don't like my blood.

For much of the time, once school work was out of the way, Fiona and I sat planning our Christmas holiday. By the end of September, we already had an ambitious list of places we intended visiting: Ngorongoro, Lake Manyara, the Serengeti, Olduvai Gorge and Kilimanjaro. I'd heard that you didn't have to be an experienced climber to reach the snowy peak of Mount Kilimanjaro that we'd seen on trips to Moshi. "It's supposed to be like a hard walk rather than a climb," I wrote to my parents. For the whole trip, we would need to travel by bus and rail, then hire a car—14 shillings a day plus 1 shilling a mile for at least 200 miles, plus of course, petrol—so we knew it would be very expensive. However, how else could we get around without a car?

Half term at the end of October was spent at the Lutheran Mission, Tanga, where rooms were cheap. Bed linen and towels were extra and we had to buy our own food but we'd saved money on travel expenses because kindly parents had given Fiona and me a lift there and back. Returning after a humid, enervating few days on the coast, I was presented with two kittens by Tonki. They were both almost wild as she had raised them in the bundu for several weeks. That meant six animals to feed, as well as Christmas presents to buy and send home for the family. But my mood was soon to change.

Sunday, 14 November's letter to my parents began jubilantly, "What do you think! Fiona and I have bought a car, another Volkswagen." I went on to explain, "We first heard about it some weeks ago from Mrs Mountford, the friend of a certain Lady L who's leaving the country. Lady L has been quite a philanthropist hereabouts as her husband, after many years of hard work and scraping, made a fortune from sisal. He's dead but his wife has been good to dozens of people with gifts and help. She and her son are selling up everything and buying a property in Malta." It was rumoured that Lady L was the type of person who would suddenly decide over tea to swap her Rolls for a Mercedes.

My letter continued, "Now, Mrs Mountford found out that Lady L had had her car valued at £550 by the chief VW dealers in Tanga. That means they could sell it for £600+. Of course we said that it was out of the question for us to think of buying such an expensive car, although it's worth it because it's about one year old with only 11,000 miles on the clock—very good for out here—and has been driven only by Lady L and her driver. It also has many extras and isn't just the basic model with standard fittings."

Having put the idea of such a purchase out of our heads, we got down to the fine detail of costing our trip. To our amazement, out of the blue, came the message that Lady L wanted us to make her an offer, as she'd like us to have the car. She must have heard on the grapevine about our plans. So, we sat down and worked out how much we could afford but decided that it would be rude to offer her £350 for a £600 car.

The situation was saved by Mrs Scott. She said she'd like to help by having a share in it and anyway, she wanted to learn to drive so as to be able to go in and out of town independent of school transport. However, finally, having squeezed another £25 each out of our bank accounts, Fiona and I offered Lady L £400 which, to our utter astonishment, she accepted.

Payment was a trifle complicated. Mr Scott paid the 8,000 Tanzanian shillings (£400) into my local account so that I could write the cheque to pay Lady L. That meant that Fiona and I repaid Mr Scott but not in Tanzanian shillings.

At a time when it was impossible to get money out of the country, here was a golden opportunity to deal in pounds back in the UK. So, exploiting a loophole in the law, Fiona and I each transferred £200 from our banks at home to Mr Scott's account in London, a neat arrangement that enabled our headmaster to top up his funds in England.

The car was a beauty, pale blue with gleaming chrome bumpers and wheel hubs. We heard it coming up the hill below our house with that unmistakable VW Beetle noise, a throaty rumble as the lower gears powered it up the steep slope. We rushed down the steps as the driver brought it to a halt on the path, a dream come true. Lady L's generosity was to make an enormous difference to our lives.

Neither of us knew the first thing about engines, so the super deluxe toolkit was destined to remain in its circular case in the spare wheel. Worse still, we hadn't a clue how to change a wheel, should we ever have a puncture, but that didn't give us a moment's worry. We could drive and read a map, so East Africa was our oyster.

As Chloe had retired and gone to Spain earlier in the year, Fiona and I arranged the programme of Christmas carols and plays that brought the term to a close. It was a joy to have children able to sing in such a variety of languages and to lead into the hall a candlelight procession singing 'The First Nowell'. Outside, crickets and other night creatures set up their noisy accompaniment in the warm darkness.

The next day, parents who had been at school for the concert collected their offspring for the holidays, a bus left with the group of pupils for Dar es Salaam, and I escorted 13 children on their ten-hour train journey back to Moshi. Kilimanjaro came out from its clouds to greet us, and the children were beside themselves with happiness at the thought of Christmas at home.

Fiona met me off the train in Moshi. She had endured a bone-shaking journey by road from Lushoto to Moshi in the Beetle and was exhausted, so we decided to stay the night in the best hotel, the Livingstone.

Next morning, we were preparing to set off on our planned road trip, stopping first at Arusha to get out of the sweltering heat when Mrs Churcher, one of the parents, met us and invited us up to Mweka, an African Wildlife College on the slopes of Kilimanjaro where her husband taught.

The couple treated us to a trip out in their Land Rover, up to Bismark Hut, the first stop in those days on the trail to Kilimanjaro. The track was rough and stony and, in some places, we had to bail out and rebuild bridges. We were amazed at the size of the tree heathers and the giant plants, some towering way over our heads.

The Churchers were keen to know what preparations I had made for my proposed trip up Kilimanjaro and what I intended wearing on the 19,000 feet summit. I'd given some thought to the walk and had decided that lace-up shoes, a pair of old trousers, a sweater and a duffel coat seemed perfectly adequate to me.

For the lower and, I assumed, warmer slopes, I was going to pack a denim skirt and cotton blouse. I didn't think I'd need socks because the shoes, my mother's cast-offs, were lined with soft leather and, anyway, I hadn't worn socks for years.

Mrs Churcher insisted that I borrow a pair of warm trousers, a bush hat, mittens and tights, thick woollen ones, to add to my wardrobe, which I could tell didn't impress her. Black boots, something like old-fashioned canvass hockey boots, were also added to the equipment before we left.

The following evening, Fiona and I were tucked up under blue candlewick bedspreads in a log cabin, part of Ngorongoro Lodge above the famous Ngorongoro Crater. We had left Moshi for the 170-mile drive at 8.15 a.m., stopped at Arusha to cash cheques and fill up with petrol, and then promptly took the wrong road. Realising our mistake, we turned back and found the Dodoma Road, the last 50 miles of which were wonderful smooth tarmac. On either side, the grass grew tall and white-blonde, a pale sea stretching away as far as the distant mountains. Masai with their herds completed the dazzling scene. When we finally reached the famous crater, we sat down at the first viewpoint and read to each other from a book of extracts from Dr Bauman's Diary describing his discovery of Ngorongoro: 'At noon (18 March 1892) we suddenly found ourselves on the rim of a sheer cliff and looked down into the oblong bowl of Ngorongoro.' We were doing just that and felt like explorers ourselves.

At 8 the next morning, a group of us from the lodge were taken down into the crater by Land Rover. The road was hair-raisingly steep but sensibly only one way: down in the morning and up in the afternoon. The dizzying view was of a gigantic enclosed arena, a caldera measuring 10 miles from North to South and 12 miles from East to West, a floor area of 102 square miles completely isolated from the rest of the Ngorongoro Conservation Area and shut in by an unbroken wall of rock rising 2,000 feet in places. It was awesome. I was glad when we reached the bottom of the descent and could look up.

"Now we should see some animals," someone enthused, as the Land Rover engaged a different gear and returned to the horizontal, but we had to be content with donkeys, a most disappointing start. I had expected to see the place overrun with gnu, but we had to drive for miles before seeing only a few gazelles. However, the ancient volcano was just teasing. There were animals aplenty and our impatience was soon replaced by that feeling of wonder and fear that comes from observing wild creatures living in their natural habitat, completely independent of human beings. Our list at the end of the trip included Thompson and Grant's gazelle, ostrich, zebra, wildebeest, a rhino and baby, hunting dogs, hippos, hyenas—one about to have babies—eland, and of course cranes, sacred ibis and all those other species that today would set you reaching for your book of African birds.

Of all the creatures that we saw, the lions were the most exciting. Not having had much luck at first with our game spotting, we stopped to speak to the guide on another Land Rover to find out if he'd seen any big animals. Following his tip, we drove more slowly along the river bank hoping that the bushes might conceal a king or even a queen of beasts.

These days, wildlife films bring intimate pictures of big cats into our living rooms but, if such pictures had been the norm, even in black and white, over 50 years ago, they would not have prepared me for the experience of seeing, close up, the lions in Ngorongoro.

My diary recorded, "First, we saw two youngish ones, all yellow and brown, then we looked down into the clear amber eyes of the mother." We circled round and round, each time going deeper into a clump of bushes. On our last circuit, we glimpsed a dark maned lion moving off to the other side of the river, so we crossed the nearest ford and searched for him.

There he was, peering out from the shade. When he saw that it was only a Land Rover, he turned his eyes elsewhere and refused to look in our direction so that we could take his photograph. Finally, after we'd rudely thumped the roof and made cat calls, he strode off to his former spot. It seemed unfair to disturb him further! An ancient Masai who was filling his water gourds in the river nearby was quite unconcerned when our driver got out and warned him about the lions.

The hyenas, dirty, smelly, rough haired creatures, were much bigger than I'd imagined. Those we disturbed near the lake really stank! As if ashamed to be seen close to, they dragged themselves away across the white patches of salt, then sat on their haunches and stared. I was to come into closer contact with a hyena on a later occasion.

Speeding along on our way back, we frightened a jackal. It ran away from the Land Rover towards a gnu, which, in turn, lowered its horns and took up the chase with great energy for a few yards. All the while, dust poured in through the open top of our vehicle so, by the end of the day, arms and faces unprotected from the drying heat were burnt raw. We were glad to sit down in our seats for the ascent back up the track to the hotel. Then, after such a day, it was bliss to relax in a bath, have dinner and sink into bed.

Olduvai Gorge where six years previously, in 1959, Dr Mary Leakey had dug up the fossilised remains of a prehistoric man, was our destination when we set off in our VW at 8.15 a.m. on Sunday morning. It was another of those wonderful trips. The smooth rolling green hills reminded me of the South Downs in Surrey until we spied a solitary eland grazing near a group of zebras. Towards the Serengeti, the clumps of wild sisal with stiff pointed leaves, that give Olduvai its name, became dryer with every few miles and the road stonier.

Rounding a corner, we came upon four giraffes amongst the thorn trees. Actually, I saw only one at first but as he started his graceful rocking canter, he was followed by two more and a baby. They streamed out until they were a safe distance from us, then they stood on the skyline, looking back at us. We left them, bending their long necks, daintily picking the only tasty leaves to be found in that parched landscape.

From there onwards, the countryside was hills, acacia trees, dust and stones, a never-ending expanse. We passed the sign to Seronera and I wished that we could have been going there too, but it wasn't to be until the following year that Fiona and I would venture out onto the Serengeti in our, by then, hammered Beetle. So, we followed the main but very rough road, too stony really for a saloon car, even a VW. Avoiding the aptly named Shifting Sands, because some Americans had warned us 'if you break down there, no one will find you,' we carried on to the old airstrip, and from there, roared across the sandy countryside towards the gorge.

Arriving at Olduvai, a bright yellow straw hut caught our attention. Here we had to sign in and pick up the guide, a Kenyan who spoke good English. "I worked in Nairobi, in the National Museum, before I came here," he explained. "We'll start by looking at some of the things that have been found recently in various digs here." We followed him to another big airy hut to look at pictures of the finds, bones and tools. There is something sensuous and satisfying about the feel of an ancient stone tool that fits into the palm of your hand, ready for use, scraping flesh from animal skin. Perhaps, it was some prehistoric energy, transmitted from a more leathery palm than mine into the round stone, that travelled up my arm and into my brain awakening some long-lost sense. Whatever it was, throughout our tour, I had the strange feeling that the dried out water course at Olduvai was crowded with unseen people who had lived there for millions of years.

From the second hut, we stepped out into the heat. The coloured layers of rock on either bank of the ancient gorge reminded me of the landscape in a Mantegna painting I had seen some years before. Rising from the flat ground between the two banks were two eroding towers of red soil, which stood out from the surrounding grey volcanic debris like strange terracotta edifices. We crossed the stony river bed and walked along the opposite bank. Suddenly, the guide stopped and pointed. "Rhino," he whispered, indicating tracks on the path. "They're fresh." It was scaring to think that we might come upon the animal itself round the next bend, so we were thankful for the shade and relative safety of the third hut, where we found more bones and tools.

Round about, there were digs where workers had been trying to follow the lines of bones in the soil. Here you could see the join between the volcanic material and the ancient river bottom. "We gently scratch about on the lava until we uncover bones. Then, we carefully pull away the surrounding material and dig down another section till we reach the line," our guide explained. "The gorge is 12 miles long, so there are plenty of places to dig."

At the second archaeological site, our guide pointed out a prehistoric living place, complete with water-smoothed stones, rounded quartz hammers and the bones of giant animals. Nearby, were the tins and equipment being used by people excavating a large hole, the sides of which were held up with sacks filled with earth.

"We dig up all sorts of tiny pieces of bone," our guide said as we handled some of the finds. "Everything has to be washed and sent up to Nairobi to Dr Leakey. She and her husband are very good at piecing them together." As we moved from one site to another, we disturbed grazing gazelle and dik-dik. "We see all kinds of animals down here," our guide remarked. "Many poisonous snakes too," he added, making us feel even more apprehensive about continuing our tour.

Finally, we made our way to the place where Dr Mary Leakey had unearthed the skull of Zinjanthropus, Nutcracker Man, six years previously. The site was marked by a concrete slab at the foot of a wall of earth showing the different layers revealed by digging.

As at all the other sites, this also had an oppressive atmosphere. The heat was quite intense, the volcanic rocks, hard and cruel. (Was someone watching us from behind a boulder?) It was easy to imagine primitive people living there before the gorge had been formed one and three quarter million years ago.

Back at Ngorongoro, the lodge was full, having been taken over by a convention of travel agents, a rum collection of Africans, Indians and Germanic Europeans, plus one very loud woman, obviously a high-powered secretary.

"I bet she'd never put the wrong person on the wrong plane!" Fiona quipped. The manageress of the hotel appeared, a gaunt woman in a long straight dress, and crisply brought calm to the foyer, already noisy with the raised voices of a large party of Americans. They had seen herds of elephants and some forty lions in the crater and wanted everyone to know.

The next morning, we awoke to mist and heavy cloud. Having argued and come to no conclusion about where we should go, we posted Christmas cards, filled up with petrol, and set off along the road round the crater. Soon, we found ourselves sandwiched between two Land Rovers on a narrow forestry trail, wheel deep with elephant dung.

There was no way that we could turn round should we meet the herd. However, we saw no animals all morning, just beautiful views when the mist lifted. By lunchtime, we had had enough of Ngorongoro so, after studying the map, we decided to take the road to Manyara, to the hotel built high up on the side of the Rift Valley, above the game park.

"When I get married, I'd like to have my honeymoon here," Fiona remarked dreamily. She was sitting in the bath looking out of the window at a vast verdant expanse of forest, grassland and marsh spreading from the foot of the Rift wall to the shores of Lake Manyara.

However, after a terrifying thunderstorm that night with the noise of trumpeting elephants adding to the din of wind and rain and tossing trees, Fiona changed her mind about her honeymoon venue. She pointed out, "You couldn't relax if you were worrying about the hotel being struck by lightning or swept over the edge."

For half a century, Manyara had been one of the most popular hunting grounds in East Africa. In 1957, the 123 square miles were made into a Game Reserve and three years later 'elevated', an apt word as it is 3,150 feet above sea level, to National Park status. An official leaflet on how to see the game promised that 'during a single visit, you should be able to see at least three of the "Big Five".' Tourists were advised 'much of the game in the park is becoming increasingly confident'—animals had been protected from poachers for less than ten years, 'but be quiet and don't gesticulate, you will only worsen your chance of photography.' A morning recce in our car gave us a preview of the spectacular bird life on the lake: a shimmering pink line of flamingos as well as spoonbills, ibises, waders and ducks.

After lunch, we returned with a guide in the back seat who directed us to the elephants' mud bath. A mother and baby were really enjoying themselves when we drove up. Not surprisingly, the mother let out a great bellow. Poor Fiona who was driving didn't know whether to go into reverse or straight ahead. "She's only saying, 'Jambo' ("Hello")," our guide maintained.

Round a corner, we came upon an enormous group of buffalo, rank upon rank of them at a water hole, looking as if they were lined up for a Victorian family portrait. I was petrified. After we'd photographed them, the guide commanded, "Drive on through them. They're blocking the road."

Fiona gritted her teeth and accelerated. Amazingly, the animals kicked up their heels and fled into the bush on either side. Later, near the lake shore, we came upon the buffalo returning from their evening dip.

"This time," I confided to my diary, "I wasn't frightened and so could observe how they came forward, not with ferocity but with curiosity." I'm not sure that my interpretation of their behaviour was any more correct than Fiona's observation, "They're like cows."

To reach Maji Moto, the hot springs at the southern end of the park, we had to drive across the Endabash River. The guide assured us that our car could make it but the river, swollen by recent rains, looked quite wide and swift flowing, and the thick, brown water brought back horrid memories. I refused to cross, so we turned back and went to look at the sleepy pride of lions we'd seen snoozing under a tree. It was very hot. A storm was brewing, judging by the thick clouds massing over the lake.

Rain made the road down the mountains via Mbu Escarpment slippery when we left Manyara next morning. It was my turn to drive but as there weren't any edges to go over, I wasn't too scared of the journey ahead. After lunch, eaten in a field during a dry spell, we went on to Arusha.

The rain seemed to be following us, so we thought it would be a good time to go out to Tengeru, near Lake Duluti, East of Arusha, with our letter of introduction, written by a friend, to a Mrs Hall at the Agricultural Research Station there. We hoped that she'd at least give us a cup of coffee, perhaps, even a room for the night.

The 72-strong staff of Europeans on the research station was developing a community training course which aimed to introduce basic innovations in food consumption to the locals. There was an egg eating project, which was working well, and a scheme to boost meat and milk consumption. This was proving difficult at a time when Tanzania no longer augmented its limited supplies with imported milk from Kenya.

It was hoped that an improved diet would strengthen the nation's workforce. The institute's vast area of operation stretched from Tanga on the coast to Mwanza on Lake Victoria, so many field officers were employed. However, the officers had no real power; they could merely advise. It was up to the government ministers to implement the technicians' good ideas, which weren't always popular.

Mrs Hall was in bed when we arrived at the research station, but her husband, a dour Scot soon woke her up and she kindly read our letter. She promptly phoned Robert Hughes, a teacher whom we'd already met at Moshi, and arranged for him to show us round the Research Station college the following day.

After tea with the Halls, our plans fell apart. I suppose we had been so used to people offering us accommodation, it came as a shock to discover there was nowhere to stay for the night at Tengeru. Even the local hotel was full, so there was nothing for it but to drive another 40 miles to Moshi and book into Browns, a second-rate hotel.

The food, after Manyara's four-star meals, was almost inedible and even the TV, a great luxury in those days, was a disappointment. The reception was so bad that, rather than sit in front of a fuzzy black and white screen in a smoky lounge, we went to bed early.

All day, Fiona had been worried about the news that Tanzania had broken off diplomatic relations with Britain. An ultimatum had been issued by the OAU calling on Britain to get tough with Rhodesia. There had been no response and the ultimatum date had expired, so Harold Wilson found himself on the eve of his speech to the UN General Assembly with diplomatic relations with Tanzania severed. But at midnight, when I heard some people leave noisily in their car, it was my turn to lie awake wondering if anything nasty would happen. Despite all her worries, Fiona was the first to fall asleep on what turned out to be a very peaceful night.

"Saturday would be the best time to visit the college," Robert advised us over the phone the following day. It was Thursday. Two more nights at our crummy hotel would be unbearable so we left Moshi and headed over the border into Kenya for Tsavo National Park. The wet roads were reminiscent of that near-fatal journey of Easter 1964. However, December's relatively benign rain is unlike the big rains in April. We stopped on the bridge and leant against the concrete parapet where my car had been launched into the whirling flood waters.

Below, we could see only peaceful boulder-strewn banks covered with lush vegetation sloping down to a dry river bed. Nevertheless, I now knew that heavy rains on the nearby slopes of Kilimanjaro could soon change all that. I thought how lucky I was to have survived and to be standing there telling Fiona the tale of the flash flood and the floating beetle.

Chapter 10
A Mountain to Climb

Tsavo National Park in Kenya is over 20,000 square kilometres of semi-arid woodland country, divided into West Tsavo National Park and the slightly larger East Tsavo National Park, and it straddles the Nairobi-Mombasa Road. We headed for Kitani in West Tsavo where we hoped to hire a banda for the night. To our dismay, the African warden turned us away; no booking, no banda. We were absolutely downcast until another visitor, a complete stranger to us, who had arrived in a VW crowded with tourists, went round the back and had a word with the warden. Just as we were leaving, he rushed out and said we could stay.

Our banda was a thatched-roofed, six-berth, mud brick house set down the path away from the other bandas. Outside was a stone fireplace so when the fire was lit for us by a boy, one of the warden's band of helpers, we could heat a debe (can) of water for a wash.

Later, he lit the lamps—we had two to read by—and let down the mosquito nets, which were essential with so many flying creatures about. Geckos had a rare time catching insects from the outside of the netting on the windows whilst the rather smelly resident bat hoovered up the insects inside. There were rustlings all night!

At sunset, we watched the impala and zebra wend their way towards the river, then three startled kongoni galloped down the track just as darkness fell. Earlier, while we had been having our soup on the veranda, a black animal with a humped back and long tail trotted past with its nose to the ground as if it were following an invisible railway line.

Next day we drove out to Poacher's Lookout and spoke to the African Ranger there, a very interesting man obviously keen on his job. He invited us to look through his telescope at the rhino and explained that there were no elephants because they had gone up into the mountains. It was too wet on the plains for them.

The Ranger's banda was at the foot of the hill. He told us, "I can't have my wife with me because I'm always on the move." She had to stay at home in the Tesla district. "She is allowed to visit me sometimes though. Once, she stayed in one of the Rangers' rest houses for three days."

Meanwhile, he was on watch for the month. It must have been a lonely existence. We imagined he must have had a radio in his hut, so he could contact HQ if he saw any poachers and summon up the Park Warden, who would go out in his plane with a group of armed men and arrest the offenders. It was difficult to see where the plane could land in such countryside but, later in the day, one came down on the tiny airstrip at Kitani.

Mzima Springs, one of the stopping off points in Tsavo, was noisy with the aquatic neighing of hippos looking like enormous Greek war-horses with their flared nostrils and bulging eyes. We stood in the hippo-viewing tower with an enthusiastic group of Americans.

One woman kept saying, "Get your cameras aimed in case one opens his mouth!" which we found amusing at first, thinking that she must be exhorting us to snap the open-mouthed gasps of the menfolk as they watched the cavorting animals in the water. But we decided to move off before we disgraced ourselves by giggling out loud.

In the fish viewing tank, there were more Americans. When we remarked that the sleek blue bodies of the tilapia looked positively gross when viewed through the glass walls, we were treated to a long pedantic explanation about the angle of refraction.

It had been hot and stuffy in the underground room and Fiona wasn't feeling too well by this time, so we returned to Kitani and asked if we could stay a second night. The warden confirmed it having radioed Nairobi and said we could have No. 1 banda, which had a bath, hot and cold water, separate kitchen and cushioned chairs; the Ritz after our previous night's accommodation.

At sunset, after we'd eaten up all our oddments of dried fruit, tomatoes and biscuits, Fiona went to bed. I tried to write at the table on the veranda with one lamp in front of me and two hanging up, but it became impossible.

I felt alive with insects; in my hair, down my nighty, on my bare feet and legs and on the page of my book. When I stood up to brush dozens off the table,

I crushed scores underfoot. In the end, I gave up and went to bed too. At least I'd kept them out of the bedroom and we had only the smell of bats to contend with.

Fiona was feeling much better when we got up at six. Dawn in the bush is a time not to be missed, when every sound, smell and colour has a sharpness and freshness to it, as if everything has just been created anew. We were off by seven and saw more game than we'd seen on Thursday and Friday: impala, kongoni, giraffe, water buck and enormous marabou storks with powerful beaks and blue jackets—we came upon some three dozen of the birds crowded over the road. When they heard the sound of our Beetle, they heaved themselves up and flapped down on the grass on either side—like men landing with parachutes—to resume the grave business of jabbing for insects in the ground. Further along, there were elephants busy powdering themselves with Tsavo-red dust, a whole herd of eland charging across the road at top speed and an obliging hartebeest that allowed itself to be photographed before scampering off.

Back in Moshi, our first priority was to go to the bank to cash cheques in order to buy some Christmas presents. Some we took to the African Wildlife College at Mweka where the Churcher's ayah, happy as ever, was waiting for us. After lunch and a freshen up, we went out to Tengeru to shake up Robert Hughes.

Robert must have quaked at the thought of having to entertain two nosy women. He looked quite haggard when we arrived, but he made tea and gave us some cake before taking us round to the Research Station. The well-fed, approachable domestic animals—pigs, cows, sheep, chicken and rabbits—were in sharp contrast to the wild animals of the nearby bush. "It's amazing what could be achieved," Robert confided, "if only farms were well run. Just look at the crops, too. There's no end to what can be done out here. We have a big community, a good research centre and training schools run by keen officers. Now it's up to the farmers. They hold the country's future in their hands." By the end of our visit, Robert was keen to show us every aspect of a project that was obviously more than just his everyday work. As I drove away from Tengeru, I nearly killed one of Robert's precious calves. Surprisingly, it was loose on the road and difficult to identify from a distance. The animal ran straight towards us and, despite the fact that I braked hard, it chipped the front wing of the car with its hoof. Fortunately, I hadn't swerved to avoid impact or more damage might have been done to beast and machine. It was a sobering lesson in the meaning of braking distance.

Up to this point, our holiday plans had been somewhat sketchy, more a tick list of places to explore and people to visit en route rather than a fixed itinerary with pre-booked accommodation. Decisions about whether to stay or move on were made on a daily basis according to the weather and or how we felt when we got up. The only firm date in our holiday was Saturday, 18 of December when I needed to be at Marangu Hotel on the eve of a five-day hike up Mount Kilimanjaro, nowadays affectionately known as 'Kili'.

Marangu was a good startling point for the climb to the 19,000 feet summit, as the hotel was built on the lower slopes of the mountain. You could walk out of the gates and immediately get into your stride up the trail, confident that the management—well experienced in organising trips up Kili—had engaged a knowledgeable guide and equipped the porters with appropriate quantities of food and bedding to ensure your comfort for the next few days.

For someone like me, whose only experience of ascending a mountain was by cable car, the organised safari from Marangu was, and probably still is, the best way of attempting such a trek. However, the cost must have been considerably less than it is today or I should not have been able to have afforded to book my place in the group leaving on Sunday, 19 December 1965.

The hotel manageress, Mrs Bridges, a shrewd Scotswoman with a love of gossip and fun, was a friend of ours. She enlivened many Lushoto parties. Now, it was her turn to invite us to sit at her table for dinner, the rest of the tables in the dining room having been taken by a large party of tiny Japanese men.

In the bar, we heard a newly-down party of climbers talking about being sick in the snow and the only woman in the group hobbled out on her husband's arm. Suddenly, what I was about to attempt so light heartedly sounded very alarming. However, it was too late to ask all those questions that I should have asked months before. One thing was clear, it was not going to be a walk in the park.

Fiona had decided to accept the hospitality of the Churcher's for the next few days while I was away up the mountain. She left immediately after dinner as she was a little apprehensive about returning to Mweka in the dark by herself, so it was an early bedtime for me with long hours to worry about how I would get up to the mountain top that I'd seen only from the sun-bleached plains below.

Sleep was shattered in the small hours of Sunday morning by the arrival of a rackety car without a silencer. Doors banging and men's voices, raised and tetchy after a long drive, put paid to the prospects of a peaceful few hours before dawn.

Unbeknown to me, my climbing partners had arrived: three young Irishmen from a seminary at Sikonge in the south of Tanzania, and a maths teacher from England. It must have appealed to Mrs Bridge's wicked sense of humour to arrange for me to be the only female in the group. She knew all about my shy, prim and proper image.

Ten o'clock on Sunday morning and I was still waiting for the men to sort out their clothes. What a time they took, each minute making me itchier and itchier about the trip. At 11.15 a.m., we set off wearing bush hats and clutching walking sticks—four-foot long, wooden poles decorated with dark brown Chagga poker work and tipped with a metal sheath. The sticks were a gift from the hotel.

Porters carried our bed rolls and clothes and food, in bundles on their heads, leaving us the luxury of walking up the stony road towards the lower slopes unhindered by baggage. We followed the guide, a tall, handsome African who had done it all before and knew how ill-prepared and sometimes unfit his charges could be. It rained, so our first test was to eat our picnic lunch sitting in the wet.

It would have been a dismal start to a five-day trek without the company of Nial, Paddy, Patrick and Stephen. By the time we reached Bismark, the first hut, their jokes, gentle teasing and just the sound of the three Irishmen's banter had me smiling and less stand-offish than I had been at the outset.

Our route had taken us along the road previewed for me by the Churchers on our Land Rover outing, then upwards through thick rainforest climbing to a height of 9,000 feet. The walk took about four hours, so we were glad to sit down on the veranda of the rustic accommodation that we had to ourselves that night.

When Nial saw me writing my diary for Day One, he looked over my shoulder, read what I had written, and asked if he could add a footnote. "You're quite correct about the time it took to get the men's clothes ready," he wrote. "We were so excited at the thought of being accompanied by a shapely and very pretty girl, that we didn't know our socks from our hats, signed one of the men."

Such wicked flattery!

Day Two, Monday, 20 December, we left Bismark at 8.30 a.m. Following the guide, I first walked uphill over trails made firm by the gnarled roots of trees, then through a belt of giant heathland plants. Half an hour or so later, we came to a clearing and stopped.

Before us were the two peaks, Mwenzi to our right and Kibo to our left. Smooth snow coated the rounded top of Kibo, rivulets of snow on craggy

Mwenzi. It was a truly awe-inspiring view. For the first time, I realised what I was about. From being just 'something to do for a few days before Christmas', a casual but long walk up a mountainside, it had suddenly become a serious challenge, and something quite outside my experience.

We moved on across the moorland along a path that had been worn deep into the dark soil by the many climbers who had followed the route up and down the mountain. The four men trailed behind, taking photographs, so I had no one to talk to until Nial caught up with me.

Soon, the mist began to blow across the hillside and I was glad of the loan of his anorak. I didn't care if he had an ulterior motive for lending it to me. It was just such a pleasant relief to have someone to talk to as the climb got tougher.

So we continued, plodding upwards, breathing heavily and trying to get a conversation going. Up hills, down slopes, over rocks, pebbles and mud, across soft earth and yellowish green grass we went, pausing only to take close-up pictures of flowers, for a drink from a stream fed by melting snow, or for a brief rest on a boulder.

I began to think we'd never get to the next hut. "Cheer up!" encouraged my companion. "Even if it's not over this ridge, it's bound to be over the next one." He took my hand and together we struggled from the bottom of yet another steep incline.

Eventually, in the distance, we spied our goal, Peters, which consisted of two huts and two gleaming, new choos, long drop toilets housed in tiny corrugated sheds that glistened in the bright cold sunshine. We ran downhill, up a short slope and into the nearest hut to bag our bunks. Nial demanded a kiss so I happily complied.

Ten minutes later, the rest of the group arrived weary, hungry and chilled to the bone after a long slog to their 12,000 feet destination. Coffee, made by the porter who had come on ahead, was like nectar. We stood in the space between the bunks, drinking and eating sandwiches until our bed rolls were laid out.

That completed, I reluctantly went outside to wash in the icy water of the stream that ran down the gully behind the hut, just a quick wash of my face and sweaty parts without exposing too much flesh to the rapidly cooling night air.

Gentlemen-like, the men stood outside the hut in the freezing darkness whilst inside I changed, climbed up to the top bunk and burrowed down into the blankets. Of course there was no electricity on the mountain. Porters had to carry lanterns and cooking stoves up from the hotel and fuel was used sparingly. The warmest place was bed.

"Kibo Hut tomorrow, then the top," someone muttered from a lower bunk.

"I wonder how far that manic German got on his bike?" queried someone else.

"We'll probably meet him on his way down. What about that group of Americans? Some of the girls looked a bit cold."

"What d'you expect, wearing sandals and not much else!" With that image to conjure up, I expect the male majority in the hut must have had pleasant dreams.

Surprisingly, it wasn't too cold when we left the hut to walk the final upward stage on day three, Tuesday, 21 December. Again, we had a marvellous view of Mwenzi and Kibo, which looked for all the world as if they were painted on the skyline and that all we'd have to do to reach them would be to go over the next hill. But it wasn't that easy. To begin with, we had a steep climb up and around a number of escarpments, Mwenzi all the time on the right. The ground in places looked as if it had been freshly turned but after a while, you could see the line where the concentration of grass ended. The plants now consisted of tiny yellow daisies and what looked to me like an Alpine cactus.

After several hours, we reached the saddle, a massive expanse of desert-like territory between the two peaks. Here, there were boulders strewn over the yellow-brown volcanic soil. Bright orange lichen highlighted some of the stones, whilst the sparse grass looked burnt, presumably by frost. Much of the path up the climb was still covered with ice crystals despite the shimmer of a heat haze that rose off the ground in front of us.

It was a perfect day for walking across the saddle; blue sky down to the horizon on our right and Kibo with its bright cap of snow in front. However, although very warm, there was a keen wind that made me shiver, and Nial insisted that I wear his jacket again as mine was packed away in my bed roll. Sometime later, we came upon the American group, which had left earlier from the second of the two huts at Peters. They were sunbathing, stretched out on the dirt, so we too stopped for a rest and a chat before continuing on our way.

It was a pleasant walk until we reached the last slopes up towards Kibo Hut, which had been in sight for some seven miles across the saddle. Paddy arrived an hour before us, and Patrick and Stephen came heavy footedly an hour after us. It was still comfortably warm in the sun, but snow—hard-packed stuff—lay in the shadow of the hut, which a group was just vacating. They had rested there after their ascent and were just beginning their return journey.

We went to bed early with the prospect of breakfast at 1.30 a.m. With my usual enthusiasm for food, I enjoyed the hot chicken stew for supper prepared for us by Mpisha, the assistant guide, before going to bed, but the men picked at theirs as we sat in the shadows beneath the bunks.

I can't honestly recall that we knew anything about the effects of altitude, how it can sap your energy, leaving you sick and unable to sleep. I suppose I had a slight advantage over the others because I had lived and worked in a mountainous area, 4,000 to 6,000 feet high. But that altitude was a mere hill compared with the mighty 19,000 feet of Kilimanjaro.

Patrick and Paddy were both ill during the night, so when Mpisha brought food in the early hours of Wednesday 22, Day Four, Patrick stayed in bed, too weak to get up. What a pantomime it was, seeing the others, Nial, Paddy and Stephen dress! We all put on our warmest clothes; for me, trousers over woolly tights, a blouse and sweater, my navy duffel coat, bush hat, mittens and canvass boots.

Sunglasses were safely stowed in pockets. Armed with our individual walking poles, we set off with the guide at about 2 a.m. to grind our way up to the mountain top. The sky was bright with stars and an air of mystery hung over the whole venture as we walked in single file up the frozen scree, following a lantern in the dark.

It wasn't too steep at first so we walked a good distance before stopping to rest. Later, the stops became more frequent as the gradient increased so at the cave which is half way up, we had a really long rest. After that, Paddy became increasingly sick, and finally, he had to abandon his attempt to get to the top. He reluctantly returned to the hut with the assistant guide who had been following us.

The scree became much steeper and Stephen began his special breathing techniques to maximise his air intake. In the dark, I could hear him gasping. Now we were having to haul ourselves up giant sized steps, I found it challenging and inspiring to follow the tall confident man in front, our guide.

By the light of the dawn, we could see how far we had climbed up the crater wall. Soon, the three of us were standing on the lip of the ancient volcano. We were on top of the world, or so it seemed as we looked out from our snowy perch to see the sun rise over Mwenzi and the distant plains.

The amazing vision and the sensation of just standing there are still very strong memories. However, cold and fatigue soon made us shiver. We hastily wrote our names in the special record book kept in a metal box secured to the ground and considered what to do next.

Our guide returned from his inspection of the trail round the summit and decided that we should go no further because the snow was dangerously icy. All that remained for us to do was to photograph each other and then set about the descent.

By now, the sun had melted the ice binding the scree, so we found ourselves skiing rather than walking down ash-covered slopes towards the dot of a hut from where we had started. How we screamed and hooted with each death defying slide. It was very dusty and great fun.

I can't remember much about the rest of the day when we retraced our steps to Peters, the middle hut, nor about the next day, Thursday, 23 December, when we returned to Marangu Hotel. My diary writing lapsed. I have photos of myself wearing the customary hat band of pink everlasting flowers made for us by the guide, and group snaps taken outside a hut. Paddy and Patrick had recovered, Stephen's careful preparation had paid off, and Nial and I were happy to have had each other as walking companions.

We all enjoyed our achievement of having reached the top—or almost the top in the case of Paddy and Patrick—of the highest mountain on the continent. It wasn't until years later when having tea at a colleague's house that I realised how special the achievement was.

My friend and her family were high achievers, with a string of academic successes behind them, so when they asked me if I'd climbed Cader Idris in Wales, as they recently had, my answer in the negative made me feel quite inadequate until I remembered and offered, "But I have been to the top of Kilimanjaro." They were impressed and envious.

Fiona was waiting for me at Marangu Hotel. After all the promises to write had been declared, the goodbyes were said and the kissing was over, she whisked me off to our next venue, Momella Game Lodge in Arusha National Park, where we were to spend Christmas.

On arrival, we installed ourselves in our rondavel, sampled the spicy Christmas biscuits left for us by our host, and when it was dark, set out for the dining room in the main building. "Watch out for buffalo as you cross the lawn," we'd been warned. "Back off if you meet any."

The family who ran the Lodge were German so we were to have Christmas Dinner on Christmas Eve. At the table, there were several other guests, military men from a central European state, who stood to attention as Fiona and I took our seats, and then stiffly sat down themselves, as if not wanting to crease their uniforms.

The room was brightly lit and the windows open, as it was a very warm night, so the area where walls met ceiling was alive with insects lured in by the lights. I remember that the first course was chilled, red cabbage soup. White bowls of clear carmine-coloured liquid were placed on the table in front of us but, before we could spoon up the first mouthful, there was a fluttering overhead, and dozens of white swallowtail butterflies floated tablewards to land in the soup.

It was most disconcerting, quite surreal. But even more extraordinary was the composure of the military gentlemen who set about their first course as if it was an everyday occurrence to share your soup with crowds of elegantly winged visitors who had literally dropped in.

Fiona and I didn't know where to look, in our own dishes or across the table, certainly not at each other or we would have broken down in hysterics. That certainly would have upset the guests. It was another torturous hour before we could return to our rondavel, relive the extraordinary incident—one of the more extraordinary highlights of my time in East Africa—and laugh ourselves to sleep.

Momella Game Lodge was run and owned by the Singer family who had moved there in 1907. We had heard stories about a grandmother who had been one of the first women white hunters in the area, but since those early days, the family had set up a ranch and game sanctuary at Momella, taking shots of animals with a camera rather than shooting them with a gun and encouraging visitors to study and cherish Tanzania's wildlife.

I remember sitting in a chair on Christmas morning with a dik-dik, a Bambi-like creature, on my lap. I'd seen this tiniest of antelopes—it stands only 35 cm at the shoulders—springing about on the lawn and marvelled at its fearlessness when approached by the family dogs.

On my lap, its minuscule hoofs were razor sharp but its reddish-brown, tail-less body and tiny head, topped off with a tuft of dark hair, made it more precious and desirable than any expensive, cuddly toy.

Before we left, there were more animals to see in nearby Ngurdoto Crater, a mini Ngorongoro, its highest peak 6,000 feet above sea level. This extinct volcano is surrounded by forest while the crater floor is swampy. Away to the west, Mount Meru and more interesting country tempted us to extend our trip, but Fiona and I were running short of cash, so we left Momella and headed for Arusha and the road back to the Usambaras.

Chapter 11
Weddings

Looking back over letters and diaries of 1966, events seem to have been punctuated by weddings. Sandy's was the first. He'd gone to Australia and was returning home via Johannesburg, when, according to his mother, he had met a lovely girl from Ireland.

We learnt this news from Mrs Scott when she invited Daisy, Fiona and me to a pre-lunch drinks party one Sunday. We had driven from our house up to Magnulla, where the headmaster and his wife lived, in high spirits. We didn't very often get the chance to see inside their house. My mood changed dramatically when I realised that we were there to celebrate their son's wedding in South Africa.

When Sandy had left, he'd promised to write to me. Over the previous year when he'd been managing Balangai, a tea estate in the Usambaras, we'd become close friends, although in retrospect, I suspect most of the romance must have existed in my head as usual. He let me drive his brand-new car, invited me to stay with him on his estate and always called on me when he was in Lushoto.

To be fair, he had written a couple of letters to me from Australia, and I secretly hoped that the Scotts would be toasting their son's safe return to the Usambaras. It was hard to share their joy at his having bagged a beautiful young wife on his travels. "She's from a very good family," Mrs Scott confided with a final twist to my already overstretched emotions.

It wasn't until I was back at the wheel of the car on our way home that I gave vent to my disbelief and anger through my right foot, pressing it down hard on the accelerator. Cries of, "Steady on! Slow down!" from my passengers prevented what might have been a nasty accident as we sped down the dirt track away from Magnulla and back to our bungalow.

Over the following weeks, the hurt I felt inside was rubbed raw by a bitter suspicion that fate was paying me back for the pain I must have caused Tony when I broke off our engagement. It took a little while to recover my equilibrium, but it was a long time before I persuaded myself that I didn't care.

Daisy was the next one to be married. When she wasn't helping out with the teaching at Lushoto, she was in Dar es Salaam with her father, house-sitting for expats who were on leave. It was in Dar that she met Bill, a dental technician from Surrey who was on a year's contract, I think, with a dental company there. I remember him as a kind, level-headed man who had a calming influence on Daisy whilst loving her free spirit.

They decided to have their wedding ceremony in Lushoto at St George's Church on Saturday, 12 March. The weekend before her wedding, Daisy arrived at school carrying her cake and dress in cardboard boxes, having travelled the 340 odd miles from Dar es Salaam by bus. Despite the hot, bumpy journey, both cake and dress were undamaged.

On the big day, Daisy looked the happiest I'd ever seen her, and very pretty in a dress that she had designed and made herself from material given her by Bill. One of the matrons had organised Daisy's veil and Mr Schmidt, the manager of a nearby tea estate, had made her a bouquet of roses, cut from his own garden.

He also made my pink carnation buttonhole. I was surprised when Daisy asked me to be her bridesmaid a few days before the 12th. Fortunately, the fundi in Tanga had just finished making me a new dress, so I wore that.

The night before the wedding, we had gone through the agonies of sleeping in rollers so that our hair should look 'done'. Next day, the weather was perfect with clear blue skies and gentle warmth. It was a wonderfully relaxed, informal ceremony in the tiny church on the slopes overlooking Lushoto.

Bill was especially happy because his mother had flown out from England to be there, together with Daisy's mother and a gathering of friends from school, Lushoto, and the surrounding hills. After much genteel feasting at an open-air buffet, the couple drove off in their Mini Cooper, racing green of course, back down the twisting dirt road to the coast.

In May, at the end of the half-term holiday, I was in Dar es Salaam staying with Daisy and Bill. They were house-sitting for some expat friends and looking forward to returning to the UK—home for Bill—in June. For Daisy, it was to be an exciting new experience, to begin with anyway, as she'd been born, brought up and educated in East Africa by her English mother and father. (Sadly, the novelty wore off and, some years later, she returned to Africa to live in Jo'burg.)

Included in her preparations was the knitting of a windcheater, although I suspected that she'd need something warmer than that, come the winter! On Friday evening, when the temperature had dropped enough for us to be able to move about without the constant need to change our clothes, we went out to dinner to celebrate Daisy's 21st birthday. The next day, I would have to do escort duty, accompanying a bus full of children back up to Lushoto for the start of a new term.

Fiona and I had spent the first half of the May half-term holiday at Thika, just north of Nairobi, with some relatives of Fiona's. Tricia, Eddie and their teenage children really made us feel welcome. It was good to be with such lively, vivacious people. In common with many expat's wives, Tricia seemed to have a flair for making the place attractive without spending out on expensive things. Even corrugated iron and boiler pipes can be made to look special with a touch of silver paint.

As always, the movement of money out of the country was a constant worry. Economies such as those Tricia practised meant that savings could be accrued, but special application had to be made before one could post home any cash in the form of cheques or postal orders.

A good reason had to be given for sending away even small amounts of money. That constraint, as well as hefty taxes and the need to present our passports every time we crossed from Tanzania to Kenya and back again, made us feel insecure, on the one hand like prisoners, cut off from the rest of Africa yet, at the same time, aliens who needed to renew our work permits every year.

Mr Scott had had to put up a £200 bond for each of his staff but, even so, he couldn't be sure that the powers that be, would honour the agreement to let us teach in his school. Without teachers, Mr Scott would have no school, so he would simply be 'relieved' of his establishment. That situation almost came about late in May.

Our neighbour, Mr Peterson, was beginning to enjoy his professed status as a 'world citizen' and had taken to writing letters to national newspapers setting out his views on current affairs. The Tanzanian Standard had published one, stating his view that Britain must blockade South African ports.

This was quite a sensitive issue at the time and not an altogether surprising demand for Peterson to make, as his wife's family were committed to bringing about the end of apartheid in South Africa where they lived. However, Peterson's outspoken challenge must have gone a long way towards raising his profile in the political circles in Dar es Salaam.

In Lushoto, it was a different matter. The local doctor, a well-educated Tanzanian who was off to London for further training, considered Peterson mad, whereas our young African clerk called him a bore. In truth, on a personal level, he came across as nothing more than a self-righteous bully.

After he'd twice used threats and intimidation to order the matrons out of the bathroom whilst he was supervising the boys after a games lesson, Mr Scott had had enough of the man's reckless behaviour. I think the Head feared for the well-being and safety of the children in school since Peterson's discipline had gone from bad to worse. He tended to excite his classes by asking provocative questions that called for vociferous answers.

It doesn't take much to stir up a group of 10 to 11-year-olds. From the quiet of my classroom, I sometimes heard him trying to calm them by shouting "Shut up!" Quite a novel command in such a well-mannered school. The children thought it highly amusing and continued enjoying their noisy Geography lesson. So, he was dismissed and relieved of his post.

Of course, Peterson took umbrage at this and immediately sent off a letter to TANU, the most powerful political party of the time, condemning Mr Scott who, he claimed, had sacked him for mixing with Africans. I'm not sure whether Mr Scott was tipped off about the damning contents of the missive but, as soon as he heard about Peterson's claims, Mr Scott flew immediately to Dar es Salaam and went straight to the appropriate minister in the government, and presumably gave his version of the sacking incident.

No one was supposed to know, but Lushoto was abuzz with the news. Fortunately, when the chips were down, Mr Scott could call upon his contacts who included several high-powered MPs, diplomats and businessmen whose children were on the roll at school. Mr Scott was a wily survivor. Together with his family, he had spent the war years in a POW camp in the Far East and not lost his zest for life. He wasn't going to let a parvenu like Peterson get the better of him.

Meanwhile, Fiona and I had noted the sound of our neighbour's typewriter working overtime and its silence when the typist disappeared up to the local council offices. The crazy thing about the whole issue was that Peterson really needed a job. He and his wife Jane now had two young babies to provide for, but very little money. They certainly couldn't afford the journey home. So it was Jane, never in robust health and at a low ebb after the birth of the twins, who had to toil up and down to school until the end of the second term so that they could accrue enough cash for their return ticket.

As neighbours, we continued our daily exchanges as if the contretemps had not occurred, and tried to conceal our relief when the offending party was laid up with a bout of malaria. Illness made a perfect cover for his ignoble climbdown. The affair was killed off but it was time for Petersons to leave Tanzania.

For Fiona too, it was time to plan her trip home. Her year's contract was up at the end of the summer term, so by June, we were talking about selling the car. I hadn't enough cash to buy the other half-share in the vehicle, and anyway, I thought that I might be leaving the term after Fiona. A German couple who lived in Lushoto had expressed an interest in purchasing our VW for their daughter who was due to arrive in Tanzania in October to take up a nursing post.

Our asking price was £400, exactly the amount we had paid for it. Remember, we'd bought it below market value, thanks to our kind benefactor. Even so, £400 was a good price to pay for a 2-year-old VW, a deluxe model that had only 19,000 miles on the clock.

True, stone chips were beginning to appear on the paintwork and, more importantly, it needed a new exhaust, but it looked beautiful when it was all polished and shining. We felt that the Kurtmans wouldn't be able to resist such a bargain. The only problem was that before we sold it, we wanted to go on safari and that meant using our car.

"Our insurance says we're not covered for driving in the Congo," Fiona pointed out when we were considering our holiday destinations.

"Well, we'll just go down to the border and see what it's like," I suggested. It wouldn't take us long to cook up another journey. A road map of East Africa always presented exciting possibilities—such mountains and lakes, such plains and forests teeming with animals and birds. As long as we had money to fill the petrol tank, then we were sure we'd arrive safely wherever we were headed.

Summer photographs of the English countryside taken when I'd returned home the previous year made us nostalgic and long to be back there. But it was only the usual drop in temperature experienced 4,500 feet up in the Usambaras in June that made us dream of green lawns and apple trees.

Our little gardener, who every day waited outside my window for instructions, was making our garden neat and tidy, even if he did grow rows of lettuces between the flowers and a few plants for himself under the poinsettia bushes. I hadn't a clue about how to advise him and mostly left him to sort things out. Goodness knows, he asked for such a minimal reward at the end of the day that I hadn't the heart to turn him away and say, "Look, we don't really need you."

Eventually, the cold weather made it difficult for anything to grow, so in the end there was nothing he could do in the garden. To my relief, he failed to turn up at the usual time before I went down to school one day.

"He's not coming any more, Memsahib," Saidi told me that evening when he came in to light the fire and draw the curtains. I was glad, in a way, that he'd taken the initiative and found something else to do without my having to go through the hurtful process of dismissing him.

Misty mornings turned into warm afternoons, clear bright evenings, and nights cold enough for hot water bottles. When we weren't planning our August trip, Fiona and I learnt to play Bridge—or at least we tried to master the rudiments of the game.

Our tutors were two young Americans, Joe and Luke, teachers at Magamba African Secondary School. We'd met them one afternoon shopping in Lushoto. They invited us to dinner and surprised us with a table set with wine and candles as well as a very good meal they'd cooked themselves.

We found it difficult to emulate their culinary skills when we invited them back to our place. However, we whiled away many evenings either at Magamba or in our house paying Scrabble and Bridge or just chatting over a beer or two. Joe and Luke were Peace Corps workers, but they knew that when their teaching tour was over and they returned to the States, they would be sent out to fight in Vietnam.

The United States had first become involved in the Vietnam War in 1955 when they went to the aid of South Vietnam. The campaign against the Communist North Vietnam turned into a long, costly conflict for the US which didn't finish until April 1975. US combat troops had been drawn into the war in March 1965 after Joe and Luke had embarked on their tour at Magamba as Peace Corps workers.

They would sit and talk about their future, sometimes cynically, expressing contempt for the system, but always with quiet resignation. For the four of us, it was an uncomplicated, good-humoured friendship. Unsophisticated, yes, but there were no other distractions; no television, cinema, dance hall, night club or even a local pub at which to spend our evenings.

An invitation to visit a family, soon to be moving out to the Serengeti, was to set us rushing for our previous road map and reviewing our plans. We had been having drinks with Sheila and Paul, the last remaining English couple in the township, when we met the Latimers, whose son and daughter were at our school.

Dr Latimer was to take up a post at Seronera, the Research Institute on Serengeti. His charming wife had said, "Come and stay with us during the summer holidays if you like."

We replied, "Thank you, we'd love to," but could hardly contain our excitement at such an invitation.

In 1960, Dr Grzimek the zoologist had published his book 'Serengeti Shall Not Die', alerting people to the perilous state of what one reviewer called 'this last stronghold of African game'. Inspired by the book, Fiona and I were keen to have a close-up look at the herds of wildebeest and antelope that he had described and photographed from an aeroplane.

However, soon others wanted to join our much discussed safari, an American Biology teacher, two German mechanics, and an English VSO who taught at Magamba Trade School. Then, at the end of June, we received another exciting invitation from a friend to visit Bujumbura in Burundi. On paper, our projected tour was becoming more and more ambitious and set to cover many more miles on the ground than we'd originally intended.

For several weeks, I'd had no news from my sister. I presumed that Louise was busy with her end of year exams at college. I was looking forward to seeing her when I returned to the UK in December and had begun to think about looking for a teaching post near Loughborough where she was studying.

As the end of the summer term approached, Fiona began to change her mind about leaving and decided to extend her stay until Christmas. We'd both leave then. The only snag was, we'd agreed to sell our VW at the end of July. However, after some hard bargaining, the Kurtmans generously agreed to postpone their purchase of the car until the end of August after we'd been on safari in it. It was an ideal arrangement for us, apart from the fact that, for our last term at Lushoto, we'd have to manage without our own transport.

All looked settled until a letter arrived with the news of another wedding. My sister's. She was to be married on the 24 September and I would be her bridesmaid. What a surprise! How I longed to know the what, where and when of the lead up to the decision. In an era before ease of communication by E-mail or even phone, I desperately needed to get home to have my questions answered, but there was another snag.

I would have to wait until the car was sold before I could afford the fare back to England. When I calmed down and thought about this totally unexpected turn of events, I figured that I could still go on holiday with Fiona and be back in England at the beginning of September to help with the wedding arrangements.

Summer term was something of a misleading name for the three coolest months of the year in Lushoto. We looked forward to having eight weeks of holiday away from the daily round of school and the constraints of life in a small community.

When the last exam had been given and marked, reports written and pupils escorted home, we were free to set off on our last safari in our blue Beetle. First though, Penny and Tim had to be taken to kennels in Dar es Salaam and money handed to Saidi to buy food for the cats, Tonki and Grey.

Three of the would-be travellers who had expressed an interest in our trip had cried off. Their battered old VW Kombi had failed to respond to radical surgery, despite the skills of its mechanically minded German owners, and it was not fit to travel out of the mountains. Fortunately for us, the English VSO worker, Ted, also a mechanic, said he'd like to join us. So, at the beginning of August, off we set.

After months of trouble-free motoring, we were to experience a series of minor technical faults such as the speedometer cable breaking and, more seriously, the horn losing its voice. Ted fixed these. Then we had a series of punctures. One was a dramatic blow-out on a front tyre when I was driving along a newly graded, straight stretch of gravel. The car careered all over the road whilst I tried to kill the speed.

Eventually, we veered off up a soft bank of earth denting the bumper and offside wing before stopping. Fiona leapt from the front passenger seat, gripping her handbag and shouted at me from the safety of the bank. "What the hell do you think you're doing, Sylvia?"

Before I could retort, I remembered poor Ted stuck in the back seat, unable to get out until the front seat was pushed forward. I don't know what he thought of us but he soon had the car off the bank and the wheel changed. He was excellent at mending punctures but in the end, we had to invest in new tyres.

The first stage of our trip took us to North to Moshi where we visited our old friends, the Churchers, who'd lent me the extra gear for the Kilimanjaro expedition. From Moshi, we drove West towards Arusha but turned off right after a few miles to Momella Lodge to arrive there just before dark at about 6, having stopped to look at giraffes on the road.

It was good to be back at the Singers' farm and game sanctuary again but there were no butterflies in the soup that evening! The following night saw us at what Fiona considered to be the most fabulous accommodation in East Africa, Manyara Hotel, some 100 miles West of Momella. It was expensive but worth the money if only for its swimming pool and magnificent view over the National Park, Lake Manyara and the Rift Valley.

In contrast, the game park was disappointing. It was so dry that the great herds of impala and other game that had been so visible on our previous visit had gone elsewhere. We had to be satisfied with one reticulated giraffe, some elephants and the ever-present flamingos on the lake.

Having three of us to take turns at driving made the trip less tiring. However, Ted's limited funds meant that he had to camp in his borrowed tent at our next stop, Ngorongoro, whilst we were safely tucked up in the nearby lodge. He had to endure an uncomfortable night under canvas, kept awake by the cold and the hippos snacking noisily nearby.

He arrived for breakfast looking drained and not at all ready for the Land Rover drive down into the crater. I thought that the highlight of that day was being taken into one of the Masai homes, a low mud hut full of flies and rich smells, but Ted and Fiona were less enthusiastic.

I can't recall why Ted returned to Lushoto at that point. Perhaps his holiday was shorter than ours or maybe he'd spent all his money. I have a sneaking suspicion that it might have been because he'd had enough of our company en route, since both Fiona and I were incorrigible back seat drivers. I liked and admired Ted and could easily have fallen for his boyish charms, if I hadn't been so reserved.

He was always cheerful, fun to be with and never grumbled like we did. It must have been quite a test of character for him to live in relative austerity at the Lutheran Trade School after his more affluent lifestyle in England where his father owned a jam company well known in the food industry.

Ted sometimes spoke about his family, but not to brag, although he confessed he was looking forward to driving his sports car again when he returned home. "I put it up on blocks before I left," he explained. "I didn't want anything happening to that."

Leaving Ngorongoro, Fiona and I set out to drive North across the Serengeti alone. Although it was so dry, there were still small herds of antelope and zebra to thrill us, their bright markings so vibrant when seen close to. Otherwise, the vast plains looked bleached and empty. No other vehicle passed us until we drew near to the Research Station, a collection of buildings to accommodate a resident team as well as visiting wildlife experts.

The last occupant of the bedroom that Mrs Latimer showed us to had been studying hyenas. There was a stuffed one at the bottom of my bed. It seemed to leer at us as it stood there, that horrid ingratiating stance belying the power of its bone crunching jaws. Not the sort of thing you want to wake up to. So I kept it covered and out of sight under my dressing gown.

Looking for lions among the kopjes, lion-coloured outcrops of rock rising up from tawny sun-dried plains, took us all day. We did come across a man in a Land Rover monitoring a particular family of big cats but he wasn't too keen on having a noisy Volkswagen disturbing the peace, so we gave up and returned to base. We were disappointed.

Perhaps we had expected too much from such a short visit. After all, the Serengeti is a huge area. Although I have no clear memory of our two days there, the name, Serengeti, still conjures up strong images of dusty plains and distant animals.

Our next port of call was Mwanza on the southern shores of Lake Victoria. The Wyngate family, as generous as ever, had invited us to stay with them when they collected their two children from school. Mr Wyngate, who managed the Mwanza power station, treated us to a tour of his establishment soon after we arrived.

He ran the place with military attention to detail but succeeded in making the visit a surprisingly interesting—even entertaining—experience, despite the fact that Fiona and I were dead tired after our long drive. Who would imagine that a power station could provide material for jokes!

After a relaxing day with the Wyngates, who were all as cheerful as their father, we set out on the next leg of our safari, a route that took us North round the Eastern shores of Lake Victoria and through Kenya.

Once we were in Uganda, we struck out for Jinja and Entebbe. On this trip, there was time to enjoy the arboretum that I had failed to locate on my previous visit and to take an afternoon cruise on Lake Victoria. It's difficult to appreciate just how vast this mini inland sea is, covering an area of 26,828 square miles, that's 70,000 square kilometres.

From the sun deck of a little cruiser, it was impossible to make out landfall in any direction once we'd left our point of departure. At an altitude of 3,720 feet above sea level, the lake is higher than Snowdon.

On our map, Entebbe didn't look too far from the Ruwenzori, the Mountains of the Moon, on Uganda's border with the Congo. So, lured by their romantic name, we headed away from Lake Victoria towards Fort Portal and onwards towards the jagged, snow-capped mountain range. We had set out early and driven towards the Congo border, along a road that skirted the Northern slopes of the Mountains of the Moon, before descending onto the plain.

Above the Semliki River and the forest hung a great cloud fed by columns of steam. Down on the river plain, hot springs bubbled up from grey-green soil making round pools, each a tiny crater. Two young Africans were cooking their bananas and cassava in the boiling water. They stood without speaking to each other, enjoying the warmth of the steam, which in some places was as thick as smoke from a damp, wood fire.

The atmosphere of the quiet, undisturbed morning, the tall, yellow grasses heavy with moisture, the flat river area and the rugged mountains rising above jungle on either side of the valley, made us too suspend our usual chat. Here was one of those unique moments to be treasured. We tiptoed about looking deep into each pool, marvelling at the mysterious liquid cupped within, then quietly withdrew to our car and set off, back up the twisting road.

As we drove, we noticed snow on several of the Ruwenzori peaks and caught glimpses of Lake Albert away to the North before swinging round yet another corner, taking us above the height of the low flat cloud and away from the Semliki.

The road south led to Goma some 225 miles away. It's difficult to equate the peace and isolation of that segment of our safari with television pictures of thousands of terrified, miserable refugees camping out round Goma and news of brutal wars, for we saw no one coming or going along the entire length of that long, red route.

Grazing herds of some kind of antelope, eland maybe or kudu, with twisted horns, were the only life form that we saw from our dusty car windows. Sadly, we knew that once we reached the border of Rwanda, without a visa, we'd have to turn round and drive back home without seeing anything of Goma. Bujumbura in Burundi and the magical Congo whose mountains and forests we'd glimpsed across the Semliki River would have to remain a mystery.

By the middle of August, Fiona and I were back in Lushoto. The travel agent in Tanga had confirmed the booking for my flight back to England, so we had about a fortnight of holiday left before my departure on September 1. Money was short but we decided to borrow a tent and head for the beach at Malindi.

The weather was perfect, the deep blue sea and coral reefs as beautiful as when Sylvia and I had stayed there, three years previously. In fact, the sea front remained unspoilt. We spent our days sunbathing and swimming, our evenings eking out our dwindling cash resources at the nearby hotel. Soon, we were joined by a group of American teachers from the school at Magamba. I envied their surf boarding skills but was too scared to venture out into the waves myself.

Back in Lushoto, we found that the extra mileage we had put on the clock of our VW had taken its toll on the pale blue bodywork. The constant hammering of stones on rocky roads had split the area below the back bumper. Thank goodness for Ted! Using welding equipment and paint from the Lutheran Trade school, he transformed the jagged metalwork and returned it to its former strength. Despite being known for his ability to drive a hard bargain, Mr Kurtman paid us the £400 asking price for the restored Beetle. He and his wife were very pleased with the gleaming vehicle that we drove up to their door at the end of August. It would be perfect for their daughter. "Would you like a VW toolkit?" Fiona asked. "Actually, it's never been used."

"Brand new you might say," I added.

"Well, of course," replied Mr K. So a price for the accessory was agreed, cash and goods were exchanged, and we left, two women well satisfied with our profit and our business acumen.

"I leave Tanga on September 1 and arrive in London on the 2nd at ten thirty in the morning. That means I can easily get home by train so don't worry about meeting me," I wrote to my mother. Of course, both my parents were at Heathrow to greet me and brief me on the wedding arrangements. It was like stepping into another world.

119

It was stepping into another world where dresses had to be tried on, a cake made, a reception room booked in a local hostelry and accommodation sorted. Photographs taken on a sunny September day show a smiling group: Louise, tall and graceful in white standing beside her new husband, his mother in pink, my mother wearing a flamboyant red hat and red carnation to set off her grey outfit, and the menfolk in dark suits. The little bridesmaid dressed in a long, apple green satin dress, a mini replica of mine, and her younger brother, uncomfortable in a kilt, complete the picture. The newly cleaned white stone blocks of the Parish Church, and a freshly painted vestry door, blue with elaborate black lock and hinges, were other colourful details to be savoured when I later received the photos back in Lushoto.

Tony, my ex-fiancé, attended the wedding. I was rather taken aback to see him sitting in the congregation when I followed Louise down the aisle, and I hoped that he would have left before I needed to make my exit. However, when I saw him standing alone in the vestry, my curiosity overcame my initial dread of meeting him again. He smiled and walked round me as if trying to assess the damage that living in Africa had wrought. How I must have changed! Very politely, he declined an invitation to attend our evening party for the newlyweds.

"I've promised to visit someone in hospital," he declared rather loftily. It came as a surprise to feel a little hurt but, in my heart of hearts, I couldn't blame him. It was to be the last I ever saw of Tony. I just hope that the proceeds from the returned engagement ring had bought several footballs for his youth club.

Chapter 12
Making the Best of It

The beginning of October saw me once more in Lushoto after yet another farewell to my family in England. Fiona picked up Penny and Tim from the kennels for me when she went to Dar es Salaam to collect the children for the start of the new term.

My month at home had been exciting but tiring. In contrast, life at Lushoto seemed gloomy, a feeling made worse by the combination of a vicious flu epidemic amongst the children and Mr Scott's financial worries. "I think the school is very near being on the rocks!" I confided to my parents in a letter. "We only have 75 children instead of 100 and that makes a big difference, at £85 per term for each."

There was a certain tension in the air on the political front. You had to be very careful about what you said and did in public places, especially if you were an expat. I was made very aware of just how cautious you needed to be one afternoon at the Lawns Hotel in Lushoto. Paul and Sheila had taken me and a VSO worker there to have a drink and to play snooker, after our weekly game of tennis.

The radio in the room was churning out African music at full volume, so Paul put his head round the bar door to see if anyone in the other room was listening to it, an innocent enough gesture. If there had been no one about, he would have switched off the radio or, at least, have turned the sound down. Perhaps, his face had displayed his irritation when he saw that there was indeed an audience or he might have made a flippant comment to us that was overheard.

Insignificant as it was at the time, we soon forgot the incident, put up with the loud music, and got on with our game. However, some time later, an African woman, the wife of the local Police Commissioner, appeared in the doorway and accused Paul of violating 'Bar Rules'. "I'm going to take a case out against you, right now," she threatened. It was an unpleasant end to our game of snooker.

Father Grant was the person to go to when you were in trouble. Being a charming Irishman and Catholic priest who had a large congregation every Sunday meant that he heard and saw most of what went on in the township. So, as soon as possible, we rushed round to his house to tell him about the incident and discuss its possible outcome. We felt that we were all implicated. News, especially bad news, travelled fast in such a small community. We were reassured by his observation, "Nothing has come of it—yet." Indeed the 'case' never materialised. It had been an empty threat.

October ended with the wedding of a Dutch couple, Ilsa and Kit, with Father Grant as the priest in charge. First, Kit collected his bride and took her into the church with his two men attendants. There were no bridesmaids or close family to accompany them. We all waited outside until we were given a signal, then followed the couple into the church. The ceremony concluded with a short mass making the whole procedure last about an hour. At the reception, we drank our way through a whole fridge full of champagne with only crisps and savouries to mop up the alcohol. There was no ritual cutting of the cake because there was no cake to cut, and our enjoyment of the champagne was interrupted by only one speech made by the best man. That evening, everyone was invited to a barbecue at the couple's house in Lushoto. As with most upcountry parties, once the eating was over, most people began to dance. 'Twist and Shout' echoed round the hills late into the night.

Apart from being great fun, such gatherings gave us the opportunity to talk to new arrivals in Lushoto or to find out more about the people we'd only passed the time of day with on shopping trips. There were two Czechoslovakian families, one Czech, one Slav—whose children had recently been enrolled at our school as day pupils. Both fathers worked for the Forestry Commission and were housed in the township where they soon picked up the lingua franca as well as improving their English. A Seychellois couple, also at the barbecue, explained why their young son and daughter had problems with speaking either English or French correctly, having come from a Junior School on Mahe where they conversed in a mongrelised mixture of both languages. I'd often seen the father, a tall, skinny man, on the road, supervising the repair of the precious tarmac stretch through Lushoto. He was employed by the PWD (Public Works Department) and lived comfortably in one of the little town houses, but both he and his wife were looking forward to returning to the Seychelles. Even Father Grant, a frequent visitor to our staff room and someone who always cheered us up with his lilting accent and lively blue eyes, revealed, that evening, his longing to be back in his home town in Ireland.

Going home was a theme that ran through the last part of the autumn term, 1966. Chloe had decided that it was time to quit, so her first task was to send her old horse, Socks, off to retirement in Nairobi. The poor old animal had to walk the 20 miles down to Mombo at the foot of the mountains because there was no reliable horse box available. It took him two days, being led gently by Chloe's faithful seis. Mercifully, the rest of his journey was by train. Chloe took off for Spain at the end of December, having made gifts of all her excess baggage— various artefacts collected over the years, books and an enormous box of artist's pastels, which she presented to me. A riding school in Malaga was to be her retirement home.

Fiona was busy planning her journey home, including stopovers in Ethiopia, Cairo, Turkey, Austria, Germany and Edinburgh. Maisie, the leading matron, had also given in her notice to take effect from Easter 1967, and having been persuaded to stay on for a further term, I decided that I too had to leave at Easter. The feeling that the whole country was beginning to close down was depressing. Even the little shops in Tanga, where we bought material and had our dresses made, were in difficulty. Import permits were almost impossible to obtain, so new fabrics could not be brought into the country. Eventually, with stock dwindling to nothing, store holders would have to close. True, the Prime Minister had cut officials' salaries by a mighty 10%, but we knew that it was only the middle-income group that would feel the pinch. As we saw it, the top officials got high salaries plus free houses, free fuel, free water, free lighting, free servants and free goodness knows what else, so 10% would mean relatively little to them. This information came to us via a friend who was quoting an African Forest Ranger. As first-hand news about the political situation was hard to come by, it was little wonder that expats, worried by rumours, gathered in corners to complain about the government and the way the country seemed to be going downhill fast.

Warm weather does wonders for flagging spirits. We couldn't feel miserable for long when the November sun shone down on us from clear skies, making us wonder how we could think of leaving such idyllic surroundings. The garden was beginning to show its summer colours under the management of our new gardener. He was an old man. He knew how to clear away the encroaching bush and plant our flower seeds, some three dozen packets of them, as well as lettuce, cucumber and tomatoes. We were a trifle ambitious. However, the mzee watered the seedlings, made many shelters for them out of palm fronds, and coaxed them along. He came three times a week but he always found something to do. It was a pity that Fiona would be away by the time everything was at its best. I had begun to realise just how much I was going to miss her company.

In the middle of November, we had an interesting glimpse of the academic side of the African Boys' Secondary School, eight miles further up the mountain at Magamba, when Mr Scott took Fiona and me to their Graduation Ceremony one Friday evening. Everyone involved in education from the surrounding area was there to witness the boys' achievements and to applaud when each boy collected his certificate. Then there were speeches.

One very good speech extolled the merits of National Service, something that the President had recently initiated. (In truth, we had heard that the University students in Dar es Salaam had expressed their strong dislike of the idea by staging a demonstration in the city.) Our evening finished with a very late tea at 10 p.m.—after which the boys entertained us with original songs and dances. There was a wonderfully relaxed atmosphere to the whole event.

After such a pleasant evening, meeting old friends and enjoying ourselves, it was quite alarming to come home at 11.30 to the news that there was an armed gang of robbers in the district. Fiona slept on the sofa in my flat after we had put together an armoury of heavy objects with which to hit any unwelcome visitors, or simply to hurl at them.

I think we barricaded the two doors before we were finally satisfied with our defences, by which time, it was almost dawn. Fortunately, there was no school the next day. Saturdays and Sundays were devoted to catching up on lost sleep after late night parties, especially when the temperature was in the 90s. We heard no more of the armed gang, so perhaps, they found it too hot to engage in their nefarious activities!

On Friday, December 9, there was a public holiday so that everyone could enjoy Tanzania's Independence Day Celebrations. I walked into Lushoto with ten girls and got caught up in the crowds. There were droves of people milling around. The main attraction was a group of dancers, some wearing tall, waving ostrich feathers and bead skirts, others with elaborate beaded headdresses and bells on their legs. The heady mixture of noise, colour and heat made the overall

124

experience seem unreal. We staggered back, too late for school tea, so I had to feed ten hungry girls in my flat.

'Uhuru na Umoja' (Freedom and Unity) was the slogan chanted by everyone on that day in 1961 when Tanganyika gained its independence. Julius Nyerere, who became the country's first president, had gained political stature in the 1950s for his role in bringing together the Tanganyika African National Union, TANU, making it the dominant political party.

Unlike some other African leaders, he chose to present himself as an ordinary, somewhat humble man, his chosen title being Mwalimu, teacher. Official black and white portraits depicting a serious and schoolmasterly president looked down at people from walls in shops, offices, schools and public places.

I have since read that at independence, there were only 120 university graduates in the whole country, a statistic that surprised me at the time, because my first encounter with anyone from East Africa was in 1959 when two Tanganyikan girls joined us at the Teacher Training college in Salisbury where I was studying.

In my ignorance, I had imagined that Tanzania's scheme to send students abroad was part of a much larger educational programme in a country where education was high on a list of priorities. However, in one of those moments when your preconceptions, certainties that have been in place for years, are stripped away, I realised the significance of the President's choice of title.

Tanzania has never been a wealthy country, either as a colony under German then British rule or, sadly, as an independent country. To this day, education to any level is still something of a luxury there. However, that overview was not available to me when I was living in Tanzania. Rumour and gossip suggested that Independence simply meant that expats would no longer be welcome in the near future when there were enough trained Tanzanians to take over.

The last week of the term saw Fiona and me rushing around arranging the Carol Service and trying—in between listening to readers and soloists, looking through costume boxes and making crowns—to write reports. However, it was great fun to work with children who loved singing and acting.

Whilst I dealt with the music, Fiona prepared the crib scene with little figures made from clay dug out of the river bed, decorated the hall, organised candles for the children to carry and helped with the dressing up. We were a real team right to the end.

There was one more surprise left before term ended. My mother wrote to tell me that Tony was getting married. His bride-to-be was a young girl I remembered having taught at Sunday School when I was about 20. Speculating, as one does, on age differences, I realised that I had never actually known how old Tony was and, on further reflection, I concluded that I'd learnt very little about him during our brief engagement.

It wasn't until the following year that I could bring myself to put all his letters on the boiler fire. Curling flakes of blue airmail paper mingled with the bitter-sweet smoke until there was nothing left but white ash.

After Fiona's departure, I longed to be out of the mountains. Lushoto could be a lonely place at the end of term. But I was lucky. Mrs Weiss had invited me to spend Christmas with her and her family at their beach house near Dar es Salaam. Three of her four children, Robert, Ludovic and Ileana, were amongst the bus party of 27 children whom I accompanied down to Dar on the first day of the holiday. It was a gruellingly hot journey.

One poor little boy was sick all over a box of sandwiches, part of a picnic provided by the school kitchen for our 300-mile trip. As luck would have it, we were near a hotel, so I stopped the bus, rushed in, and managed to stir the sleepy staff into finding me a bucket of water. A very kind young man, quick to assess our needs, bought us a bottle of Dettol out of his own money at a nearby duka, then persuaded the hoteliers to lend me a cloth.

All that remained was for me to swab out the bus. Fortunately, we had so much food that we didn't need the sandwiches that had been spoilt. No doubt the insects and bush scavengers enjoyed them after we'd gone.

At the bus station, we were met by parents all eager to gather up their children and drive off to cooler places. Mrs Weiss was there too with her youngest daughter, six-year-old Ann-Marie, as blond and as lively as her siblings, whom she greeted with hugs and kisses.

At the end of any school trip, there is always one child left waiting after all the rest have been collected, and so it was that steamy December afternoon. However, once the apologetic parents had relieved me of my tearful charge, it wasn't long before I was packed into the Weiss Land Rover along with the four junior Weisses, their mother, my two dogs and all our end-of-term luggage. Soon, we were heading towards Kunduchi Beach.

Christmas passed with a whole round of feasting beginning on Christmas Eve. First, all the children lined up to receive their presents. Then, it was the turn of the grownups, including several couples who had come round to join our festivities.

After all the presents, the children went to bed and we sat down to a superbly cooked simple meal of hors d'oeuvre, roast lamb with bacon and vegetables and a chocolate and nut pudding topped with marron glace for dessert. Judy Weiss's culinary skills were well known.

On Christmas Day, we visited another family for drinks and an exchange of festive greetings, and then in the evening, when it was cooler, we enjoyed a tremendous meal at the Timpson's, a family who lived just down the road. On the menu, there was duck cooked with prunes and eaten with rice. First though, was the hors d'oeuvre of lobster. I had seen the fisherman carrying freshly caught lobsters from door to door when I arrived in Kunduchi, but it was my first experience of eating such a delicacy. Of course, there was Christmas pudding to follow, great helpings of it smothered in brandy flavoured cream, and then there were nuts, raisins, chocolates, crystalised ginger, liqueurs and coffee. All the while, we had wine to drink, and I even smoked a cigar when we were sitting down, full to bursting, watching the children twisting and dancing till their socks and feet were completely black.

Judy and her husband, Greg, had an evening barbecue on their lawn later that week. It was the perfect setting; tall, stark palm trees and a full moon rising over the warm ocean.

Rain came at the end of the year. It poured. I remember standing in the Weiss's backyard in my bathing costume, shampooing my hair in gouts of heavenly, cool water. A whole new year lay ahead. It would be a fresh start, with new people to meet.

Chapter 13
Stuck

"Yes, we're stuck," the driver assured me. Clearly, the bus full of children wasn't going anywhere that afternoon early in January 1967. Outside, on the muddy embankment, there were cars and lorries in a similar predicament. Ahead lay miles of water-logged soil churned up by roadworks where the original, unmetalled route was being graded and transformed into a tarmac highway, thanks to aid from Yugoslavia which was then, a communist regime in Europe.

Behind, and to either side, was traffic which had given up the struggle to find a way past the already bogged down wheels of heavy vehicles. We were about 150 miles north of Dar es Salaam, and I was in charge of some 30 children, ranging in age from six to thirteen, returning to Lushoto for the start of term. It was hot and sticky inside the bus, but the children were used to putting up with humid conditions and took them as the norm without fussing.

They all had plenty to eat, and games, books, paper and pencils with which to amuse themselves. Apart from little six-year-old David, the children had all experienced the tedious journey several times before. It was to be little David's first term at Lushoto, so thank goodness he had his two big loving sisters, as well as their friends, to cuddle and comfort him.

My first priority was to reassure everyone that, although the road was blocked, we'd soon find a way out. "Mr Scott will come and collect us," I declared optimistically. "Meanwhile, I want everyone to stay on the bus."

The driver and I weren't the only grownups on the vehicle. There was also Bashir, the new secretary from school, who pretended he didn't have anything to do with the children, until I sent him off in search of a telephone. He was a young man and very particular about his appearance. He didn't relish the idea of having to squelch about in red mud on an impossible mission. Indeed, the prospects for getting a message through to Lushoto were very poor. On one side of the embankment, there was a tropical forest as far as the eye could see, and on the other side, down a steep bank, a small village. You could just about make out the thatched roofs of huts amongst the palm trees.

Time was ticking on and soon there were the inevitable toilet trips to be supervised although, thankfully, there was no squeamishness about going behind the bushes. All the children were used to relieving themselves in the bundu. The only trouble was, with all the coming and going of little feet, it was impossible to keep the bus clean. Red mud stuck to shoes and was immediately transferred to the metal floor. Thirty years on, I would have been equipped with plenty of wipes and tissues, but back then, I didn't even have any bottles of drinking water. That was my next priority.

Bashir returned. "No one in the village has a phone," he reported despondently. He was hot and dirty from climbing the bank. "Perhaps, one of the car drivers is going up to Lushoto and would take a message. Some people are getting through on the track down there," he observed before slumping down into his seat and becoming invisible again. By this time, our driver had disappeared.

"I'm going down to look for something to drink," I announced. "Keep an eye on the children please." It was my turn to brave the mud.

The only drinkable liquid that I could find was some unlabelled cola in little bottles, so I bought a small crate of it at a duka which passed for a shop but was in fact, someone's front room. By this time, cars were tentatively finding their way along a narrow track through the village. It was dusk and they had their headlights switched on. As a vehicle slowed down, I managed to speak to its driver and received his assurance that he'd do his best to get my message to Mr Scott. "Tell him we're all right," I urged.

Darkness descends early in the bush, so back in the bus it was time to do something about settling down for the night. I talked to the children and sat with each of them checking to see how much food and drink there was left. No one minded sharing. It had been an early start for most of them so the younger ones were already drooping and just waiting to be told to go to bed. The fact that we weren't at school was something of an adventure, I suppose, a novel situation akin to camping out, with the suspension of normal routines. Where adults might complain and waste energy on being angry when the going gets tough, children can be marvellously adaptable and resilient when it comes to the crunch.

I can clearly remember the two sisters, Susan and Sarah, making a bed on their laps for their 'baby' brother, David. There were no coats or extra pieces of clothing to soften the sharp angles of the coach but everyone managed to get comfortable by either stretching out on the spare seats or by curling up close to a friend. I slept on the floor in the middle.

The uncarpeted, muddy walkway was hard but even harder was finding somewhere discreet to go to the toilet. To make matters worse, it was 'that' time of the month for me. So, I sought refuge from prying eyes down the forest side of the embankment and discovered how difficult it is to squat down on a steep, muddy slope.

Sunrise is a magic time on the plains. I think it's the best time of day. The feeling of rebirth and newness is augmented by birdcall and the gentle warmth that bathes your bones, making you feel it's good to be alive, especially after a surprisingly chilly night on the floor of a bus.

There were no curtains to blot out the first light, so the children, all 30 of them, were soon up and wanting to go outside. For breakfast, we shared around our remnants of food and assorted drinks. Now, by chance, someone had given me a basket of limes before we left Dar es Salaam. At the time, I expressed my gratitude but secretly wondered what I could do with about two pounds of the little green fruit.

I didn't know what they tasted like and supposed they were as sharp as lemons. However, having tried one and enjoyed the refreshing juice, I realised that they would be perfect for the children. The basket was placed on the front bumper of the bus and we were all sucking limes when someone spotted a group of people walking towards us along the empty, muddy wasteland of what passed as a road.

On they came through the cutting from where all the soil had been dumped to build the embankment. A voice called out and we realised it was Mr Scott and a group of people from Lushoto, African staff from school and several parents. What a relief!

During the long return walk to where Mr Scott's bus was parked, I lost my shoes in the ooze of a spongy rut. Trailing along after the eager children, I must have wandered into it, not thinking and suddenly very tired. Both elegant, black suede shoes sank without trace.

My once beautiful new linen dress, a pale apricot colour with dainty embroidery around the scooped neck, was filthy and, worse, I was aware that I was in desperate need of a bath. Still, it was wonderful to hand over the welfare of the children to others and relax for the rest of the journey.

At Lushoto, the new recruit, Fiona's replacement, had arrived. Her name was Vanessa. Goodness knows what her first impressions of me were when I emerged from the bus, smelly, shoeless and streaked with mud. The children were scooped up by matrons and staff to be bathed and cosseted, but it was Mrs Scott who sensed my distress.

She stepped forward, gathered me into her arms, and kissed me as if I were her daughter. "We're so glad you're back safely," she murmured in her soft Scottish drawl. Fortunately, there were no ill effects from our night in the bus down on the plains, but the children delighted in relating their experiences to their dormitory friends after lights out.

Vanessa soon made herself at home in the flat next door to me. A small, neat girl, she had a quiet air of authority and spoke with the sharp, clipped accent of a Northerner. Her home was in Middlesbrough. During the first weeks of our acquaintance she tended to name drop when talking about her social life back at home but, when she realised that I didn't share her enthusiasm for politics, she stopped referring to Harold (Wilson) and Barbara (Castle) as family friends.

However, I was always impressed by her resourcefulness; she cut her own hair, prepared beautiful work cards for her class, and loved making her favourite, unobtainable cottage cheese. There was always a dripping mesh bag full of curds hanging up somewhere in the dining room. I learnt a lot from Vanessa about making the most of my figure, having slimmed down from nine to less than eight stone.

She'd brought out with her some M&S children's dresses which fitted me, so I wrote off to my mother asking her to buy me some summery frocks size 10, as well as sandals and underwear. Vanessa had come equipped with three or four dozen pairs of brightly coloured nylon knickers, which she showed me arranged like piles of rose petals in her drawer. Not surprisingly, a few were spirited away by the African staff when they were cleaning, going the same way that all of my best underwear had in previous years.

With a diminished full-time staff, Mr Scott had drafted in Mr Perry, a retired teacher whose wife had volunteered to help with the matroning. With so many changes there was need of a new timetable. For the first time, I found myself having to teach French, which included preparing candidates for the 13+ entrance examinations that many of our children took in order to continue their education in public schools in England. I also acquired four piano pupils and the musical appreciation classes that Chloe had taught.

Then, there was all the nature study, biology, English, singing, arithmetic, geography and games to be fitted into the week's schedule. Mr Scott was even less inclined to invest in new text books or teaching materials, at a time when the political scene looked uncertain, so I soldiered on, thankful that the blackboards were large and there was plenty of chalk.

However, despite our limited resources, our classrooms were always buzzing with children at work, examining a new find for the nature table, compiling books of stories, practising reading aloud for a literary event or looking up information in our few reference books.

Towards the end of February, the heat grew unbearable. It was far too hot and humid for work, even at 8 a.m. when school started. There was no air conditioning or even a fan to cool the classroom. The gardens were bleached white, plants shrivelled up and died and even magnificent well-established trees began to look desiccated and old.

Drought was widespread and things were becoming serious. The shambas, little plots of ground where local people grew maize, had become sterile dust bowls and on the tea estates, after months without rain, the bushes were not giving enough leaf to keep up production.

In addition to the drought, there was the threat of a government takeover. Almost overnight, many small, private businesses had been nationalised, together with banks, some of the most prosperous sisal companies, a tobacco group, shipping firms, overseas traders and several insurance companies. Trade in Dar es Salaam, it was reported, was virtually at a standstill and a dejected air pervaded the city.

Tanzanian currency had been rendered almost worthless outside the country, even in neighbouring Kenya and, because of the restrictions on taking money abroad, expats preparing to return home found it difficult to scrape together enough cash to get them back to Europe. At one point, it was practically impossible to obtain travellers cheques. It was time I left.

Back in November, I had started pestering the travel agency in Tanga for information about ships returning to Europe from East Africa. I had hoped for a berth in April 1967 but there were no vacancies. Going by sea, I thought, would be cheaper than flying and would enable me to transport all the stuff I had acquired over the years, at a reasonable price.

Air freight would have been too expensive. As my contract did not terminate until July, I would have had to pay a percentage of my fare, as well as a £45 personal tax and a huge lump of income tax. It was no use asking Mr Scott for a loan because he himself was on the rocks and relying on an overdraft. So, the only option was to stay until July and leave at the end of the Summer Term.

Families were leaving the country and taking their children home. Hence, the future for Lushoto Prep School looked bleak, with numbers of pupils at an all-time low and the imminent threat of being 'restructured' by the Government. For some time, there had been talk of Africanising education.

After all, our school was something of an anomaly, a private school in an increasingly Socialist country. That year, 1967, The President's Arusha declaration set the seal on things to come when he singled out education as an essential part of his plan to replace the old order with a new cooperative endeavour. Ideally, social equality would be achieved through education.

With a good education, no one should feel inferior or feel obliged to cow tow to intellectuals or to wait for orders to be handed down. All Tanzanians should then be prepared to take part in the reconstruction of their country.

It was a wonderful dream and the first step to realising it was to withdraw European staff from recently nationalised banks. Some would simply decamp to Kenya, the end of July being the deadline.

In state junior schools, all teachers were obliged to become Tanzanian citizens, and eventually, all European heads of secondary schools were to be replaced by Africans. Surely, Lushoto Prep School wouldn't be allowed to survive! There were no African teachers on our staff and our only African pupils were from Nigeria, Zimbabwe and Ghana, not locals.

Perhaps, some of the Indian children, Sikhs from families owning sawmills in the Usambaras, and sons of business men in Dar held Tanzanian passports, but most of our pupils were from America and Europe. It was a worrying time for the Scotts. They must have realised that they would not be spending their retirement in Lushoto and that they might have to leave empty handed without being able to sell their property or their land.

"Only another five months and I'll be on a ship," I promised myself, but I still didn't know which one it would be. "If it's the 'British India', it won't be till the beginning of September, then there's the Kenya, a super, duper boat. It leaves Tanga on August 11 and should be at London Docks on September 3" I told Vanessa. The idea of "camelling" over to the pyramids and sightseeing in Cairo whilst the Kenya made its way through the Suez Canal was quite exciting.

Then, there would be the stops at Gibraltar or Malta. "Can't you imagine how gorgeous it will be at that time of the year in the Med!" I enthused in my letter home. However, secretly, I was hoping for a much more original return journey.

The thought of having to endure the social demands of life on a liner didn't fill me with enthusiasm so, when the travel agents wrote at the end of March to say there was a guaranteed berth on a boat, a cargo boat, sailing from Tanga to UK on August 6, I booked it without waiting to find out any more details.

There was a surprise visit from the Weiss family. They called in on their way up to Nairobi. Mr Weiss had a new job in Kenya so they had sold their beach home in Dar es Salaam and had bought another house near Kisumu on the north-eastern shore of Lake Victoria.

During our conversation, they invited Vanessa and me to spend Easter there with them, the end of term plan being for us to accompany their children as far as Nairobi where they would meet us and drive us all to Kisumu by Land Rover. It was something to look forward to on days when we were feeling low.

The Easter term, however, was certainly not all doom and gloom. Vanessa was soon initiated into the life of impromptu parties, surprise visits and midnight motoring that I had become accustomed to in Lushoto. Letters home must have been read with incredulity by my parents. I spared no details about an evening Vanessa and I had spent with Dot, Vic her Dutch husband, and Dot's grown-up son James.

We thought James needed deflating with a good-sized pin as he was one of those pompous types who go out of their way to let everyone know just how flush they are. He couldn't resist the opportunity to boast about his new car with its top of the range radio that cost £100, a lot of money at that time, and more than a month's salary for us.

When he started to speak about his work in a copper mine in Zambia, his obvious contempt for his African workers made me feel even more apprehensive about the evening ahead, but James turned out to be even worse than we'd imagined. He found fault with everything and seemed to go berserk every time he saw a black face. He was despicable. We were in for a rough weekend!

First, we went to the Lawns Hotel for drinks where James downed several strong Amstell beers and Dot and Vic started on whiskeys. Bored with the ambience at the Lawns, a scruffy place at the best of times, the couple drove us several miles up into the mountains to the Jagertall Hotel, where they were staying, and had more drinks before dinner at 8.30 p.m.

Afterwards, there was coffee laced with brandy, then horror of horrors, it was decided that we should all return to our bungalow in Lushoto back down the dark twisting dirt road. Having served our guests their drinks, Vanessa and I were careful to take plenty of soda with our shorts and to drink slowly so we could see how the other three were gradually deteriorating.

We had had a new bottle of whiskey delivered with the groceries on Friday but that was destined to be emptied by the thirsty threesome. By the end of the evening, they had drunk every drop.

Angus and Norman, our tea planter friends from Herculu, arrived unexpectedly at our bungalow late that evening at about 11 o'clock. They had been to see some Indian timber mill owners and were annoyed about a disagreement they had had. Both men were spoiling for an argument to vent their anger and quickly stirred up the inebriated Vic and James.

It looked as if we would have a fight on our hands as Vic lavishly helped himself to glass after glass of spirits, and then became increasingly morbid about the Japanese and all that he and other Dutch people had suffered from them in Indonesia during the war. It's strange how men seem to resort to fisticuffs to express their emotions when they are drunk.

At one point during the fracas, James leapt up and cuffed my innocent dogs because he didn't take to them de-fleaing each other in his presence. "You're lucky not to have had your hand bitten off," I remarked, calming Penny and Tim.

"Don't worry. I'll kill 'em if they bite me," he retorted breathing heavily as he sank back down into an armchair. It was all a bit rich, having to put up with such tiresome, uninvited guests!

As the evening lurched on, their conduct grew worse. James kicked the dogs every time they got near his feet and even took off any record he didn't want played. He was indeed an ill-mannered bore but he was also big enough and tall enough to beat up and overpower anyone in the room, so his behaviour continued unchecked. Neither of his parents was in a fit state to object.

By this time, Dot's speech was becoming slurred and Vic was almost in tears, egged on by Angus. Afterwards, Angus confessed that he'd tried to make other Dutchmen tell about their wartime tortures in Indonesia, but they were always too proud and too strong to give away any terrifying secrets.

At 1.30 a.m., after many hints, Vanessa and I finally persuaded Dot and her two men that it was time to return to their hotel. Vic drove up and down a bank outside our house before he managed to find the road back down the hill. But it was another half hour before the other two men got away. Angus, in backing out to let the other car past, reversed into our open sided garage and straight into the inspection pit, which the notorious Peterson had dug under the thatched roof.

I'm sure that all the shouting and screaming that went on, together with the flashing of lights and revving of engines, didn't go unnoticed by the Scotts who lived across the valley, or the Parrys who were in my former bungalow at the bottom of the drive.

The evening didn't end there. By 2 a.m., we had pulled the car out of the pit, then, after big debates about whether or not we should accept Angus and Norman's invitation, Vanessa and I packed our bags and set off, plus two dogs, over the mountains to Herculu Tea Estate where Angus and Norman worked, having convinced ourselves that anything was better than having to meet Vic and Co the next day—perhaps in town or back at our bungalow if they called on us again. The two bachelor tea planters had no spare blankets so, by the time they had roused another planter and made up our beds with borrowed covers, it was almost time to get up.

Sunday morning, Vanessa and I explored the estate, walking Penny and Tim along hillside tracks between neatly clipped rows of tea bushes. The Schmidts—Mr S was the manager at Herculu—hospitable as always, invited us in, and I came away with two guinea pigs to add to my menagerie. Astrid Schmidt, a weekly boarder at Lushoto, assured me that she would look after them during the holidays. The two white, ginger and black animals were bedded down in a cardboard box and carted back to Lushoto on Sunday evening.

Vanessa liked animals. Having been impressed by Norman's Dobermans, she thought she might have one of their puppies in addition to the budgerigar and cat that she fancied. At about this time, Tonki and Grey produced seven kittens which had the freedom of the house until they learnt to climb onto the breakfast table. Vanessa put up with the guinea pigs in the bathroom until their hutch was made, but understandably, she quickly went off cats. In the end, she settled for a quiet life without pets of her own.

When Pete Johnson, the local carpenter, had made me a light portable hutch for the two guinea pigs, they were installed in the back of my classroom during the week. Lessons were sometimes interrupted by scuffles and squeaks. The children loved feeding and holding them at break times, but cleaning them out was a rather more tricky operation and needed adult supervision. At weekends, the noisy pair would sit on my lap whilst I wrote home letters full of plans for the Easter holiday.

Before the end of term, there was the excitement of the East African Safari to raise our spirits. Usually, the drivers had to battle their way through roads deep in mud and awash with the Big Rains of Easter. But Easter was earlier that year, and the weather had been more humid and hot than wet, so even the most technically difficult parts of the course, tortuous back roads through the Usambaras, as well as on the Northern leg in Uganda, were slightly less hazardous.

The Safari route came right past the school and, for a month before the actual race, cars roared along the road. The tarmac stretch started opposite the end of our games field, so the drivers let themselves go after all the bumps of the dirt road up the mountain—on practice runs. The children, of course, were full of it. Every playtime, Dinky toys were trailed round winding tracks made in the red dust of the playground.

On the Friday night of the Safari, there were loud cheers from dormitory windows as each bank of headlights heralded the approach of the battered cars. As always, it was exciting. Everyone wanted to be out there, taking part, shattering the stillness of the night, braving unexpected hazards and to win the prize of coming first.

On Saturday, there were tired children and crotchety matrons but plenty to talk about. Mr Scott had even decided that his pupils should enjoy an extra hour in bed. We heard later that Soberstrom, a Swedish driver, had had bad luck, going into a ditch dug across the road for drainage.

Apparently, all the drivers had been forewarned about the hazard but it was believed the Swede was touching 90 mph at the time. Victory for Bert Shankland and Chris Rothwell driving for Tanzania in a Peugeot 404 injection was captured on film by BBC TV. It was the first time that the East African Safari had been televised, and I hoped that my parents would watch the programme back in England.

The five months until I could pack my bags and sail away seemed an eternity. The rains came, the temperature dropped, and there were times when, surprisingly, I felt homesick. Letters from England were always a joy to receive; my parents, sister and friends certainly kept me up-to-date with events. April's mail was full of Easter holidays and reminded me that, although I was remembered, I was missing out on being part of a family with all the quarrels and problems as well as the happy times that shape and develop relationships.

So, I sat on my favourite fallen-down tree, up in the maize field, looking out across the eucalyptus plantation towards what I considered as 'our' beautiful mountains, my head filled with rosy dreams as I read and reread letters from home. Admittedly, I was in a comfortable rut but government constraints were beginning to irritate. Soon, European-ness would no longer protect us from the real Africa of hardship and poverty. Vanessa, I believe, was the last European to be recruited by Mr Scott to teach at Lushoto Prep School. He was desperate to engage another member of staff so he was very pleased when Sherbanu, a young Indian woman from Tanga, agreed to fill the vacancy. During the week, she lived in the top house in the Peterson's former flat. (What parties we had enjoyed there when there were six of us in our twenties on the staff!) Sometimes relations and friends visited Sherbanu. On one such occasion, she introduced Vanessa and me to Sanju and Ravi, two lively young businessmen. Sanju had been educated at a public school then at a college in Sussex, having failed his university exams. His excuse was that he had been badly taught. Although from one of the wealthiest Asian families who owned most of the Tanzanian sisal estates, he was having to work up through the ranks to win his Mercedes. Meanwhile, his means of transport was a humble scooter. In contrast, Ravi had gained a Pharmacy degree at London University so he could take over the family business in Tanga. However, he had been accepted by an Oxford College to study for a second degree. It was his ambition to become a politician and finally a Tanzanian representative in the United Nations. He was a great flatterer whereas Sanju was more direct. Both were travelling in the area selling powder, medicine and cosmetics to African shops.

Vanessa and I were soon made welcome by the families of both men, as well as by Sherbanu's relatives in Tanga. It was a new experience to sit down for an Indian meal with so many chattering friendly women, and to stay overnight in a house where the grandmother had the final word on the daily programme of events. Before the end of term, Ravi lent me his movie camera so that I could film the animals on our proposed Easter holiday trip to Murchison Falls Game Park in Uganda.

Chapter 14
An Easter Safari

For Vanessa, our proposed jaunt up to the game parks in Uganda was to be her first safari. She was very excited but I had different feelings. Before we set out, I had to arrange for Penny and Tim to be collected from school by Father Grant's friend, Father Maddon, who lived in Mazinde, some miles from Lushoto. It was an anxious time for me because Father Maddon had agreed to take my much-loved pets to stay at his Catholic Mission somewhere near the foot of the mountains.

Not only would they holiday there, they would spend the rest of their lives there because to take them home to England was not an option. The Mazinde fathers would take good care of them, I felt sure, but nevertheless I was very sad to have to part with them. No longer would I be 'The lady with the brown dogs'!

Reluctantly, I had decided on an Easter handover rather than wait until the end of the summer term because I wanted to ensure a safe future for my dachshunds, before the business of packing and winding up at Lushoto distracted me. It would be one less thing to worry about.

As it happened, Father Maddon didn't collect Penny and Tim at the appointed time on the day before we set off on holiday. Despite much running back and forth up and down the hill to school to make phone calls in the office, I couldn't contact him at Mazinde. I later discovered that a tree had fallen on the line, but at the time, I felt very bitter about priests who spent all day in church, or so it seemed, so as not to be disturbed in their devotions by phones ringing.

Early next morning, in desperation, I took the dogs round to Father Grant in Lushoto hoping that he would be able to help me out, maybe even look after Penny and Tim until Vanesa and I returned from our trip to Uganda. I was in a terrible flap and the dogs were just as agitated by now but, wonder of wonders, I found Father Maddon there.

He cheerfully scooped up the two little sleek, brown animals and was soon on his way to Mazinde. The giving away of Penny and Tim was all over in a few minutes but I was to miss them for many years. In retrospect, it was the beginning of the end for me at Lushoto. I never saw my dear little dachshunds again.

The following day, Vanessa and I set off, our luggage light, and with Sherbanu's letters of introduction, one to a family in Entebbe and the other to the town clerk in Mwanza, just in case we needed somewhere to stay. Our first duty was to escort a group of children home to the Moshi area, first by bus and then by train.

It was a hot, tedious journey which took most of the day. That night, we stayed in a hotel with the three Weiss children, then at 7 a.m. the next morning, the five of us flew up to Nairobi. As always, we had to be very careful to have up-to-date visas and re-entry permits when moving between East African countries.

Over the years, I had collected pages of those official purple stamps in my passport. At Nairobi Airport, however, I was astonished when the Immigration Officer scrutinised my passport and announced, "Your re-entry permit into Tanzania is invalid."

"But it lasts until next year," I countered, being careful to remain polite whilst standing my ground.

"Oh but that was issued a year ago and things have changed since then," he assured me. Perhaps, he was feeling magnanimous that morning or maybe, he just wanted to remind me that Kenya had the power of allowing or denying entry to such as me, but in the end, he let me join Vanessa and the children. "I can't imagine why anyone would want to return to Tanzania, anyway," he concluded, registering his contempt.

That, from an African about fellow Africans, was quite a surprise. Had I been travelling by road, I would have had to return to Moshi to get a new re-entry permit. Things had come to a pretty pass when documents issued a year previously were rendered invalid after any political upheaval.

The long safari by Land Rover from Nairobi travelling West to Rapogi reminded me just how treacherous East African weather can be in April. We set out with the Weiss's driver after lunch, then ran into a tremendous storm. At one point, a car careering along in the middle of the road nearly collided with us. In such weather, headlights and windscreen wipers were practically useless, even at walking speed. We arrived at 11.30 p.m., after what had been an exhausting two days, especially for the children who were longing to see their new home.

At their beach house in Dar es Salaam, Judy and Greg had installed electricity and were about to put in water mains before they had left. Their new home in Rapogi was quite different. Candles, Gaz and paraffin lamps provided heating and lighting, and rain carefully stored in big tanks was their only source of water.

It was no use even considering spending money on improvements because the Weiss's lease ran only for a year. After that, the property was to be requisitioned by the government as housing for extra teachers for one of the many expanding schools in the area.

What the house lacked in mod cons, however, it more than made up for in location. In the far distance between dips in the hills, Lake Victoria was just visible and in whichever direction you looked, there were low, rounded slopes, mostly wooded. In the middle distance, beehive shaped huts, thatched with brown stalks, rose from green shambas planted with maize.

Just down the road, a Catholic Mission with its church, school and Fathers' houses completed the little community. Four VSO brothers, an American Peace Corps worker and a British VSO worked in the school, swelling the number of European teachers in the district to some 150. We ruefully agreed that it was a somewhat different matter in Tanzania, where the authorities couldn't boot out non-Africans fast enough!

Vanessa and I would have been happy to have lingered longer in such a peaceful haven, although peaceful didn't mean boring with the Weiss children around. Cycling, trips out, energetic games and usually animals were involved in a day's fun.

I think that it was at Rapogi that Judy had her geese which kept the grass in trim and, led by a fearsome gander, protected the house. When you are wearing shorts, there's plenty of bare leg to be nipped, so Vanessa and I always took care to give the birds a wide berth when we saw them patrolling the grounds.

Changing Tanzanian shillings for Kenyan currency necessitated making a long journey up to Kisumu. The best exchange rate that Greg Weiss could ferret out from a back street money shop was a miserly 15 Kenyan shillings for 20 of our Tanzanian shillings. He was lucky. Banks paid less. The deal done, we could then proceed on our journey up to Kampala where it was relatively easy to buy Ugandan currency.

Undaunted by our lack of wheels, Vanessa and I hired a taxi from Kisumu to take us to Kampala. The 270 miles cost 35 shillings, a bargain, compared with the 140 shillings we were charged for a double room in the only hotel in Entebbe, our next stop.

As it was Vanessa's first visit to the lakeside town, we followed the usual tourist trails as well as looking up Sherbanu's friends, using the letter of introduction she'd given us. We had come north to avoid the worst of the long rains of April, knowing that the only game park we could safely visit at that time of the year was Murchison Falls in North-western Uganda. So, it was back to Kampala to search out some means of transport.

By chance, as we sat over our drinks in a bar that evening, we fell into conversation with the Ugandan Minister of Culture. He asked us where we were heading and when he heard of our search for a vehicle, he gave us the address of a travel agency just round the corner from our hotel.

By the following evening, we had hired a car, a smart Vauxhall Velox and a driver who would take us on our three-day safari. The price for the trip was well within our budget, thanks to the friendly—and slightly tipsy—government minister.

Murchison Falls on the River Nile gives its name to Uganda's largest National Park. When Vanessa and I went there in 1967, we stayed at the new and very swish Paraa Lodge where, as in other National Park lodges, much use was made of wood, local stone and thatch.

We were impressed by the high standard of decoration in our room and especially in the public areas where, it seemed, a great deal of thought had gone into creating an African 'feel' with wooden carvings and stone mosaics of animals on all the floors. In a separate building, there were rooms for drivers and hotel staff as well as garages for the many coaches and cars that arrived daily.

Sadly, the luxurious lodge was destroyed during the decades of upheaval in Uganda after I'd left East Africa. Rampaging invaders and armed gangs bombed and looted the area, making it unsafe for tourists, and decimated much of the wonderful wildlife that had so excited us. However, Uganda's National Parks have since recovered following the cessation of hostilities, populations of game have increased, as have numbers of visitors and accommodation has been built.

Tourists can again take the boat trip, as Vanessa and I did, to the foot of Murchison Falls and experience the thrill of being in such close proximity to bathing hippos and gaping, yellow-mouthed crocodiles sunning themselves on spits of land jutting out into the Nile.

Before the area became a hunting ground for poachers and retreating armies, in the 70s, 80s and early 90s, there were so many elephants that they were becoming a threat to the ecology. Such is a pachyderm's zest for pushing over trees to reach the succulent parts that the once-forested entrance to the park had been reduced to acres of sandy scrub. I remember our driver nodding towards the desolation then turning his head and saying over his shoulder, "Tembo" (elephant).

"Their numbers will have to be reduced," we declared with visions of a ring master cracking his whip to drive several thousand tons of elephants out of the park. Culling, that smug euphemism for killing, was not in our vocabulary.

Vanessa and I had been invited to spend the last part of the Easter holiday at a coffee estate at Ruiru, just outside Nairobi. We travelled there by bus and were met by the Sorensens, a Danish couple who managed the business. Their son, Peter, and daughter, Margarethe, were boarders at our school. At first, the children were on their best behaviour. It must have been a pain to have had their teachers invading their privacy, especially during the precious last week of their holiday. However, meal times changed all that. It's easier to relax and engage in friendly chat if you are all gathered round a table sharing a meal at the end of the day, and Peter and Margarethe were soon treating us as normal human beings, a favour not extended to all teachers in such circumstances. Mrs Sorensen took a close interest in the welfare of the local people, as many estate managers' wives did at that time. She talked to Vanessa and me about the work that her own country, Denmark, was involved in, in Tanzania, but she expressed her doubt that the right sort of help was being given.

"Do you know," she added to amplify her point, "I heard of a Danish nursing college built not far from here where the girls had to be taught to use the bathrooms and toilets. Washbasins and lavs usually get mixed up, especially if the basins are on the low side! I think it's all rather sad. These organisations have such good intentions but they get bogged down in sentimentality and idealism instead of keeping things simple and practical at first." Stories abounded of expensively equipped colleges which came to nothing for want of staff or suitable students. "It's not enough to simply pour money into the country without consulting the people who live here to find out what's best for them," she concluded passionately.

Our holiday ended with another bargain-priced journey. The bus fare for the 320 miles from Nairobi to Mombo at the foot of the Usambaras cost 30 shillings. We arrived late at Mombo, as the dirt roads had been rather slow going, and we were wondering how to get up to Lushoto, a further 20 miles, when a man drove up to the petrol station where the bus had dropped us off.

"I'm going as far as Soni," he said in reply to our question. That would be only half way to our destination but we knew some people who worked at the Press there and thought they might give us a bed for the night, if we could find their house.

As luck would have it, the boy who was also waiting for a lift up to Soni knew where our friends lived and said he could point us in the right direction. So, all three of us, plus mountains of luggage, piled into the man's Ford Anglia.

By midnight, two beds had been made up for us and we were sitting drinking coffee with Walt, a young German. Vanessa and I had invited him and his friends to dinner at our house on several occasions, so we knew him fairly well. Ezra, with whom he shared his lodgings at Soni, had returned to the States, so there was a spare supply of everything, sheets, blankets and towels, in the house.

The next morning, we were delivered to our own front door in the Vuga Press Combi, which was going into Lushoto for supplies and the mail. People were just so amazingly kind.

Back in Lushoto, our house was damp. The big rains had turned our garden into a dank jungle of weeds and grass. Firewood was so wet that it would only smoulder and not produce enough heat to air our rooms or give us hot water. However, there was no time to sit down and succumb to the gloomy season; the new term, my last at Lushoto was about to start.

Vanessa had to journey up to Moshi to collect and escort children back up to school and I opted for the Dar es Salaam run. I needed a new passport and I wanted to buy some souvenirs and presents. There had been no further news about the boat trip home that I'd booked earlier in the year, but I was confident that come July, there would be a berth for me on a vessel travelling north.

Why is it that passport photographs are so cringe-mackingly embarrassing? My first, taken in a hurry one afternoon in 1957, shows me dressed in school uniform of tie, shirt and mac with hair still wet from cycling through a rainstorm. Ten years on I was glad to be rid of that image, but no better pleased with the new picture.

My glazed look and damp hair were achieved this time by having got up at 4.30 a.m. to make the long journey to a very hot and humid Dar. There was no British Embassy in the capital in 1967, so I had to take my photo to the Canadian Embassy and queue along with hundreds of others for my passport forms, which then had to be completed and quickly returned.

It was a nail-biting wait for the vital documents to be processed. I was full of admiration for people who could work under such stress in such heat, knowing that there was an ever-lengthening line of people eager to secure their right to a British passport.

Back at the Lutheran guest house where I was staying, I found it fascinating watching Dar stir itself as I sat eating breakfast. First came the office people, smart women in straight dresses and high heels, going into the block across from the dining room. The offices must surely have air-conditioning, I concluded. Then, there were the builders who had started in the cool of the morning, pounding away on a site somewhere, digging out foundations, hammering in poles and churning up the soil.

Silhouetted against the sea, as they walked along the promenade, were the less hurried ones carrying on their heads baskets, jembes (hoe-like tools) and even huge palm leaves. They were digging something down on the beach. It might be worth going and having a look later on, if I had the energy. Several cyclists passed by, their shirts flapping out over their trousers, some wearing little white Muslim hats.

The harbour had been busy with shipping for the past few days, so I expected there would have been plenty of parties and partaking of duty-free drinks. I looked forward to the time when I would be on one of those ships sailing out into the Indian Ocean.

Chapter 15
Final Term

Water was our chosen and certainly the most appropriate topic for the new term. The games field was flooded and our steep drive, newly graded, was an impassable quagmire, so there was plenty of stimulus for creative writing! Tonki produced her umpteenth brood of kittens outside under a bush, but some of them must have perished in their sodden den because she brought only two into the house instead of the usual half a dozen little bodies.

I had a box prepared for her in the corner of my bedroom but she really wanted to make a nest in my bed. From time to time, she trundled the babies out of their cardboard creche, jumped up onto the bed and tucked each kit under my pillow.

If I said, "No, Tonki!" when I caught her practising her porterage, she would respond just like a dog and replace the little dangling body in the box. However, she was a determined mum and claimed the daytime slot, figuring that I would not need the pillow until I went to bed.

Vanessa's health seemed to deteriorate in the cold damp of the mountains. Children and staff often developed coughs and mysterious aches during the wet season but Vanessa, not having had time to build up her resistance to African bugs, needed penicillin injections and pills to cure sores on her face, a septic finger and a chest complaint that degenerated into the early stages of pneumonia.

It was about a month before she was strong enough to put in a full day in the classroom. Fortunately, Sherbanu had agreed to work a further term at Lushoto so we shared Vanessa's class between us.

At the end of May, I had a strange phone call from Tanga. "Which missionary society do you belong to?" I was asked. "We have a parcel for you to collect from the Post Office." It was the long awaited dresses posted a month previously by my mother. She'd followed my instructions to crumple them up and mark the package 'used clothing' to avoid having to pay excessive taxes.

What fun it was to put on a fashion show for Vanessa! By then, she was on the mend, although still unable to tolerate noise or the company of visitors for very long before having to retire to bed.

Despite the fact that we lived off the beaten track at the top of a very steep hill, Vanessa and I never wanted for callers. For example, one Saturday morning we were visited first by a young man, a friend of the Weiss family, who had called in on his way to Dar es Salaam to take out their four children and to look us up. Judy had given him our address.

Next to arrive was a group of girls from Form 5. They wanted to listen to our LP of 'The Sound of Music' whilst they drank coffee. Mrs Parry was the next person to call "Ho di" and knock on the door, closely followed by Angus, the lively Scot whom we affectionately referred to as 'that dreadful tea planter'. He had called to enquire about Vanessa's health.

Bertha, a young Goan who worked in the school kitchens, sometimes escaped from her chores at weekends to join us. Her bright chatter and laughter often cheered up a gloomy morning. She smiled when she talked about her brothers and sisters back in Margao and always wanted to hear about our families.

"You must come over to Goa," she urged, but it wasn't till a few years ago when I and my husband, Mike, spent our first holiday, one of many, in that wonderfully laid-back Indian State, that I kept my promise. I think that the Margao of the 1960s must have been quite different from the present day town full of elderly vehicles filling the air with choking fumes, but I could recognise Bertha's outgoing, warm nature in the people I met in Goa.

Not everyone in the school was blessed with Bertha's good humour or capacity for making others happy. One such, was a woman whom Mr Scott had recently appointed as matron in charge of the senior boys. Too late it was discovered that she was a tyrant. She made the 12 year olds' lives a misery, until they became so desperate to get away from her brutal tongue that a small group of them planned their escape.

The oldest boy in the school ran away at morning break, an easy feat with so many places to hide in the school grounds until he could slip away undetected. That night, he was followed by four more senior boys. They must have left their dormitories in the small hours when it was very cold. Without fear of leopards, which were known to roam the area, they had taken the eight-mile short cut down the mountains to the plains then set off along the main road towards their homes. It would have been a very long trek.

Next morning, when the news broke, everyone was on tenterhooks. I think we all felt responsible for having failed the boys by not speaking out against the bitchy matron. Mr Scott spent the morning on the telephone to the boys' parents who, being business people, were at various meetings up and down the country.

How much easier it would have been with mobile phones to co-ordinate the ensuing search. However, there was a happy ending. The five runaways were picked up by one of the boys' fathers and driven back up to school. It was a tearful time for all concerned and very disturbing for the rest of the boarders.

The runaways soon recovered and, apart from a few scratches and bites, showed no signs of damage, mental or physical. After talking to them in his firm but understanding manner, Mr Scott had them write letters to the governors of the school, apologising for their foolhardy misdemeanours.

I don't think it was a punishment, more an exercise in soul searching to help them to assess what they had done. They completed the task without truculence but I wonder what they told their friends at night in their dormitories and whether they still remember their adventure.

Of course, the matron, the cause of all the unhappiness, was sacked. She left immediately and within a week, the school was a much happier place. Unfortunately, it wasn't possible to find a replacement for her, so members of the teaching staff found themselves volunteering to act as temporary assistants to the one remaining matron.

After Vanessa had taken a turn at looking after the boys' dormitories one Friday evening, she returned on Saturday morning looking ghastly and went straight to bed. She'd been unable to sleep in the ex-matron's room, convinced that something sinister was lurking there, with so many moths in the room, a toilet that kept flushing itself for hours, dampness, bats at the windows and lights going off as if everything was conspiring to frighten her.

In the end Mrs Harper, Daisy's mother, took on the task for the rest of the term. With a stiff pink gin in her hand, she soon chased away the evil spirits.

By half term, there were four big packing cases standing in the dining room. Pete Johnson, the carpenter who had made my guinea pig hutch, had sized up the possessions I wanted to ship home and had made boxes big enough for a rocking chair, a cedar chest, several stools and a table. A large rug, books, baskets and wooden souvenirs would have to fit round the bulky items. How to move and transport them to a ship in Tanga was a problem I had to address at a later date.

There was confirmation of a berth aboard the Dutch 'M V Nijkerk' in June, but there was still a worrying silence from the tax office. Tanzanian income tax was paid in a lump sum at the end of the year and only then was one's passport stamped with a Tax Clearance Certificate, signed, in pen, by the Assistant Commissioner and embossed with his official seal. Woe betide the expat who tried to slip over the border and head for a new life in South Africa without that all-important purple stamp in his passport.

Half-term saw me in Tanga yet again, doing battle with the tax officials and trying to establish from the travel agent when I might be arriving in England. The Arab-Israeli conflict, known as the six-day war, in June, had left the Suez Canal badly damaged and littered with sunken ships and so, the Nijkerk would have to sail via South Africa. I was to be denied a trip to Egypt yet again.

The vessel was due in Tanga on August 3 to pick up cargo and begin the return voyage on the 6th, so I expected to be home by the end of September. Any thoughts about future employment were at the bottom of my list of priorities at that stage. Never having been 'career minded', I had a vague notion that something would turn up.

Sherbanu was also in Tanga with her family at half-term. Much to my delight, she took me to an Indian wedding, first to the ladies' part on the Friday afternoon when we met the Italian bride, dressed in her beautiful sari, then to the wedding feast.

There were so many new tastes to savour like halwa, a kind of jelly and nut sweet, and Arab coffee. I was thrilled to have my hands decorated with delicate interesting patterns painted on with a stick dipped in a henna mixture. The smell of the red paste laced with lime juice lingered on my palms for weeks afterwards until the finely drawn lines vanished.

The weekend of partying was overshadowed by a sobering tragedy. On Friday evening, Norman, the gentlemanly tea estate manager, booked into the hotel where I was having dinner with some friends. He was accompanied by a young woman.

Everyone had heard about Norman's engagement to a doctor from Bumbuli Hospital. He briefly mentioned it just before he went on leave, but no one thought that Norman, the perennial bachelor, would actually see the business through to the end. "Meet Frances, my wife," he invited. "We were married this week," he added with a smile.

The following morning, I saw them again with Jack, another young man from the tea estate. They were doing some shopping before driving up into the Usambaras, later in the day. That was the last time I saw them. On Sunday morning came the news that all three had been killed in a really horrific car crash on Saturday night. The crushed vehicle was still beside the road when Sherbanu and I travelled back up to Lushoto. An oncoming timber lorry had slaughtered the three friends as it careered along, out of control, some 20 miles out of Tanga. Jack had a wife and three children, one newly born, back in England. Norman and Frances had been married just four days. Our sadness deepened during the following weeks as we discovered the morbid details of the accident. As for Angus, Norman's friend, the accident brought about a profound change in his life. He was never again as cheerful or as outgoing as he had been.

The cold season was upon us. It was hard to keep my mind focused on the lengthening list of things I had to do before I could leave the country whilst teaching, writing reports and generally trying to come to terms with the fact I was about to quit a way of life that had wrought such radical changes in the way that I viewed the world. My whole outlook on life had been challenged and subsequently, changed. It would be a wrench and, as with all radical changes, it would be painful. But it had to be done. I knew that I was in danger of ending up in a rut, stale and disillusioned. It was time to move on, to go back to my roots and test my grown-up self in the real world. Items placed in the four empty packing cases would be my only tangible links with four years of incredibly rich experiences. The pictures and images that were crammed in my head have had to wait much longer than my treasure chests to be unpacked.

One of the most difficult decisions I had to make during those last weeks of term was what to do with my two cats. The guinea pigs would holiday with the carpenter and his family, and then Vanessa would take them on as her form's pets since they were classroom trained. But Tonki and Grey were a different matter. Yes, they were good hunters but they invariably slept on my bed, heavyweights the pair of them when they were expecting kittens, and after a long struggle, they were house trained. They were more domesticated than wild. Mother and daughter had been with me almost from the start and no homecoming after a safari was complete until they had raced from the garden to rub themselves round my legs and purr their welcome. I had cursed them when the pong of a really smelly mess deposited under my bed had woken me from a deep sleep during our first years together, but I could forgive them all of their misdemeanours when they were curled up on my lap. I, and the cats too, had missed the dogs terribly at the start of term, but I knew Penny and Tim were together and being cared for. Who would want two female cats though? I couldn't bear to think of them going wild, to grow thinner and scrawnier with each successive litter of kittens. They would steal food and be chased away into the bush. There was only one sad but humane solution. I would have to have Tonki and Grey put to sleep. Standing waiting for the school car to take me to the vets with each frantic cat zipped into two separate shoulder bags was one of the bleakest moments of my life.

"Today, Vanessa and I were nearly killed when we were walking into town," I chattily wrote to my parents in July. We were passing a high bank topped with evergreen trees, just nattering as usual, when there was a cracking noise and a very tall conifer began to totter towards us, gathering speed as it fell.

We both experienced almost paralytic fear before we could move, only to race with great bursts of speed across the road, right into the path of the tree. I can only remember being absolutely hypnotised as I ran in circles, all the while keeping my eyes on the tall, falling trunk.

The whole event lasted only a matter of seconds but afterwards, we both swore that we could feel the blow which never actually came since the tree's fall was arrested by other trees bordering the road. Jokingly, we agreed that if we had been squashed flat, Mr Scott would have had to have closed the school for lack of staff. Meanwhile, the gung-ho axe man up on the bank continued chopping. We hoped that he would be finished by the time we walked back.

Saba Saba day came round again and, as usual, there was an ngoma in Lushoto with wild dancing and plenty of drinking late into the night. That evening, I was in the bath when someone knocked on the front door. Vanessa opened it and I heard her say, "Come on in."

"Would you like to walk into Lushoto with us?" I recognised Bertha's voice. She was with Bashir, our school secretary. "We're going to see what's happening."

It was a beautiful, crisp, starry night, so we needed to wear thick sweaters, warm trousers and shoes. Outside the so-called Police Hall, really only high walls surrounding a roofless, concrete dance floor, Vanessa and I had second thoughts. What if the crowd inside, local people from the town and surrounding villages, objected to two white faces?

It was Bashir who persuaded us to go in and we were soon enjoying ourselves dancing a rumba to the music of a very good group. Osman, whom we knew as a former school secretary, was there too, so we danced with him and his young brother and another man who used to attend the English classes for locals I had held in town some years previously.

They were all good looking, well dressed young men, about the same age as Bertha, Vanessa and me. "Naturally we didn't dance with the more scruffy types brandishing bottles," I assured my mother in my letter home. (She was always exhorting me to 'behave myself'.) "We wouldn't have done in an English dance hall," I added defensively.

Altogether, Vanessa and I didn't feel at all odd being the only Europeans amongst so many Africans, dancing under a sparkling sky, on a cold night to celebrate Saba Saba day. We were all one vibrant group of people. Then, it was back to school, shrieking our heads off over ridiculous Goon-type jokes, walking in the middle of the road, of course.

It was the closing of a circle of events which had begun for me with the sound of distant drumming, a ngoma in the Usambaras which had made me feel threatened, an outsider, who had no place to hide in the dark should the night revellers descend from the hills. What ignorance! Four years in East Africa had changed all that.

Chapter 16
At Sea

The intervening weeks between the end of term at the beginning of July and embarkation in August were an emotional merry-go-round. I longed to be back in England but couldn't bear to do things for the last time in Lushoto. The children's farewell messages, drawings and verses, all so disarmingly affectionate, made me laugh, cry and revise my self-image.

Some pupils continued to write to me for a long time after they too had left the Prep School and returned home or started school in England. They must be domiciled all over the globe by now. Mr Scott saw me off with two champagne parties, both highly emotional affairs, and a parting kiss, which came as a great surprise one starlit evening, standing on his veranda.

The venue for my own private dinner party was again at Oaklands where Mrs Abbot produced another of her exquisite meals. Discussing the menu over the telephone, I had tentatively suggested duck as the main course.

"Just a minute," interjected Mrs Abbot. "I'll go and see how many ducks I have in the yard."

"You mean you'll have to kill them for us to eat?" I squeaked horrified.

"Why, of course!" Mrs Abbot laughed.

"Then, can we have something else, please?" I'd changed my mind. I'm not a vegetarian, but I still can't bring myself to eat duck.

Before boarding the Nijkerk, I finally got to settle my debt with obstreperous aficionados at the Income Tax Office, an operation that required a week of form filling and officialdom. Fortunately, I had been invited to stay with a Danish family on their sisal estate during that period, so what might have been a frustrating seven days was transformed into a week of hectic socialising and leave taking.

I was quite relieved to sit down in a quiet cabin on board ship after the last goodbyes had been said and I'd seen all my boxes safely lowered into one of the holds. After the disappointment of not being able to have Vanessa to spend an afternoon on board—we had been misinformed about the departure time—I tried to make the cabin look homely with photos and gonks made by girls at school as leaving presents. It felt strange to be cut off from everyone that I knew and yet still be on home ground, or at least in home waters.

For the next ten days, the Nijkerk plied between Tanga, Mombasa, Zanzibar and Dar es Salaam, taking on freight, mostly sisal and four more passengers. The six who were already installed were elderly folks. Mrs McGraw and Miss Bonner, two retired American teachers from Detroit, immediately took me under their wings. They bemoaned the fact that there were no young people on board to keep me company although both were alert and sprightly enough to make them interesting shipboard companions. Their sheer exuberance and love of noisy verbal communication was to lift our spirits when the going, literally, got rough. It took a little longer to penetrate the outward reserve of the four Germans, especially as Mr Muller, who seemed very straight laced at first, would hardly speak to me for the first few days after my embarkation. His wife kept her distance too. Mrs Ahern hid a kind and extremely canny nature behind her well dressed, dignified exterior. Small, with thick white hair, she followed the married couple around on her bendy, bad legs. I was surprised to learn that she was a business woman and owned a baby clothing factory in Brazil. Later, when she knew I was a teacher, she offered me a job in her factory school. On board though, she, as Mrs Muller, left everything to the man of the party, the dour Mr M. One evening, from my corner where I was pretending to read a book, I observed the trio playing cards and noticed that they soon thawed out, showing a much lighter side of their characters and, obviously, enjoyed each other's company. The fourth German, a woman in her late 50s, positively ancient to me in my 20s, was Mrs Inge Rüdmann. Her figure hugging clothes and bright lipstick accentuated her sexy image and she definitely had a way with men. Her voice, especially when she spoke in broken English, reminded me of Marlene Dietrich. Mrs McGraw told me in contemptuous tones, "Frau Riidmann has simply boxes and boxes of clothes in her cabin."

Having made its way north from Tanga, the ship spent five days hove to just outside Mombasa. There was no berth for us at first, so journeys ashore took 25 minutes by launch. It was quite a novelty for me to feel like a "foreign" tourist on shopping trips to the Kenyan town. So that we shouldn't be bored, the shipping company arranged for us to go up-country for a few days to visit a game park. It was a wonderful and unexpected opportunity for me to revisit Tsavo, the first reserve I'd driven round in 1963. It was almost like an eleventh hour reprieve, a gentle protracted leave, taken before severing my links with East Africa.

Wonderful weather was laid on for our two-day safari to Tsavo. Rumbling elephants impressed us, zebras dazzled and giraffes well, I wonder if I saw them today whether they would look as newly washed, all soft yellow and burnt brown, as they appeared on that August trip in 1967. I remember a child's picture book scene with six long necked twiga grouped round a pool backed by blue sky, green flat topped acacia trees and deep red soil. There were antelopes and gazelles aplenty, of course, even the secretive water buck with their long dark fur coats, but no amount of leaping limbs and flicking tails would satisfy the travellers. Their eyes probed the plains for a glimpse of carnivores.

Philip, the African driver, must have realised that the trip for the old people would have been ruined, or at least rendered less memorable, if they went away without seeing lions. After much jolting along dusty tracks, Philip located a pride up on a rocky outcrop overlooking a waterhole where zebra were grazing. We could only make out the forms of the lions in the distance and had to be satisfied with that for the time being. However, Philip later picked up tyre tracks leading off into the bush, following the route made by another Land Rover and finally there was mama lion and three middle-sized babies. What more could one ask for? Being in close proximity to such beautiful animals is dangerous. You almost feel compelled to step out of your vehicle to engage with them, to stroke the fur and look into their amber eyes. However, we all stayed put in our seats and returned to Mombasa to process our photographs.

Piet, a young Dutchman, had joined our safari party. In port, he was a passenger on the Nijkerk, but at sea, he was a member of the crew working in the engine room to pay for his holiday. His parents were acquaintances of the director of the ship's company. The two American ladies and Mrs Ahern had grown fond of Piet (having already vetted him for several weeks) so he was deemed a worthy escort for me and I was allowed to go to the cinema on shore with him.

Mrs Ahern liked to call us her son and daughter. When she quizzed me as to whether or not I was engaged, I got the impression that she might have been sizing me up as a possible daughter-in-law, as her youngest son was still unmarried. However, after she showed me his photograph, I avoided the subject of marriage in her presence.

Mrs A could be very persuasive. I had observed how abrasively she dealt with the young man in the shipping office when he protested that he was unable to refund her money on the round trip. She had decided to fly from Dar es Salaam to Cape Town to pick up a ship going direct to Rio de Janeiro instead of staying on board for the return voyage to Europe and then having to wait in Amsterdam for a flight to South America. The young man's resolve cracked and the cash was handed over. Mrs Ahern was not to be trifled with, so I made sure I kept in her good books.

The short journey from Tanga to Mombasa had made me feel queasy, but I soon adjusted to the gentle motion of the moored vessel and could lie on my bed and read, or from the porthole forward facing down across the long deck, watch netfuls of sacks being lowered and piled up deep down in the holds, the cranes like giant arms feeding handfuls of cargo to the workers. The goods were Kenyan, the cranes made in Bath, England.

On board, my cabin was beginning to feel more like a boudoir to which I could escape and relax. It was sheer luxury compared with the economy class accommodation on the Jean Laborde. My single room was equipped with an ample wardrobe, dressing table, desk, big sofa, plenty of drawers under the bed, shelves, little chairs and lights in every conceivable place.

Air conditioning made the cabin a perfect refuge from the heat during the day and chilly enough at night to need a cosy Dutch blanket to snuggle under. The en suite bathroom was another luxury; no bath but a vast shower which necessitated the purchase of a big orange and yellow shower cap.

Hans, the cabin steward, was in charge of the cleaning. He was always discreet and only appeared if he thought I was unwell or if something in the cabin had been damaged in a storm.

One afternoon, whilst we were still in Mombasa, I went up on deck for some air and was standing watching the cargo, when a man approached me. He introduced himself as Captain Munroe. At first, I assumed he must be an unexpected passenger, newly embarked, but after a long and interesting chat, I realised that he was the elusive Dutch captain of our vessel.

At last, I could obtain a firm date for our arrival in Europe and so, plan my onward journey. We would be in Antwerp on September 4, but Captain Munroe suggested that I stay on board until the Nijkerk reached Rotterdam from where I could more easily cross to Harwich.

The new voyagers who had joined the ship at Mombasa had a party on board. Loud laughter, the taped sound of accordion and strings playing tango music, and people talking in la-de-da voices filtered down to my cabin from upstairs. The noises, coupled with an occasional "Bye bye" as someone left, sounded like an excerpt from a radio play that repeated itself throughout the day. When the Nijkerk slipped from its moorings at 11.30 p.m. on Tuesday night, I was fast asleep and only came to as the ship's movement grew more noticeable as we steamed into open water outside the harbour. I rushed up onto deck. It was dark, but I strained my eyes for a last glimpse of the Kenyan coast.

It had been a long day. A 2 a.m. bedtime that morning had been occasioned by a long session of babysitting. Piet and I had had to leave the party in the officer's bar to go and look after the children of some old friends in Mombasa. After a few hours of sleep back on board, we had walked into town a second time to buy records for some of the crew. Then, on the way back, we had called in at the Mission to Seamen for a refreshing swim in their pool. It was a 45-minute walk from our number nine berth to the end of Kilindini Road, along a route we knew well having trekked in and back again every day we had been in port. Whenever my legs ached, I countered the pain by reminding myself of those 21 days we would have at sea, when I might welcome the chance to walk a leg aching distance. However, it was not yet time for the high seas. The Nijkerk was first and foremost a cargo boat and its holds still had spare capacity.

"Today, we went to Zanzibar," I wrote on Wednesday, 9 August. I had only seen the island once before and that was but briefly from the deck of the Jean Laborde, but on my second visit, it looked as beautiful as I had remembered, like a Venetian scene, the buildings growing out of thick, green-blue water. The soft yellows and pinks of the little houses and the crisp white of the public buildings, with the many archways and Arab-style architecture set me dreaming, my senses already drowsy with the spicy perfume being given off by the hot land.

We all went ashore in a motor boat and the older folk set off in two taxis to tour the island. The company agent and the Chief Steward went to visit the ship's representative in town, leaving Piet and me to wander off by ourselves into the maze of alleyways that make up Zanzibar town. It was new ground for me and potentially dangerous for a lone European woman, but with a big, tall Dutchman by my side, I felt well protected.

Piet had a girlfriend back in Holland for whom he wanted to buy some bracelets, so we first sought out a shop selling silver and antiques. For my parents, I found a set of spoons, each with a different Zanzibar motif, a clove, a dhow or a door, on the handle. For myself, I bought some jewellery, a charm bracelet, earrings and brooch, all of Arab silver and made on the premises.

It was cool in the old streets, the tall shuttered houses acting as a barrier to keep out the burning sun. Everyone we met was so polite and, despite all the stories that proliferated on the mainland, no officials stepped from shady doorways to prevent us from taking photographs. Arab doors, their huge timbers encrusted with mystical Arab carvings, made irresistible subjects.

A heady combination of smells, odours emitted from dark bazaars and the perfume of cloves borne on breezes, conspired to transform the streets into a magical labyrinth. It was easy to be lulled into forgetting the sinister presence, if we were to believe the reports, of the Communist faction on the island.

That evening, the Nijkerk anchored off Dar es Salaam, awaiting a berth the following morning. Before we left Zanzibar, I had had another chance encounter with Captain Munroe who had quietly approached me as I was standing on deck alone. "What did you buy on Zanzibar then?" he enquired with a smile.

A friendly chat ensued until, from an upper deck, two officers called down something to him in Dutch and he left to take charge of operations. A little later at dinner, Mrs Hacker and Mrs Shelley, the new passengers from Mombasa, Frau Rüdmann and I were speculating as to when the captain would occupy his chair at our round table for five in the centre of the dining room.

"We haven't met him yet," complained the newcomers.

"Nobody sees him," snorted Frau Riidmann. "And I know most of the officers on board."

"Really?" I asked naively. "Well, he's just been talking to me. He seems such a friendly man," I added. Was it incredulity or something else in the look that the three women flashed me? The fact was, as Piet reported to me, Captain Munroe was not keen on getting buttonholed by the older people.

They shared that tendency of people of more mature years to be inquisitive. Indeed, they always wanted to know where I had been and what I had done when I went ashore with Piet. Their nosiness was quite endearing really, but I can imagine why the captain kept out of range. He had a ship to run.

From the sea, Dar es Salaam harbour looked beautiful, as peaceful as the name suggests, when our big cargo ship carefully negotiated the narrow entrance on Thursday morning. Immigration rigmarole took ages and then, we were allowed to go ashore. Again, it was strange to be a tourist with a time limit on my stay.

That afternoon, I paid a visit to the Mission to Seamen to have tea with the Padre and his wife. Their son had been in my class at Lushoto. On Friday, Piet played in our ship's football team against a team from another Dutch vessel. Then, after a good-humoured draw, we all went swimming before returning to the Nijkerk for dinner. It had been a perfect day for a valedictory visit to Tanzania.

The number of paying passengers had risen to eleven with the embarkation of Mr and Mrs Granger, Betty Shelley and Jill Hacker at Mombasa, but then Mrs Ahern left us at Dar es Salaam. It was good to have another married couple in the group. Younger than the Mullers, the Grangers were more relaxed and ready to take the lead in shipboard merrymaking, instigating several parties.

Jill, some ten years older than me, a vivacious woman, became a lively friend but never gave anything away about her private life, though, later in the voyage, she admitted that she had left her two children with her husband back in Mombasa.

Mrs Shelley, the fourth new passenger, had the bearing of a lady accustomed to 'colonial' standards but prepared to tolerate the changing world of the 1960s. She preserved an old-fashioned dignity that her more garrulous contemporaries on board lacked. However, over our evening games of Scrabble and perhaps, a glass of gin and tonic, another Betty emerged.

She would laugh as she recalled her life in Kenya in the 'bad old days'. I do not remember the details now, but I am sure that she once let slip that her first husband was Lord Montgomery's brother. As a sister-in-law, she claimed to have known 'Monty' well, a disclosure that gave her celebrity status and somehow explained her abrupt, sometimes crusty, manner.

The ten of us, two men and eight women with ages spanning some five decades, made up Captain Munroe's passenger list, when with hatches battened down, we slipped from our berth at Dar es Salaam and set sail for Cape Town.

Chapter 17
The Boat Party

The first morning of the M V Nijkerk's journey back to Europe, I was up at seven feeling marvellous after my first real night's sleep aboard. Surprised at not experiencing even the slightest pangs of seasickness, as I had on previous occasions when we started moving, I decided to venture up on deck. It was a grey, misty morning. Below, on the foredeck, some half a dozen men were heaving lumber overboard, tidying up after the last cargo had been stowed, preparing for the long voyage home. I wished I could have been down there, throwing wood into the waves; it looked a very satisfying task. Later on, the men rounded up all the odd oil drums that were lying about and put them down into the hold nearest our cabins, before finally lowering the ship's cranes. When the deck was washed and clean, the passengers would be able to walk there in safety.

Establishing a routine in any given situation in life takes some time and effort even when there is the rigid structure of, say, an academic course, working hours, or the constraints of family commitments to impose parameters. The prospect of whiling away some three weeks, at least 21 nights and days, with nothing specific to do, nowhere to go other than the confines of a cargo boat, and no one of my own age to commune with, offered a unique opportunity to dispense with dull old routines and timetables. I could drift through each day doing pretty well, exactly as I pleased. So day one at sea began with a game of table tennis with Jill (Mrs Hacker). We kept losing the ball and had to call on Freik, the chief steward, and a pantry boy who had been idly watching us, to fish it out of the outer edge of the deck, under the lifeboats.

The Captain and First Officer chose day one to make their debut in the dining room. However, conversation was not exactly sparkling as several passengers were unwell, feeling seasick, no doubt. Even I felt a little queasy when presented with a plate of brown beans, fried onions, fat pork and leeks, all swimming in a greasy gravy. I was ashamed at not being able to tackle what had been recommended as a Dutch speciality. However, Jill came to my rescue and asked the steward for something plainer, having realised that I had been set up. As the youngest passenger, it was permissible to tease me.

The highlight of the afternoon was a visit to the bridge. The First Officer, a big booming Dutchman, had invited several of us up to see how everything worked. The wheel was fixed on automatic whilst the Second Officer was writing up the log prior to going off duty. I looked at our position on the chart, and then the First Officer showed me how they took bearings with the compass.

The instrument measuring the depth of the water was registering 570 fathoms, where we were, six miles out from the coast, and about to enter the Mozambique Channel. With wind and current against us, we were making 13.5 knots. Radar had been used to navigate through the morning mist but the weather had improved. The sky was a crisp, bright blue, whilst the strong, cool wind whipped up a stiff lace edge to the waves.

The ship cut through them with a purposeful movement, not rough but a firm up and down. On the bridge, there seemed to be plenty of room, with all the flags and charts neatly tidied away into pigeon holes and drawers. A coffee pot stood on a little stove in the chart room and reassuringly, the Engine Room Telegraph was set at Full Ahead.

After dinner that evening, activities in the passenger lounge began quietly enough with reading and games of Scrabble to occupy us till bedtime. That was until 9.30 when the Chief Officer asked Betty, Jill and the rest of us to join him at the bar. From then until the early hours of the next morning, we really enjoyed ourselves.

The officers danced with us, then instigated a hilarious session of dressing up, which involved wearing hats from their amazing collection and boot polish moustaches. The Chief Steward, in his role of makeup artist, blackened my eyebrows and round my eyes.

Then later, after we had exhausted ourselves with so much cavorting, he cleaned off the makeup with alcohol, probably gin. Everyone drank a lot. During the evening, I unwisely downed three sherries, an advocaat and vodka, then two more cocktails with vodka.

Freik, in his element behind the bar, produced scarves for us ladies and, propelled by the officers, we all danced in a conga line through the lounge. The merrymaking finished with Freik dressing up as a hula-hula girl complete with bra and grass skirt, which he magically produced from under the counter.

Sunday morning was a subdued affair. I awoke with a cardboard mouth and burning skin. Everyone drooped around deck before settling down in a quiet corner to drop off to sleep. The ship was rolling its way down the coast so, not surprisingly after coffee and biscuits at 11 o'clock in the upstairs lounge, I suddenly felt the need to make a quick exit to be sick in my cabin.

After that, I felt better but Kathleen (Mrs McGraw) stayed in bed and Jill retired to the deck as she had been 'overcome' while trying to do some ironing in the laundry. Inge Riidmann was still not well but the other travellers, Mr and Mrs Muller and Betty Shelley, were fit enough to play Canasta with me in the evening.

Of course the crew members, all experienced late night party-goers, were unaffected by such riotous evenings, many more of which were to liven the monotony of a long voyage.

Monday began with a fire drill. Seven blasts of the siren set us scurrying to muster stations on deck wearing life jackets. I understood that number 3 position was where I should join the group but the Chief Steward soon changed that. He towered over me, retied my life jacket, and redirected me to number 4 on the other side of deck, to an all-male group, as he pointedly remarked.

I suppose there were some perks to being the smallest passenger. I was glad when the exercise was over and we could retire to our respective sunbathing places on our own chaises lounges until lunchtime. Digestion after lunch was aided by another spell on the sun deck.

With the foredeck clean and tidy, we were allowed to take a stroll up to the prow. By 5 o'clock, the temperature had dropped and it was cold, with a roaring wind, when Kathleen, her friend, Ann Bonner, and I, went to explore an area that had hitherto been out of bounds. No doubt, if we had seen the film 'Titanic', we would have been inspired to emulate Leonardo Di Caprio and Kate Winslet's antics, but it was exhilarating enough just to look down through an opening in the deck and see the prow cutting a track through the water below. It was a unique sensation intensified by the powerful sounds of the sea and wind. Distanced, as we were, from the throb of the engines, we could imagine that we were alone on the ocean, skimming over the waves. .

That evening, the lights of Durban shone out of the darkness to starboard. From a distance, that troubled corner of the continent looked so peaceful. I wondered if anyone looking out would see us steam past, just another ship out at sea on a dark night.

The observer on land would have been surprised by the deafening noise emanating from the crew's bar where passengers and officers were shouting their heads off just like school children. We were playing horse racing, and prizes were pink chits that could be exchanged at the bar for glasses of beer. Of course, the volume of noise increased in proportion to the amount of alcohol consumed.

Early morning skipping was a good antidote for late-night lethargy as Jill, Inge and I discovered. We decided that we needed some vigorous exercise and, obligingly, Freik had provided us with skipping ropes. Table tennis was becoming more demanding on an unpredictably sloping floor but despite the big waves, we still played outside on the sundeck where duty officers sometimes challenged us to a game.

Dancing became another favourite way of exercising, starting one morning when I took my records—I must have packed them in my hand luggage—to the bar. Even a little hand washing of clothes and hairdressing made the day pass more agreeably. Inge proved to be quite a stylist with a few hair rollers and a comb. Conversations with one's fellow passengers provided plenty of mental stimulus; everyone had tales to tell and experiences to recount on such occasions.

Some evenings, we socialised with the officers, but it was only when we were invited into their bar that this occurred since crew, apart from the Captain, First Officer and stewards, were not allowed into the passenger areas.

However, because Piet, the young Dutchman who had accompanied us on our on-shore excursions earlier in the trip, was neither a passenger nor a full member of the crew, he was given special permission to talk to me in the crew's bar.

He had been unwell since we left Dar es Salaam and I had not seen him for several days, so I was delighted when he hailed me on Tuesday evening and asked me if I would like a tour of the engine rooms the following day. Jokers, who threatened to put out all the lights down there at some stage, had to be bought off at a cost of five beers.

At 2 o'clock on Wednesday afternoon, I followed Piet down into the depths of the ship. The floors were treacherously slippery with grease whilst the noise of the pistons was ear cracking. First, I was shown a machine for extracting water from oil to cut down the cost of buying ready cleaned fuel oil.

Most of the statistics about oil consumption and speed drained out of my brain as I tried to concentrate on following Piet's explanation of how the maze of pipes, valves and rods, generators, boilers and check cocks powered the Nijkerk on her home run.

Educational as it was, half an hour in such searing heat was enough for me. Back in the fresh air, I felt sorry for the engineers toiling away below decks; so much noise, so much heat, so much oil. No wonder they consumed so much beer!

That evening, flocks of birds paid us a surprise visit as the ship was travelling within flying distance of the coast. We could see sand dunes on the beaches before the light faded. The sea was calm when we went inside for dinner but it was the lull before the storm, which began with bright lightning before bedtime. Spray sounding like hailstones crashing against my porthole woke me at 1.30 a.m. I looked out onto a deck lashed with jagged spray as the ship nose-dived into each mountainous wave. It was a terrifying scene of tumbling water. The vessel seemed to tremble with anticipation as she sat at the bottom of each trough between waves, waiting to be flung even higher on the following roller. How could we stay afloat? There was no more sleep to be had and soon, I was battling with water pouring through the tightly screwed up porthole. What a relief to see the light of day, grey as it was!

Hans brought tea at 7 o'clock. Fortunately, I had finished a first cup when the tray was flung off the table to land in a messy heap of broken crockery, tea, sugar and milk. At breakfast, another great roll of the ship sent me and Jill skimming backwards on our chairs across the dining room away from our table amidst spilled coffee and cutlery. By this time, I was sure we were about to die, each lurch and crash winding my tensed nerves one notch tighter. There was nothing to do except sit helplessly in the lounge and watch the menacing waves gather to even greater heights before crashing down onto the foredeck below the windows. I have never felt so numb with fear as I did during that storm which harried us all the way round the Cape.

As the day wore on, we passed some half a dozen ships all lurching along and we wondered how their sailors were coping. Our crew busied themselves hosing down the passenger decks aft as they were unable to work below where everything was awash. Later, after I'd had a nap and some tea, Mr and Mrs Muller gave me a German lesson. We had started these lessons when we left Dar es Salaam where I had bought a German course book, hoping to teach myself on the long journey. The Mullers were sticklers for good pronunciation and dutifully marked my written work, but I was a poor student when it came to learning vocabulary. However, whilst the storm raged, it was good to have something to take my mind off the present danger.

Drinks to celebrate the Chief Engineer's birthday and dinner, excellent as usual, despite what must have been impossible cooking conditions in the kitchen, put us in a calmer mood for what was to be another terrifying night. Great crashes again awoke me in the early hours. The ship was rolling heavily and suddenly, I found myself on the floor along with drawers, clothes and other loose objects that had been shot across the cabin. After such a bruising experience, it was impossible to go back to sleep so I put everything away and longed for the dawn. I later learnt that most of the noise from below was caused by the bar in the officers' quarters falling across the room. Empty bottles rolled from side to side whilst full ones smashed against the walls as they were flung off their shelves. My imagination, working overtime as usual, suggested that our ship was about to fall apart. Why else would there be such a noise of breaking glass and timbers? I was even more scared than I had been on the previous night and longed to see daylight and to feel the Nijkerk steer into the bay at Cape Town.

The sun rose over Table Mountain on a crisp, clear morning. It was beautiful to see the town gradually show up, revealing its houses, factories and skyscrapers, then to watch the clouds roll back from the summit and almost uncover the flat top. Cable cars like white beads crossed the rock face. On deck we gathered, trying to make light of the storm by feeding the gulls and taking photographs. There was to be no going ashore in the rough seas but a pilot ship came out to where we were hoving to, to deliver mail and collect our letters for posting in Cape Town. Still, it was blissful to stand, like animals newly out of hibernation, with the sun warming our backs. Business completed; the crew was about to follow in the wake of another vessel rolling its way out of the harbour when the Nijkerk's anchor jammed. There was an electrical fault which had to be fixed before it could be raised. So, the bosun, carpenter, deck hands, various engine room electricians, Piet with a fire extinguisher, and the First Officer set to on the prow. The repair, difficult in the heavy seas, almost cost one young hand his eyesight when the cutting equipment exploded, but the job was completed and we left the relative calm of our anchorage.

Outside the harbour, the swell made even everyday activities impossible. A dining room chair fell on me and coffee went everywhere, a simple enough accident but it was the last straw for me after two sleepless nights and hours of pent up terror. I broke down in front of everyone and wept.

Afterwards, I felt foolish, stupid to have been so childishly afraid. Perhaps, my older companions were more stoic and better able to control their fears but they all sympathised with me and encouraged me to cheer up.

I was told, "One just has to accept the sea's ways. One wouldn't expect a ship to be like a house. The Nijkerk is strong and there are forty men keeping her in order. Most of the time she behaves herself." The First Officer's words of wisdom made me feel myself again and less ashamed of my tears.

Saturday, 19 August, our eighth day at sea, began with clear blue skies and bright sunshine. It was chilly but warm enough to sit outside and watch the sea birds wheeling around the ship. I couldn't believe that some of them were really albatrosses, but compared with the gulls, their wingspan was enormous.

Against the deep blue sea, their white and black markings looked like paint work on a smooth surface rather than coloured feathers. White frills on the wave tops added to the illusion that the scene was a carefully composed seascape of great beauty. Nothing frightening there! The inner terror I had struggled to hide during the storm was replaced by a feeling of peace and freedom as I watched the great birds gliding between sky and sea.

Saturday ended with a surprise party to top all surprise parties. After dinner, Jill, Betty and I had been sitting at the bar chatting as usual. We had sensed that something strange was afoot, but we didn't discover exactly what it was until 10 o'clock when we were invited downstairs to the officers' bar.

I was singled out to be escorted by two men wearing pigtails and pretending to be girls. It was very funny. They directed me to the vacant chair next to Piet then, to my astonishment and mounting anxiety, in came the Chief Steward dressed as a priest accompanied by Jane Granger clad in a sheet and bearing a tray, followed by an apprentice officer carrying a paint brush and a bowl of water. Suddenly, Piet and I were centre stage in an elaborate practical joke.

Everything had been carefully planned, with a lot of hard work going into the making of the rings—fashioned by an engineer from a length of copper pipe—and the Wedding Day cards illustrated by one of the crew. With much splashing of water and Ave Marias, Piet and I were 'married'.

At the end of the ceremony, the Chief Steward took two rings from Jane's tray and fitted them on our fingers, upon which everyone cheered and clapped. Having to face a queue of handsome young Dutchmen lined up to kiss the 'bride' was, to say the least, quite overwhelming. Never before had I been the focus of such attention.

When the kissing was over, we all danced a conga round the bar and deck before settling down for the second feature of the evening's entertainment. Horse racing. This was much more exciting. I was allowed to call the numbers and succeeded in winning lots of beer tickets—which of course, were shared with my 'husband'.

Some time after midnight, the other passengers drifted away leaving me to kiss the officers' goodnight and thank them for an unusual evening. Their response was more fraternal than paternal but, as in everyday contacts, there was never any hint of anything improper in the crew's behaviour to any of the passengers. As for Piet, he took the evening's fun in good part.

Obviously, he was teased by his fellow crewmen but he seemed to enjoy the joke. Subsequently, we spent many evenings sitting together talking about what we would do when the Nijkerk returned to port in Holland. Piet was looking forward to seeing his girlfriend back in The Hague before going into the army, whereas I had arranged to meet Els, a long standing pen-friend, in Rotterdam before going off on a three-day tour of the Netherlands.

Captain Munroe had rooted out a little guide book for me when he heard of my plans. After that, our futures were undecided. It was 1967 and anything was possible. Thinking about it now, those three weeks at sea provided me with a perfect transition between what someone once called my 'African Experience' and the rest of my life.

The further North we steamed in the South Atlantic, the more difficult it became to keep track of local time. The hours of daylight and darkness, of dawn and dusk, were constantly changing. Temperatures began to rise and as soon as it was warm enough, we had a swimming pool on the deck aft, a construction of timbers and blue pvc deep enough to dive into.

One Sunday afternoon, some of the officers did just that in a mad display of one-upmanship, senior followed by junior ranks, all in their Number Ones, white shorts, shirts, socks and epaulettes. They had been celebrating the wireless operator's birthday and had decided to cool off.

Watching the sea became a favourite pastime. The water was never the same colour or texture from one day to the next, its mood dependent on wind, sun, spray or haze. The albatrosses had left us but then, there was a new delight provided by flying fish, some large, and like steel bluebirds as they took off and wheeled over the waves, others in flocks like tiny silver butterflies which had been frightened away from their secret places under the waves by the passing of our ship.

One afternoon, when Jill and I were enjoying a swim, the dolphins started a fantastic dance round the bows, so we hauled ourselves up onto the railing round the pool and watched the dark sleek bodies as they flung themselves two by two out of the sea. I was amazed at the height of some of the leaps and the way in which they curved their bodies before disappearing into the blue depths.

Like a gymnastic display with a line of people leaping over a vaulting horse, their movement was continuous and at the same time mysterious. We felt privileged to be onlookers at such a show of exuberance. The evening walk to the prow to savour the smells of rope and cargo spiced with fresh paint where a rusty section was being spruced up, became an integral part of our day. Kathleen and Ann, the two retired American teachers, and Betty and I were thrilled by the appearance of the phosphorescence round the bows. We watched glittering showers of star-spangled foam swirling out into the velvet waters beyond until it was too cold to stand about in the darkness.

Gulls flew round the ship again as we passed Dakar. Sight of the coast on that Western tip of Africa after so many days at sea brought tears to our eyes. The ten of us stood in silence clutching the ship's railings, each person isolated in his or her own thoughts but united by a deep yearning to walk on terra firma again. It was inexplicably moving to see land, houses and trees in the distance, so tantalisingly close yet disappearing so quickly. I realised how much I was looking forward to being home. Friendly as my travelling companions were, I longed to see my family again and to be in touch with daily events once more.

Soon, we would be passing the Canary Islands and heading for the Bay of Biscay. There would be European music on the radio and a Farewell Dinner Party, the Captain's last, for he too was leaving the ship. The company had decided to reshuffle the crew, upsetting the First Officer who did not relish the thought of having to work under a more orthodox leader after six voyages with Captain Munroe. According to Piet, on the Nijkerk, engineers and mates were allowed to mix and make merry downstairs at a bar that they should not really have had, because the captain considered it better for morale to bend the rules than to observe them to the letter and have men sitting in their cabins brooding over petty quarrels which could easily grow into fights. As passengers, we appreciated the efficiency and good humour of the crew throughout the long trip back to The Netherlands.

The end of the voyage came on a cold, grey morning. I cannot remember the leave taking apart from the discomfort of being out in the real world again, alone on the street and in charge of a considerable amount of luggage. However, once I had booked into a hotel in Rotterdam, arranged to store my cases for several days, and phoned my friend Els to invite her over for dinner, it was no problem to plan an interesting three days sight-seeing by train and coach. To some people, it might seem a strange thing to do, to be touring around The Netherlands at a time when I could have been on the ferry back to England, but my itchy feet syndrome had kicked in again, and I could not resist the temptation to look at places new. Only when my curiosity had been satisfied, could I pack up and go home, back to living with my parents in Farnham.

One cold, snowy day in December, the wooden crates that I had last seen being lowered into the Nijkerk's hold, arrived by carrier and were offloaded into our small front garden. The handmade furniture, the wooden animals, baskets and souvenirs which were eagerly pulled out, as well as all the books and papers that, in common with most teachers, I had collected, gave off that unmistakable African smell of wood smoke and red earth. It was to be another 34 years before I could fulfil my dream to revisit Lushoto and see once more the hills and plains of Tanzania.

Chapter 18
Return to Tanzania

We boarded the plane for Nairobi late on Friday evening at the end of September 2001. The flight over Paris, down past Rome, out over the Mediterranean and into African airspace, was mostly smooth with very little turbulence but, as always, I found it difficult to sleep. As we circled a brown landscape in preparation for landing, I felt none of the old emotions stirring. It was all a bit of an anti-climax.

After the excitement of my journey and returning home from Africa had worn off, I hadn't known what to do. I'd had a vague notion of attempting some further study, to graduate maybe, as my only qualification was a Certificate of Education. But first, I needed some money. The savings I had accrued from a Provident Fund set up whilst at Lushoto had been spent on a car, a VW Beetle of course.

It was a mistake to take on a part-time teaching job at the local Primary School where I'd been educated. I couldn't cope with such unruly children—they stood on their desks and shouted at me—so I left. After two challenging terms at Weydon Secondary Modern in Farnham, where I'd started my career, I was accepted for an English post at Dr Williams, a girls' boarding school in Wales. My mother had spotted the advertisement in the Times Ed and encouraged me to apply.

My two years in Wales were eventful and immensely satisfying. I loved teaching the 11 to 15-year-olds even though the boarding school duties were sometimes onerous. Who wouldn't be happy in a classroom with windows looking out to Cader Idris? An Additional English Certificate gained in a fun-packed year at Worcester College of Education brought me to Bridgnorth, Shropshire, as Head of English at the Girls' Secondary Modern. With no real desire to put down roots, I bought a bungalow so that my family could visit me.

However, I was still searching for another teaching job abroad, somewhere warm and sunny where classes might be small, when I met Mike. We were married in 1972 and the following year, started our European travels, when not teaching, in our beautiful, new VW camper van. Trips further afield began in 1999 when we were both retired.

It was my husband Mike's idea to arrange the trip to Tanzania and to invite my sister Louise and her husband Jim to join us. Although Louise hates flying, she agreed, and Jim said he would love to go if we could include a detour to Nyali Beach, one of his favourite haunts from years ago, so we combed through travel brochures and looked into the possibility of combining a standard safari with an adventure holiday in the Usambara Mountains. However, even when costs were minimised and economies made, the price always came out too high for our budget and, anyway, the logistics just didn't work. Eventually, Mike resorted to the computer and made the amazing discovery that a certain Grant's Lodge, Lushoto, had a website. The pictures showed a colonial style house set in a pretty garden. The rooms reminded me of my flat at Lushoto Prep School with dark wooden floorboards and heavy furniture. Could it have been the home of the Grants I'd known in the sixties? Old Mr Grant, the forestry commission man, had made me a camphor wood chest, a rocking chair and the mvuli coffee table which we still use in our lounge.

Further research threw up another familiar name, Kearsley, a travel agent based in Dar es Salaam. I remembered seeing their advertisement in my carefully preserved Tanganyika gazetteer of 1963. That clinched it! Mike emailed them, setting out our travel requirements; safaris to Serengeti, Manyara, Ngorongoro, Olduvai, Momella and a trip to Zanzibar and Selous in the south of Tanzania, as well as a stay in Lushoto at Grant's Lodge. Thus began our correspondence with Rita, an enigmatic fixer, who we were to meet only briefly one hot afternoon in Kearsley's head office. Rita arranged for us to have a car—which turned out to be a Toyota 4x4 Land Cruiser—and a driver to take us to most of our destinations. After many e-mails to tweak the tailor-made package, an agreeable price was fixed. Paying the final bill of some £8,000 for the four of us—in dollars, by money order to a bank in New York—without having any real assurance that the people at the African end would actually be there for us when the time came, was an act of courage!

At Nairobi Airport, there was no one to meet us. Our names weren't any of those on the hand held message boards clustered round the arrivals lounge. Our worst fears suddenly looked well-founded. However, as the various agents scooped up their travellers and disappeared into taxis and minibuses we scanned the notices again and spotted one for Mike x4. That was us! The next uncomfortable moment was at the Serena Hotel. At the reception desk, we discovered that we weren't booked in. There was no reference to Kearsley's Travel Agency or to our surnames. Things were beginning to look bad when Mike remembered that our pickup van at the airport had been a Safari Seeker's vehicle and that was the clue. The receptionist looked under the reservation for Safari Seeker and found our group's booking. Again, it was for Mr Mike x4. Feeling relieved at having side stepped the first potential problems, we were soon installed in our spacious rooms on the ground floor.

Our early morning drive from Jomo Kenyatta Airport had taken us past Nairobi Game Park close to the city boundary, with sightings of antelope and distant giraffes to excite us. The landscape looked dusty and bone dry. Further along, we came upon people going to work, on foot, on bikes and in noisy, battered old cars and trucks belching forth black smoke. Nursery gardens of plants grown in plastic bags along the banks of the drainage ditches of the dual carriageway made surprising oases in the midst of such noise and pollution. Deeper into the city, our driver pointed out Uhuru Park, a scruffy area of grass and bushes which, according to him, became a mugger's paradise after dark. Everything looked neglected and hostile until we reached the gates of the Serena Hotel. Inside, all was tasteful and well run. After a nap in our rooms and a drink beside the pool, we felt refreshed and ready for action but, disappointingly, there was to be no sightseeing outside the gates. Louise and Jim had been out whilst Mike and I were asleep and had found it an uncomfortable experience. Despite having been warned of possible dangers and commanded not to go out of sight of the gatekeeper, they couldn't resist the temptation to explore. Perhaps, it was the fact that they were constantly glancing over their shoulders on the lookout for trouble that highlighted their vulnerability, but they soon found themselves being accosted by would-be guides and street vendors. Reluctantly, they decided to turn back before they could attract even more attention. We were prisoners shut inside the hotel's well-guarded walls. Luckily, there was a big swimming pool and a pretty garden—patrolled by an askari—in which to amuse ourselves until dark. Then, the ponds and miniature waterways became noisy with tiny frogs.

The following morning we were up early in time for a stroll around the grounds. It was surprisingly chilly. Louise and Jim admitted they hadn't slept well. They hate air conditioning so much that they had turned it off and, contrary to security advice, had opened their windows. The whine of incoming mosquitoes followed by furious but ineffective attempts at swotting them had ensured a restless few hours. Late night screaming from the adjacent Uhuru Park, conjuring up scenes of mayhem and murder, was simply the last straw.

Soon after breakfast, the Safari Seekers kombi transported us to Wilson Airport. The departure lounge was full of Europeans dressed in safari clothes in dull greens, greys and stone, leafing through books about Tanzania or studying unfolded maps. (Old memories had already been stirred when I'd sighted a man reading *The Snows of Kilimanjaro* beside the pool at the Serena.) There was the feel of travellers going places and the buzz was making me feel excited. Would I recognise any of those places that had once been so familiar?

A thrilling take-off in a small plane with its four jet propellers whirring took us bumping through the clouds into the clear skies above. The pilot's door was open so you could see out through the cockpit window and really get a sense of climbing. There wasn't much to be seen below, just one or two villages glimpsed between clouds, thatched huts, water courses and brown land. Kilimanjaro was hidden in mist.

At the grand-sounding Kilimanjaro International Airport—I certainly didn't remember that from the sixties—we were speedily processed, along with sixteen other passengers from the plane and met by a cheerful young man who introduced himself as our driver for the holiday. He said his name was Fazili. He was accompanied by Jane, the Kearsley Rep, who presented Louise and me with a bouquet of long-stemmed red roses, and Mike and Jim with a bottle of wine each. What a lovely way to begin a holiday!

On the journey to Arusha, some 36 kilometres, Jane told us that her mother was Masai and her father Chagga, people from the coffee-growing lower slopes of Kilimanjaro. Fazili's home was Tanga, the small coastal town that I had visited so often in the 1960s. The two Tanzanians talked frankly about their work and family commitments, each having two children. "That's more than enough to finance," they both agreed and were genuinely shocked when we confessed to being three-child families.

We sped past coffee plantations and maize shambas, townships and markets smelling of wood-smoke. The intense blue of jacarandas and the green of the wooded areas along the Usa River made us gasp at their beauty and keep exclaiming, "Wonderful! Isn't this wonderful?"

At Arusha, we dropped Jane off at Kearsley's office and set out for our first stop, Manyara. (I hadn't fulfilled my promise to spend my honeymoon there and I don't think that Fiona has either, but at least, I was going there *with* my husband.)

Fazili raced along the good tarmac road, slowing down only to negotiate the occasional—and sometimes quite random—speed bumps, until we reached the long dirt section at the turn off. It was very dusty and suddenly much hotter. We were thankful that we had bought a box of bottled water in Arusha.

Our Land Cruiser coped well with the corrugations and we bounced along racing our own personal cloud of red dust. Fazili was skilled at keeping us entertained whilst remaining alert to the vagaries of other road users. Sometimes, we met or passed lorries, trying to keep out of potholes and ruts by steering a smooth path all over the road.

Beside the road, the bush trails were busy with Masai herding long lines of cattle and goats but villages, often only an untidy collection of mud brick huts, were few and far between and seemingly empty. Towards the end of our tiring journey, so reminiscent of those beginning of holiday trips of the sixties, we drove into Mto wa Mbu and had to adjust our speed to the pace of people moving about the township. Past the last huts, we climbed the escarpment and there at last was the view I had for so many years wanted to see again, Lake Manyara!

Serena Hotel, built on a ridge overlooking the lake, is a series of tall, round, pointed-roofed chalets. As soon as we had unpacked, we couldn't resist a dip in the cool swimming pool, cleverly built to give a 180 degree view out over the forest to the lake.

With chins resting on the edge, we watched the sun setting on the game park down in the valley below, and with the darkness came those distinctive sounds and smells of the African bush at night. It was thrilling!

Before six next morning, we drove down the escarpment to Manyara National Park, eager to enter, but the gates were locked and we had to wait for the warden to arrive. It didn't matter though, because it was wonderful to be outdoors at that time of the day, pacing up and down in the chill dawn air, cracking jokes then falling silent as we became aware of the steady increase in volume of sounds around us; monkeys beginning to stir amongst the leafy branches and the steady background hum of bees already working high in the white flowers of some big trees.

At 6.30 a.m. the warden arrived, took our fees and let us into the park. One of the highlights of our early morning game drive was being charged by a baby elephant, all gangly legs and floppy trunk. We stopped a little way behind his mother who seemed to be encouraging her offspring in his ridiculous behaviour, which made us all laugh until we suddenly noticed a huge bull elephant observing us from behind a bush next to our Land Cruiser. We withdrew quietly. Later, we were lucky enough to see a family of elephants drinking at a stream beside a wooden bridge. We stopped on the bridge and from our vantage point could look down on five heads with ears neatly folded back onto five bodies of varying size, whilst five trunks reached forward then rolled under, busily transferring water from the stream into five thirsty mouths.

I had hoped that I would recognise some of the landmarks within the park but even the lake looked different. There were no flamingos wading in the shallows and, anyway, the road no longer gave access to the shore. I should have realised that in nearly 40 years, everything would have changed. The Africa of the 1960s existed only in my memory.

Back at the Serena Hotel after breakfast, we were treated to a tour of the kitchen gardens. Here, we met a truly inspired head gardener, an old man who talked with passion about conservation. All the food he produced for the hotel was grown organically and he and his team were developing a nursery where they could experiment with new strains of disease-resistant fruit and vegetables that would also withstand the onslaught of insects and climate at Manyara. (The agriculturalists I had known in the 60s would have been amazed at such progress and at the knowledge and practical skills of the gardeners.) The trial plots, carefully monitored trees and shrubs, each in its own little stone surround, and the pit of composted leaves and vegetable matter were all displayed with pride.

At 10.15 we left for the Serengeti; another long, hard drive. I had forgotten the rocky outcrops and distant mountains that feature along the route. Nothing was as I had remembered it. I couldn't even identify on the map where Fiona and I had stayed on our first visit, although the Research Institute must have still been there. This time, we were booked into a posh hotel with no stuffed hyenas to worry about in our bedrooms.

With Fazili at the wheel of our 4x4, we were treated to a wondrous display of animals and birds. There were oribi lying in the long grass, topi away on a

175

hill, a Verreaux eagle-owl on the branch of a tree with a dead guinea fowl dangling from its foot, hartebeest, hyenas keeping cool in a muddy rut in the road, giraffe reaching up to leaves in a tall acacia, and lions resting in the shade, quietly viewing a small group of zebras.

Best of all was the sighting of two cheetahs. We spotted them stalking Thompson gazelle. The cats were completely oblivious of our slowly moving vehicle and crossed the road in front of us to sit on the top of an old termite mound which made a perfect viewpoint. Having satisfied themselves as to the whereabouts of the flighty Tommies, the cheetahs climbed down and continued on down the road behind us, passing close to our wheels as they went.

Olduvai Gorge, the next stop on our itinerary, was reached via a shortcut across a dusty plain. En route we came upon a group of young Masai boys. They looked like strange apparitions, the thick white chalk decorations on their foreheads and cheeks accentuating the deep black areas of eyes, mouth and nose. Each wore a black toga-like garment adding to the illusion that the chalked faces were unsupported by bodies or limbs.

Fazili explained that the boys had recently been circumcised and were living away from their village for a while. All together in their pain, maybe. I thought they looked rather forlorn and at a loose end, no longer children but not yet ready to be recruited to the rank of warrior. Graduation to moran status would be the next step.

At Olduvai, all had changed. A small museum had been built overlooking the gorge and we could no longer go down to the mysterious paths that I had followed some 25 years before. I had taken along the notes that the guide had given Fiona and me on our first visit, and I showed them to the museum's curator, an old man, who was amazed that the flimsy pages of typewritten information had lasted so long.

"Please send me a copy," he urged giving me his business card. "I'd like it for the museum."

Louise, Jim, Mike and I took some time looking at the exhibits, especially the poignant trail of the Laetoli footprints said to have been made by a man, woman and child 3.6 million years ago. Mary Leakey and her team had discovered them in 1976 and excavated the find in 1978, more than ten years after I'd left East Africa.

Later, we sat outside in the warm sunshine looking across the ancient, empty river bed to the rugged block of red rock standing proud of the flat sandy plains beyond. How much change there had been in my life since I'd last visited the site but, compared with all that had taken place in the gorge over the last millennia, it was a mere nothing.

Our next stop was Ngorongoro. Fazili's trusty Toyota had broken down on the way past Ngorongoro, en route for the Serengeti, and had had to be mended, but on the way back from the Serengeti to Ngorongoro, it was fit enough to take us down into the crater after we'd booked into our hotel on the rim.

Fortunately, the steep road is still one way down and on the far side, one way up. We had heard the Masai descend with their goats and cows before we'd had breakfast at the hotel, so it was just us and several other 4x4s kicking up the dust.

On the crater floor, it was cool standing up in the wind looking out of the open top of our vehicle, binoculars and cameras at the ready. Sometimes, there was nothing to see but blond grass or a distant safari car searching for one of the 'big five'.

Our first sighting was a large herd of buffaloes with a personal escort of oxpeckers to clean their backs, noses, faces and eyes. Then, rounding a bend, we came upon a lion with a bloated belly and bloody chops just finishing the remains of a zebra. Later, we caught sight of three more lions slowly moving forward, abreast of each other but spaced out, stalking something hidden in a dip in the ground.

Beautiful, yellow-barked acacias at the Lerai Forest sheltered a pastoral scene featuring gently grazing zebra, gazelle and velvety grey waterbuck, which had us reaching for extra film; none of us possessed a digital camera at that time. At the wet area, it was the birds that caught our attention; black ibis, sacred ibis, saddle-billed stork, blackscott plovers and pelicans.

However, the most memorable image was of the flamingos on the lake. Thousands of birds had gathered in a shallow area and taken formation in high-stepping, chorus girl lines, all pink feathers and pink legs bending at the elbow-like knees. The colour, the noise, and the smell of soda from the shore made for a unique experience in a unique location.

It rained heavily when we stopped for lunch but Louise and I had already decided to eat in the car, having been warned about the black kites that were partial to tourists' sandwiches. With macho disregard for potential danger, Mike and Jim had said, "Oh we'll be all right outside. We'll sit under that bush. They won't get us there."

Of course, the kites had a reputation to keep up and soon they came screaming down to dive bomb the men and beat them up with beaks and wings before snatching their food.

When we set out again, all the birds we saw were drenched and there was a strong smell of wet foliage and of recently burnt grass. We all scanned the horizon now, looking for the one animal that had eluded us so far on the trip, a black rhino. When we saw a stationary vehicle in the distance, we sped towards it and questioned the driver but no one admitted to having seen the creature we were after. Then at 3.30, we finally spotted him, a solitary black bulk, a rhino standing on some grassland a distance from the road, not grazing, but just looking.

Fog hid the scenery when we set off for Arusha at 7.30 a.m. next morning. Tall purple flowers and dense vegetation weighed down with red dust leaned towards us from either bank and, by the light of the headlamps, we could make out fresh buffalo droppings on the red road ahead. At Beauman's Point, we slowed down to look at the view but the vast crater where we'd spent the previous day was just a misty bowl.

Lower down, at Ngorongoro Gate, the mist cleared and we were soon into open country passing fields with straight rows of trees acting as wind breaks and cow-drawn carts carrying maize. At Karatu, a big township, Fazili announced, "We're stopping for fuel," so we climbed out and looked for a toilet, in this instance a little shack housing an old lavatory pan. The oil drum outside held the flush water which you scooped up in a plastic basin. There was also the luxury of a closing door.

Before we left Karatu we swapped seats. The back seat of the Land Cruiser was marginally more comfortable than the other two just in front. The passenger seat was kept for packed lunches, a big box of bottled water, Fazili's bird books and, for the first part of the journey, the roses I had been given at the airport. Each night, I trimmed their thick stems and plunged them into water until they had revived and could be arranged in a cut-down, plastic water bottle. The sturdy blooms set off with the ribbons and frills of the original bouquet gave our room a touch of glamour.

Still on the dirt road, we made our way down the ridge of the Rift Valley, past the huge baobab tree again and into Mto wa Mbu where schoolchildren were outside playing on the football pitch. Then, it was on, past houses and piles of bananas and drying maize.

We noticed that the colour of the soil was gradually changing, fading into chalky whiteness, making the dusty bushes look as if they were frost covered. Electricity pylons heralded the start of the tarmac and leaden skies of heavy clouds replaced the early morning sunshine.

Along the road, Masai, in their flamboyant dress made splashes of red on a pale background; a man cycling along clutched a dangerous looking stake; a woman striding through the bush carried a pot on her head.

Further on, we came upon a group of Masai women wearing wide, bead collars and those fantastic earrings which had so amazed me the first time I'd seen them, years before I'd even known that earlobes could be pierced.

"What's in those?" we asked Fazili after we'd passed yet more bulging sacks seemingly abandoned beside the road.

"Charcoal waiting to be collected and taken to market. Used for cooking," was the answer.

There was other traffic speeding past now. No doubt any road kill was quickly cleaned up by scavenging birds and animals, although the dead hyena we avoided didn't seem to be the flavour of the month! One truck had come to grief in a dramatic accident and was on its side in a ditch. The two white-suited police sitting beside it were, presumably, protecting it from human scavengers.

Nearing Arusha we came upon a hunting party of five Land Rovers trying to negotiate a spread of speed humps which were being repainted with white stripes. "Tanzanian Defence Force," Fazili pointed out as we too waited for the painters to finish their work.

The centre of Arusha looked almost modern with its pavement-lined street, busy shops and even an internet cafe. (It still had a 'Bata' shoe shop to bring back memories of the 1960s. I was always puzzled as to the connection between bata, which in Swahili means a duck and shoes.) The town was teeming with people who surged round the Toyota when Fazili parked outside Kearsley's Office.

We felt trapped but couldn't resist looking out on the wares that the vendors pressed us to inspect through our closed windows. Before Fazili had returned, Louise and I had succumbed and splashed out on four batik pictures of animals, purchases to be put away with other impulse buys from overseas.

Fazili's need to back the vehicle into the road acted as a deterrent to further shopping, although one or two young boys, would-be traffic police, saw us out then strained their selling techniques to the limit by running alongside us for a while until their sense of self-preservation made them give up the chase.

Momella Game Lodge was our next destination. The family home that Fiona and I had visited in 1965 had later been extended and turned into a hotel by John Wayne and Hardy Kruger, the actors. I suspect that they had tried to buy into the beauty and tranquillity of the place, having fallen in love with that corner of East Africa whilst making *Hatari*, an early 1960s film about a group of hunters who trapped wild animals for zoos. After being jolted along the dilapidated approach road for nearly an hour, the sight of the bright flowers and green lawns of the hotel was as welcome as an oasis in a desert. Unfortunately, that was as far as the hospitality went. The dark, scruffy corridors made it difficult to find anyone who could book us in, let alone show us to our rooms or rustle up some food. When we were finally seated in a big, gloomy dining area, we were made to feel that we were something of an inconvenience and that we should be very grateful to the cook for having broken into his siesta to prepare our meal. Duly chastened, we did our best with the unappetising plates set before us.

Our accommodation was out in the grounds, in individual huts, not the romantic rondavels with thatched roofs that I had been telling everyone about but, instead, chalet-like buildings. The fixtures and fittings obviously hadn't been updated since John Wayne's time and were, quite frankly, worn out! To add to our gloominess, the summit of nearby Mount Meru was in black clouds.

Our spirits were soon to be raised by Daniel; the young, local guide who was to take us on a walking safari round the adjacent Momella Game Park. During our walkabout, we were much impressed by Dan's bird-spotting abilities. White-chested bee-eaters, bulbuls, a speckled mouse bird, a flycatcher, an amethyst sunbird on its nest, a robin chat and a francolin in some dark bushes were just some of the names we noted. Then, there were several species of eagle to be tracked through binoculars.

"I once helped an RSPB official in a bird count here," he told us proudly.

His education consisted of one year at college but, for the rest, he was self-taught, using his own observations and books, mostly donated by visitors. Financed by tourism, he generously helped support local schools and several women's groups who were involved in environmental issues.

It was thrilling to be so close to wild animals without the protection of a solid vehicle although Daniel did carry a rifle. In the gloomy afternoon light, we quietly made our way past a herd of buffalo. We must have been downwind from them because we could smell their bovine aroma and hear them making buffalo conversation as they grazed peacefully.

Following Dan, we approached a matriarchal group of five giraffes browsing among the bushes and quietly spread out, taking photographs as we moved forwards. The animals kept a wary eye on us whilst attending to their business and cleverly, little by little, moved forward too, thus keeping their distance. The smallest giraffe was the last to canter deeper into the scrub.

Raucous cries set Daniel off on the trail of a big baboon high up in the trees further on. I was quite frightened as we moved along the narrow woodland paths towards some rocky cliffs, all the time thinking to myself, "Anything might be lurking here!" However, the sun was setting and we had to turn back, going via a giant strangler fig and a hidden waterfall which thundered down the back wall of a cave through a hole in the roof.

It was dark when we reached the Lodge so, back in our rooms, we had to unpack our bags by torchlight. I was upset to discover that my binoculars were missing. They were a small, fold-up pair, so I assumed that they had fallen out of my rucksack when we got out of the car.

However, although Mike searched the area where we had stopped and the path to our hut, they were not to be found then or the following morning when we set out for the Usambara Mountains.

Chapter 19
The Usambaras Revisited

Some people say that it is a mistake to go back to a place where you have spent happy years and expect it to be the same. Better to keep your memories intact rather than have them spoilt by the reality of change.

However, given the chance to revisit Lushoto and to share the experience with such sympathetic travellers as my husband Mike, my sister Louise and her husband Jim—all of whom had heard me go on about, "When I was in Africa…"—how could I be afraid that images nurtured for over three decades, might be shattered? So, it was with curiosity tinged with excitement that I set out on this stage of the journey.

An hour's drive down the incredibly stony track from Momella saw us back on the tarmac road once more. Here, traffic consisted of donkeys and bikes carrying yellow, plastic containers of water instead of the buffaloes, zebra, warthogs and giraffe we'd encountered earlier.

First, we travelled through a flat area, dotted with cone-shaped hillocks, the distant mountains still in cloud. In an hour or so, the factories, smart garages and flower-filled traffic islands of Moshi came into view. The township looked prosperous, enjoying, as it does, its position at the end of the railway line from Dar es Salaam and, being situated close to Kilimanjaro, its status as the starting point for expeditions to the continent's highest mountain.

As we drove through the hustle and bustle of Moshi, Jim pointed out a sign for 'Moshi Lions'. We laughed, then realised it was not the four-footed ones but the worldwide group of business men who do charitable works. On the outskirts of the town, we came to a turning, left towards the Kenyan border and right to Dar es Salaam, a 9 to 10-hour bus ride away, that's if you go by luxury express service. We turned right.

The Pare Mountains rising in the distance became the new backdrop for the familiar baobab trees and, closer to the road, groups of dark shade trees. We were through Kisangeru and driving alongside the railway now. At Mwanga, women carrying kikapus on their heads, ubiquitous goats and bikes bristling with those familiar yellow water containers slowed us down, as we drove past small, corrugated roofed houses tucked away in the bush.

Rows of spiky sisal plants were the next feature to dominate the landscape and then suddenly, there was nothing except bush stretching for mile upon mile on either side of the road. At Mgago, we noticed men clearing the ground to dig footings for a group of new houses and there were more bags of charcoal awaiting collection. All disappeared as the road took us to the top of a rise, giving us a better view over the plains to the distant hills. We looked out across a foreground of red-brown soil, grey leafless bushes and scattered trees.

Our quiet contemplation of the vast panorama seen from the Toyota's windows was sometimes rudely interrupted by the sudden swish of a fast-moving vehicle; a high lorry with two humans atop the cattle jammed in the back or a bus racing down to the coast. We followed a coach with a huge fish eagle painted across its back, outstretched wings where there should have been windows.

Further along, candelabra trees and electricity pylons became part of the scene, and then a lacy network of simple fencing round an isolated settlement drew our eyes back from the distant mountains. The tilled soil round the huts was blond with the remains of a maize crop.

We had been following the route on my vintage Shell Map of East Africa, the one that had been used so often on trips back in the 1960s. It had worn well, being laminated, but it smelt musty, as did the Shell books of birds and animals I had fished out of my tin trunk for our holiday reference library.

To my surprise, the new tarmac road wasn't where it should have been! The Pares, scrubby mountains rising to 8,080 feet appeared on our left when, according to my estimation, they should have been on our right. "The old road, the one that you would have used, goes round the other side of the Pares," Fazili explained.

At Makanya, there was sisal again and beehives, like long drums, hanging in the trees. Now, the endless Masai Steppe on our right stretched to a flat horizon, just bush and red soil disappearing into the heat haze that smudged the line between earth and sky.

A tiny village appeared on our left, its football pitch of sorts boasting one set of goal posts without a crossbar. Then, in the distance beyond the line of trees marking the course of the Pangani River, we could see the dark shape of the Usambaras. Thorn bushes gave way to thatched huts surrounded by banana trees, coconut palms and shady mango trees. The railway line became visible again and at the station, an ancient tractor hauled a load of sisal. At last, we were approaching Mombo.

For people living in the Usambaras, Mombo was a significant landmark. If you could get to Mombo, you could go almost anywhere; East to Tanga and the coast, South to Dar es Salaam and the interior, and North to Moshi, Nairobi and the rest of the World. You could travel by road, rail, even air in the early 1960s when East African Airlines used to land its Dakotas on the grassy airstrip at Mombo.

For all that, this regular Waterloo Station of a place consisted of just a few houses, a bar with a pull-in for travellers who weren't looking for anything more sophisticated than a Tusker beer or a Fanta orange and a sawmill specialising in sandal wood. (I'd had a crush on the mill owner's son at one time.) But, like me, everything about Mombo had changed. The quiet village had grown into a noisy, bustling circus of a place.

Fazili made straight for the filling station, picking his way cautiously between parked vehicles and crowds of pedestrians newly released from the confines of their long-distance buses, many of which were jockeying for pole position round the petrol pumps. Vendors clutching trays of greasy samosas, dubious looking orangeade, packets of biscuits and dusty passion fruit, pressed their fare on mile-weary travellers.

The resultant hubbub of so much humanity packed together in that one small spot was unbelievable, and as I studied it from my vantage point in the Toyota, I wondered if 30 years would have made similar changes to what lay ahead of us up the mountain road.

Meanwhile, Mike, Louise and Jim were having to cope with the importunate traders who were urgently tapping on the windows, imploring us to buy their irresistible goodies.

Manoeuvring our way out of the garage without damaging people or goods wasn't easy but finally, we were heading up towards the first bend on the metalled road to Lushoto. Fazili negotiated a sharp right and Mombo disappeared behind the flank of the hill. Then, a river valley opened before us.

What a shock! Gone were the lush greens of remembered trees and bushes that had covered the slopes. Instead, every contour looked brown and shaven, young crops were growing in the steepest fields and thatched, mud houses sprang up everywhere. The whole valley had changed.

I looked for the giant boulders which had been home to noisy hyrax on a higher section of the route, once made cool and damp by overhanging trees and a stream, but none of the features remained. Potholes and mud had been replaced by tarmac, overhanging rocks had been blasted away and trees had been cut down.

Half way up the road, the heights above Soni Falls make a good view point from which you can take stock of the whole of the valley below, then you are in the mountains and travelling beside high meadows and steep slopes. By this stage, I felt as if I were seeing everything for the first time. Nothing looked even vaguely familiar. It was gum trees lining the road that jolted my memory into action.

We passed Deutchy Village with its tightly packed red mud houses, then suddenly, away on our left there was the school, a long, low, white building exactly as I had remembered it. We had come upon it so quickly and unexpectedly that we were almost past before I could call out, "There it is!"

We didn't stop but drove slowly enough to read the sign 'Chuo Cha Uongosi Wa Mahakama' or Institute of Judicial Administration—Lushoto. So, the Scotts' school, old Mrs Fraser's building, had survived as an educational establishment, despite all the vicissitudes of such an impoverished country.

Lushoto, of course, had grown to be a much bigger place, with more dukas or little shops, an enlarged tannery which I had completely forgotten, and a number of solid-looking houses built into the slopes surrounding the township.

The original, expats' homes remained amongst the jumble of new constructions, as did the boma at the top of the hill, whilst the Catholic Church, always a dominant feature of the townscape, looked particularly well-kept, its white walls and red roof set off by the heavenly blue of the jacarandas.

As we began the final leg of the journey up to Grant's Lodge, we looked down onto a colourful scene to be visited later. Fazili had to concentrate on avoiding the worst of the potholes as this section wasn't tarmacked. The higher we climbed, the denser and taller the bushes and trees became and, at over 6,000 feet, it was much cooler. We arrived at Grant's Lodge, Magamba, in time for a late, much needed lunch.

Maria, the owner of Grant's Lodge, had known old Mr Grant and he was indeed the man who had made my furniture. Maria and her husband had been about to finalise the purchase of his house when they had been rudely ousted by another local family. The details clearly evoked painful memories. However, undaunted by their experiences, Maria and her husband had bought a similar house at Magamba and simply kept the original name, Grant's Lodge.

From the outside, the house would not have looked out of place in 1960s Surrey. Made of local red bricks and with a steep pitched roof and bold wooden framed windows, it looked as solid as a Surbiton business man's family home. Maria's lovingly tended gardens, where roses and other European flowers held their own amongst rampant tropical species, added to the English aura.

It was only when you noticed the scuffed grass and cracked, hard baked soil of the paths that you were brought back to reality. Then you realised that the tall trees reaching up into the clear, sunny sky were definitely not English.

Inside, everything that could be made of wood was made of wood. Much of it was dark hardwood, giving the stairs, hallway and rooms a sombre atmosphere, but this was offset by an eclectic collection of artefacts and pictures, souvenirs of overseas visits.

Our bedroom had a Himalayan theme and was decorated with prayer flags and framed photographs of mountain scenes taken by Maria's husband, whilst the terracotta-coloured walls of the dining room made a perfect backdrop for ethnic scarves, simple wooden utensils and colourful still-life paintings of wine bottles and plates of food.

Maria's love of plants extended indoors. Potted creepers roamed freely round the corners of the ceiling and, given half a chance, would have escaped through any window left open long enough to join their relatives doing their best to disguise the overhead electricity cables.

Our photographs of Maria show a small, vivacious woman, dressed for work in the house or garden in a bright purple blouse and a yellow kanga worn as a wraparound skirt or in more formal trousers and a traditional, bandana-like head scarf for outings. Her exuberance and warmth made us feel at home as soon as we met her.

She showed us our bedrooms, pointed out the fridge from which we could help ourselves to whatever wine we wanted, then sat us down to a late lunch. She disappeared for the rest of the afternoon leaving us free to explore or relax. The house was ours! After a week of early mornings and organised safaris, it was exactly what we needed.

Whilst the others had a snooze upstairs, I spent the afternoon in the back garden, reading, thinking about the trip and nodding off to sleep when the effort of trying to keep my brain active became just too much. Grant's Lodge is set on a little hill separated from the village by a narrow valley, so sounds of people about their Saturday activities drifted across to where I was sitting on the lawn.

African pop music from transistors mixed with drumming, singing and shouting. Abandoning my book for the umpteenth time, I decided to do some bird spotting, and began to scan the trees with Mike's binoculars. Being nosy, I couldn't resist training them on a group of people busy doing something on a green slope at the edge of the village.

They were working on a hidden object but it wasn't until a passer-by, curious like me to know what was going on, caused the workers to move aside that I could see that the centre of attention was a dead cow. The body was being skinned and butchered on a bed of banana leaves. How strange it was to see the gory process taking place outdoors in public and how grisly to see a man hurry off with a whole leg over his shoulder!

At 10 a.m. next morning, Fazili arrived to take the four of us and Maria back down to Lushoto. There was a market in the centre but our first call was to Lushoto Prep School, now the Institute for Judicial Administration, somewhere that I had dreamed of visiting for such a long time. Would it have changed?

Of course it would, although when we had driven past, it certainly looked the same, with nothing added or taken away. It came as a rude surprise to be stopped by a barrier and a sentry as soon as we turned off the road to enter the grounds. The askari needed to obtain permission from a higher authority before he could let us through but as it was Sunday, there was no one about.

So we were obliged to wait in the grilling heat until eventually, we were allowed to leave the Toyota at the entrance and walk up the drive leading to what used to be the lower staff house. I strode ahead, unable to believe my eyes. Instead of lush vegetation, wattle plantations and towering trees, there were razored banks of brittle, parched grass.

It was difficult to identify the building that had been 'my bungalow'. Gone were the gardens and brick boiler house with its ten gallon can for heating water. Then, I espied the familiar side door and red steps where I had sat so many hot afternoons in the shade of the overhanging roof.

The overhang had been extended to make a shelter for patients waiting outside, now that the flat had become a dispensary. I was amused to see that a door labelled 'choo' had been knocked through the outside wall into the bathroom making it into a public toilet. It was all so different from the image that was, and still is, so clear in my mind's eye.

A newly cut driveway led us up to the top house. Again, all was so bare. The little copse-like area, through which the path had made a short cut between bends in the road, had been removed. Sandaled feet dashing uphill at the end of school would no longer send snakes slithering off into the ground cover of thick vegetation. At the top of the hill, we stopped in front of the bungalow, its solid walls freshly painted white and its window frames bright blue. The red polished steps leading up to the veranda made me long to go inside but I had to be satisfied with a souvenir photograph, after I had finished reminiscing about who had lived where and what wild parties we'd had in the early years. Caught up in the past, and eager to point out all the changes that had taken place, I had forgotten that I no longer belonged to the establishment, that I was a stranger and, indeed, we were all trespassers. Our laughter and chatter must have disturbed the present occupant and Maria was immediately summoned inside. It was an uncomfortable few moments. We were very thankful that Maria had come with us. Apparently, the man had been enjoying a quiet glass of beer when we noisily burst upon the scene, so I suppose it's no wonder he was so angry. Maria had managed to smooth his ruffled feathers but she advised us to leave. "He wants you to know that it's an offence to photograph government property," she said. It was ironic to note, before we all trooped off back down the hill, that the wonderful view across to the distant mountains was now totally obscured by an ugly plantation of wattle trees growing on what was once the front lawn. The palm trees that the fruit bats had flown over at sunset and the magnificent poinsettia bush that migrating white butterflies had so loved had obviously been grubbed up years before.

The principal of the institute joined us as we neared the college. A small, neat man who spoke English well, he welcomed us, and when Maria had explained why we were there exclaimed, "But that was such a long time ago!" Afterwards, I thought he probably wasn't even born when I left in 1967!

"Would you like to have a look inside?" he asked as we tentatively followed him down the steep steps to the main building. He unlocked the side door, the familiar entrance that I had used every day for four years, and we stepped inside.

How wide the corridor looked! "It's bigger than I thought it was going to be," Mike remarked, and the others seemed impressed too. Surprisingly, the interior of the building had shrunk in my treasured memories instead of enlarging, as is usually the case.

The principal unlocked the nearest classroom, a favourite of mine from the years when Penny and Tim had dreamed doggy dreams stretched out in their bunk beds, the bottom shelves of an old bookcase, while children had busied themselves, brimming with an energy that makes 9-year-olds so wonderful to teach. "I expect the room is smaller than when you were here. It's been divided and this side's a conference room," the principal pointed out. There were now just three rows of dark wooden desks facing the long, wall-mounted blackboard. Could it have been the same one that I had spent hours covering with diagrams for nature study lessons? Chalk is cheaper than text books! However, despite the changes, including the addition of brown curtains at the windows looking up to what was my first house, the smell of hot, dusty soil pervading the gloomy room remained the same.

Metal grills at the doors of the remaining six classrooms prevented us from looking round the rest of the school. It was closed for the weekend. So we descended the stairs into the courtyard and back into the heat. Mike, Jim and Louise were keen to hurry away into the shade but I stood looking up to the closed windows wondering, "Where are the children of Lushoto Prep School now?" Scattered about the world, I surmised, some nearly 50-year-old, with children, maybe even grand-children of their own. For me, though, they will always be young. There was something dreamlike about finding myself surrounded by buildings, so solid and unchanged, that had been part of my interior scenery down through the years.

We posed for photographs on the front steps beneath the institute's 'new' name, complete with telephone and fax numbers and address. PO Box 20 does not have quite the same exclusive overtones as Private Bag, Lushoto does. The principal chatted to Maria whom he had not met before, then shook our hands and cordially invited us back should we ever find ourselves in the area again. I wonder what he thought of us, a group of middle-aged Europeans who had disturbed his Sunday morning by traipsing around his grounds and showing such enthusiasm for an empty school. As we made our way back to Fazili and the car past the silent dormitories, I noticed that there were no longer jacarandas along the drive, no moonflowers growing along the river beside the games field, in fact no games field. However, it was wonderful to see the old building looking so well cared for, its walls freshly painted with the rough, red foundation stones picked out in white, setting off the sea green paintwork of pillars, doors and window frames.

The market was a few minutes' drive away. It looked prosperous and well-attended, a far cry from the markets of the sixties. We threaded our way on foot through the shacks on the outskirts then struggled to make headway through the hot, noisy crowds. There was so much food on sale, bright piles of vegetables, fruit, and dried fish displayed in baskets or on matting on the ground, and meat in open fronted butchers' shops. One woman trader offered me a warm passion fruit which she had broken open so that I could lick out the jelly and seeds, a unique taste. Mike was enjoying himself with the camera. A group of socialising women had agreed to pose for a photograph—for a small fee of course—and several of the younger ones were laughing at his banter as they adjusted their headgear, arranged their skirts and exchanged private jokes. The resultant snap is a riot of pinks, puce, yellows, polka dots of black on white, blue and touches of lime green. Louise and I inspected the kangas, thinking that the long lengths of vividly patterned material might make summer skirts or cushion covers, although we had to acknowledge that whilst vivid colours look stunning under a bright tropical sun, at home, they don't really fit in. Still, we were pleased with our purchases.

On the far side of the market, there were piles of second-hand shoes for sale, not just the ubiquitous rubber flip-flops, but a surprising array of women's footwear, much from years ago, the sort of shoes that turn up as donations in UK charity shops. The best of these donations are sold immediately, and the rest are bagged up and sent on for further sorting, so some end up being shipped abroad to be sold to market dealers in poor countries, hence, the amazing selection of vintage shoes being picked over in Lushoto. I recalled that back in the 1960s, very few local people could afford flip-flops, let alone shoes.

Escaping from the blazing midday heat of the town centre, we drove up the deeply rutted road to Irente View Point. What a thrill it was to look out over the Masai Steppe from a great rock buttress at the edge of the Usambaras! We ate our packed lunches at a rustic picnic table on a platform which an enterprising villager had built right on the edge of the sheer drop.

The area seemed to be part of his garden. We bought cold drinks from his bar and were entertained by his young children, little tots of three and four, who played peep-bo with us from behind chairs and tables. The same villager, with an eye to business, had installed a generator in an outbuilding and ran a television which was obviously a great local attraction. As we left, a swaying truck load of people arrived to watch the Sunday programmes and, presumably, to quaff plenty of cold beers.

Next day, we decided that we had had enough car rides and needed instead a long walk, so we gave Fazili the day off. Although he had several friends to call on in Lushoto, he seemed reluctant to leave us to explore the countryside by ourselves. He had laughingly christened Mike 'mzee', old man, because of his grey hair, and joked about the fact that we all had grandchildren.

We reassured him that we would be quite safe—we appreciated that we were, after all, in his charge for the duration of the trip—and, when Maria suggested that the waterfall several miles away might make an interesting destination, he decided we would be all right.

Louise had opted for a less strenuous morning. "I want to pamper myself," she had declared. "I want to wash my hair, do my nails and just, you know, relax!" So Jim, Mike and I set out without her. To reach the trail, we had to make our way through Maria's kitchen garden, down a bank and out of a gate onto the Kifungilo Road, a wide track of red earth worn smooth by the passage of feet.

Soon, we found ourselves descending a hill leading towards the river and past the clothes washing area where several women were busy with their Monday morning wash. At the new concrete bridge, we paused, leaning on the wall to admire the enormous clumps of arum lilies growing along the grassy valley.

Turning off the road, we next made our way through a forested area, the path sometimes climbing above the river and sometimes running beside it. Our progress was slow because we constantly made detours to track down a bird we had spotted or to explore the shallows where spits of land and rocky outcrops gave access to deeper water.

The little waterfall that we had come to see splashed its way down between two shoulders of rock to land in a picturesque, green pool. Unfortunately, the tranquillity of the spot was spoilt by a ragged bunch of young men who were noisily washing themselves and their clothes in the water. We'd disturbed their ablutions. At first, they looked at us menacingly then predictably asked us for money. We got the message and hurried back to a quieter stretch of the river to continue our bird spotting.

Bright green and blue butterflies flitted in the dappled shade now that the sun had cheered up the cool morning, and I caught a jaunty, green grasshopper. Whilst the big insect clung to the back of my hand, I had a good look at its bulbous red eyes, twitching black antennae and the delicate network of veins in its wings.

Even more remarkable was the discovery of a small, purple flower growing on a damp, shady bank beside the path. (Could it be the elusive African violet?) The succulent, slightly hairy leaves and the petal formation certainly resembled those of the potted African violets I'd kept. I couldn't be sure that it was a wild version but I like to think that it was.

On our last evening at Grant's Lodge, Maria took us for a walk round the nearby villages, explaining as we went how each one organises itself. Apparently, every ten houses chooses a 'senior', a man who knows everyone, to represent them.

All the seniors report on the welfare of their individual groups to the village chief who, in turn, along with other village chiefs, meets the town boss. All the town bosses are answerable to the District Commissioner, a title which is reminiscent of colonial times. Births, deaths and land ownership are registered in each township, in this case Lushoto.

Maria pointed out the foundations of a two-roomed house. Although it looked abandoned, it signified that the land had been claimed and could not be taken back, even if the property was not completed for several years or until the owner could amass enough money to buy the rest of the building materials.

Children played noisily in the dust outside the houses, their toys made from bits of wood, a tiny football of rubber bands and paper. They were grimy but looked happy and full of energy. Many rushed up to Maria, to hold her hand and talk to her as we made our way between the houses.

She greeted villagers, older men and several women who stopped work to talk, and then, we were out on the hillside where people were tending plots, growing cabbages and tomatoes, watering and weeding before it was dark.

Further up the mountain, we could make out fruit trees. The land looked productive. It was easy to see why so many people had moved into the Usambaras where life was less harsh than on the uncompromising plains. Up here at the edge of the forests, the land did not appear to be under pressure yet but an expanding population would surely need to make inroads into the precious tree-covered heights. Then, they would take on that bare, razored look of the hills below Lushoto.

Education had come to the villages but schools were, at best, merely rudimentary, mud shacks. One, that we saw, actually had glass in the windows but no door, so all equipment—which would not have amounted to much—had to be removed at the end of the day.

In contrast, the school just outside the gates at Grant's was practically derelict with crossed sticks at the windows and old-fashioned desks crammed between the daubed walls. "They're due a new building," Maria quipped as we looked on, aghast that such a building was even standing.

I wanted to know how HIV/AIDS had affected the mountain communities. Maria spoke of the effectiveness of healers' medicine coupled with modern drugs, and suggested that she was more optimistic about the future because of a greater openness about discussing sex and the transmission of the disease.

She told us about a programme started in the Tanga region, which involved taking patients to centres by community funded transport, thereby giving some of the poorest access to treatment and advice. However, everything worked on a tiny budget and there was only one qualified doctor in charge, "And he's quite an old man," Maria concluded.

Tired but reluctant to turn in, back at the Lodge that evening, we continued our discussion huddled round a big log fire in the sitting room, finishing off a bottle of good red wine after another tasty dinner produced by the cook and his kitchen boy. Fresh vegetables and fruit came from the garden.

We were Maria's sole guests and in just three days, her house with its books, music cassettes and comfortable furniture had begun to feel like home. It was magic to get up when we were ready, open the windows and look out onto a pretty back lawn surrounded by trees and flowers. For me, it was a mixture of the Surrey of my childhood and the 'old' Lushoto.

Next morning, Fazili arrived at 6 a.m. to take us back down onto the plains. We were sad to be saying goodbye to Maria, a woman who combined youthful exuberance with mature wisdom. Her warmth and vivacity as well as her thought-provoking observations on life in her native Tanzania had made our stay at Grant's Lodge an experience to be treasured.

Perhaps, it was her friendly hug and exhortations to return soon which made the parting that much more poignant. I could quite happily have stayed on but we were due in Dar es Salaam that afternoon. I must confess that I shed a few tears as I looked back at the dusty road as we wound our way between the gum trees down to the township, past the school and thence to Mombo, out of the Usambaras and back to the plains.

Chapter 20
The End of the Trip

An excellent tarmac road took us all the way to Dar es Salaam, sometimes running alongside the railway, sometimes beside newly planted sisal estates, and often past busy roadside villages. Fazili was ever on the lookout for local cyclists and pedestrians who would meander out onto the highway without warning, although the biggest danger was from manic bus drivers intent on getting to the capital as fast as possible. There was an everlasting hooting as vehicles warned straying people and animals—and other vehicles—that they were driving by.

Near the River Ruvu, piles of pipes destined for a new pumping station were stacked along the road. Labourers were digging a trench through the bush to take water from the station out to villages and small groups of houses far away from the main road and the river. "That'll make a big difference," Fazili remarked after he had finished pointing out to us the course of the future pipeline, marked with white spray paint.

I tried to see the spot along the road where the school bus had been bogged down in mud and we had been forced to spend the night in December 1966 but there were several cuttings where it might have happened. The only stop we had was when police flagged us down at a section where white lining was going on. Boys selling bags of peanuts and soft drinks immediately dashed down the banks and offered their wares to their captive customers.

At Kearsley's in Dar, we met Rita, a small, chic Indian woman. It was good to be able to put a face to a name that had appeared on all our e-mails out of Tanzania. She briefly shook our hands, made sure that everything was going to plan and that we had no problems, and then resumed her business of running the crowded, hot office.

There were no neat racks of travel brochures or comfy chairs at Kearsley's. Instead, shelves were filled with box files, thick directories and timetables and clerks were busy on computers, making telephone calls or discussing arrangements with clients. After such frenetic activity, it was good to retire to the air-conditioned bar of the nearby Hard Rock Cafe for a cold drink before a swift tour of the seafront. Then, it was time to check in at the Old Airport for our flight to Zanzibar.

A bottle of Louise's Chanel in Jim's top pocket—where he was keeping it upright so that it didn't leak—set off the alarm when we were being body checked. Everyone was highly amused when he produced the offending bottle from his safari jacket.

Out on the tarmac, Louise was definitely not amused when she saw our aeroplane, a little six-seater. She hates flying. However, we were soon being sized up and directed where to sit; Louise and I in the back, Jim in the front next to the pilot and Mike in the middle, beside a newly married young woman. (Her poor husband had to await the return flight.) For me, it was a novel experience, flying at two to three thousand feet across the narrow stretch of sea between Dar and Zanzibar.

The pilot inspired the utmost confidence with his take-off and landing, but Louise confessed afterwards that she was shattered and had hated every moment. Jim too had found the flight nerve wracking. He had been worried in case he inadvertently touched any of the switches and admitted, "All I thought about was what I'd do if anything happened to the pilot. I kept trying to remember what I'd learnt in a flying lesson I had some years ago. It would have been my responsibility to save everyone, you know!"

We stayed at the Tembo Hotel on the sea front in Stone Town. Our room at the end of an upstairs corridor was enormous with a balcony on two sides giving an uninterrupted view of the sea. The dark woodwork of doors and furniture was in Arab style and so heavy, that we couldn't move even the smaller chairs, let alone the great upholstered pieces.

There were carved chests, oceans of floor-to-ceiling curtains, a massive bed with intricately carved foot and head boards, low tables and, surprisingly, a grandfather clock. Poor Louise and Jim had drawn the short straw because their room was nowhere near as palatial.

In fact, it was too small for a double bed and even the two, high, bunk beds left only enough room for a small cupboard and a fridge. For some strange reason, this played "Auld Lang Syne" when you opened its door but there was nothing inside, of course, because no alcohol was allowed in the hotel, it being a Muslim establishment.

Cats were eating fish off-cuts from the fishing boats pulled up on the beach when Mike and I took a stroll in the cool, early next morning. The day soon heated up later though, later when the four of us made our way round Stone Town, inevitably getting lost in the muddle of alley ways. At one point we sat down on a wall beside a school where children were being taught "I am running." The loud repetition of the verb made us feel even hotter. Louise and I had taken the trouble to dress discretely in trousers, long-sleeved tops and sunhats. Nevertheless, we were acutely aware of the looks we attracted in some quarters where women went about completely veiled in black. Some turned away when they saw us coming down the street.

At length, we were lured into a souvenir shop firstly to buy the ubiquitous clove rings. How could we leave Zanzibar without something to remind us of the island's most famous spice? Although space was limited in our small travel bags—you can't carry big cases in the back of a 4x4 or, as we discovered, in a small plane—we splashed out on a few more 'gifts'. Jim found an outrageously bright, patterned shirt, the sort you might wear on a tropical beach, and to complete his outfit, an elaborately carved walking stick. Modelling both his purchases he was transformed from a soberly suited European into—well someone quite different! Louise and I settled for some beautiful green beads made of malachite whilst Mike saved his money.

Our guide books directed us to look out for St Joseph's Cathedral, the massive Arab fort, which is so big that you couldn't miss it, and the excitingly named House of Wonders amongst the mouldering jumble of buildings that make up old Stone Town. We found refuge from the fierce sun in a nineteenth century bath house. The monument was locked when we finally located it but the guardian spotted us from his nearby shop and tried to interest us in his antiques, including the sort of coins that were currency when I was last in East Africa, before he agreed to unlock the door for us. The baths ceased to be used in the 1920s, so there was no water in the huge cisterns, but the high, vaulted ceilings and the whitewashed interior made the air deliciously cool. It must have been wonderful to come to such a place out of the glare and heat of the sun to bathe and to lie on a raised dais in one of the open alcoves set in the thick walls to be massaged. We spun out our time there, drifting from room to room through arched doorways, and lingering in gloomy corners until we had cooled down and felt ready to emerge from our haven to face the walk back to our hotel. Here, a taxi picked us up and we were driven across to the east coast of the island for two days of 'luxurious living' at Breezes, one of the most expensive hotels on our trip.

The taxi driver was obliged to stop at a number of what looked like temporary road blocks, and each time, he had to hand over something to the official. He seemed reluctant to explain why, but we sensed an element of fear on his part when he had problems with his permit at the first stop. Such excessive security, or whatever it was, soon petered out when the tarmac ended and we embarked on an ocean of potholes. Here, the driver needed all his skills to avoid wrecking his vehicle. He steered a course between troughs, all the while keeping an eye open for approaching cars doing exactly the same. After an exhausting hour, long enough to dispel all thoughts of an immediate return journey along the same route should we fancy dinner at another hotel, we arrived.

Breezes was, as promised, an exotic confection of bright tropical flowers, thatch-roofed buildings and a palm-shaded private beach set against the Indian Ocean. Petals and leaves arranged across our bed to spell out 'Welcome' and the attention to detail in our room completed the illusion that we had been elevated to celebrity status. Sadly, neither the distant sound of waves breaking over the reef, nor the gentle sighing of wind-ruffled palms managed to calm Louise's shattered nerves. Next day, she was still stressed out from her flight across to Zanzibar. She was not happy until Jim had contacted Rita at Kearsley's and arranged for them to return to Dar by hovercraft even though it meant leaving a day earlier than us. With that sorted, we could all relax with our books beside the pool, taking an occasional dip as and when required. The hotel had a selection of upholstered sun loungers to choose from, including decadent looking beds raised above the ground on tall legs, fully cushioned and swathed in diaphanous curtains, but they were usually occupied by starry-eyed young couples. In fact, when we began to look around, we realised that the place was full of honeymooners!

Mike and I started the day with a walk along the beach. The tide was out leaving rock pools where sea urchins, long limbed brittle stars and grossly fat sea cucumbers could be discovered. Distant smoke drifting across the sand attracted our attention, and as we drew closer, we could see men piling dried palm branches round their precious craft.

Using a mixture of sign language and my less than elementary Swahili, we learnt that they were burning the green growths off the hulls of their fishing boats. Each craft was handmade, put together with wooden pegs and sisal rope, so the fire, although extremely effective, had to be carefully monitored and controlled. We gathered that it was an annual practice, much the same as 'bottom scraping' on modern yachts.

Whilst Louise and Jim were installing themselves in the Cliff Top Hotel in Dar it was my turn to be nervous. There was a beginner's diving class run by an enthusiastic team of young Israelis at Breezes. In a moment of sheer abandon, I had said "I'd like to try that," as we passed the ticket office, and carried away on a cloud of recklessness, I was soon signing the necessary documents to enable me to don the gear and swim in the depths.

Of course, Mike couldn't be left out, so he also signed up. The next day seemed a long way off until we heard that the dive would go ahead at 9.30 the next morning but even then, my nagging fears were assuaged after a successful practice in the swimming pool.

There were several of us in the boat heading for a deep channel in the lagoon. It was a bright morning and the sea was sparkling. I felt petrified. Mike went first and did well, staying down for the allotted time. He is a strong swimmer and confident in the water.

"That was good," he enthused when he was back on board, drying off and watching me preparing to go overboard. He had seen a sea snake. Then it was my turn to swim away from the boat and, holding the instructor's hand, head for the bottom.

Remembering the signals I had been taught in the pool, I could give a positive O for ok with my index finger and thumb as I looked into the incredibly blue eyes of my teacher. He pointed out particular fish and picked a star fish off a rock for me to hold as we made our slow, graceful way along the underwater gulley.

Unfortunately, I started taking water into my mouth and soon my imagination was kicking in with pictures of me drowning, crushed to death by the tons of water that I had suddenly become aware of. It was difficult to breathe evenly, let alone relax as one should, so I panicked and my next signal was a frantic finger pointing up to the surface.

My dive was over as I struggled to stay afloat in my cumbersome equipment. It hadn't been a complete failure, more an expensive experiment, but as I shivered on deck, I resolved to stick to snorkelling in future.

The last phase of our holiday began at 5 a.m. the following morning when Mike and I set out on the tedious journey from Breezes to Stone Town Airport. We arrived before the officials and whiled away a surprisingly chilly half hour talking to another couple who had started even earlier than us with a boat trip from a remote island. The plane, a twin engine 10-seater, took off at eight, when the pilot had folded up his newspaper and adjusted his seat. Jim was on the tarmac at Dar to greet us at 8.30 a.m. and Louise was waiting outside the airport with Fazili. He had been home to Tanga for a few days to see his family and was now to drive us down to the Rufiji River Camp in Selous National Park. It was Saturday and we were to stay in Africa's largest Game Park, an area of 30,500 square kilometres, until Tuesday.

First, we had to get there though! Out through the teeming streets of Dar es Salaam, the roads were lined with stores selling everything; building materials, furniture, kitchen ware, hundreds of plastic buckets, as well as food and clothing. The tarmac ran straight and smooth once we were through the melee of buses and people.

The end of the comfortable part of the journey was heralded by road works, after which the surface rapidly deteriorated. We could see that in places, there had been a thin skim of tarmac but it was potholed and rutted. Finally, all semblance of metalling gave way to corrugations, then sand. Fazili drove with his usual skill but the jolting and heat were wearing, although for me, the ride brought back memories of past safaris, real African journeys which were part and parcel of living on that continent. For Mike, Louise and Jim, it was to be a grin and bear it situation.

We stopped for cokes at a roadside shack and bought bananas from a little boy. Another child offered us hard boiled eggs. He even had a bag of salt to make his wares more tasty. Further along the road, we encountered two weddings; at one, people were dancing and singing, at the other, a group with a transistor radio was providing the music as the guests proceeded down the road. Chickens scooted across, narrowly avoiding death beneath our wheels, to arrive in an indignant fluster of feathers on the other side. Goodness knows why they couldn't have waited a minute longer to cross. We were the only moving vehicle within miles!

The houses with their mud walls and deeply thatched roofs looked tidier than those we had seen up-country. Each had an enclosed area at the rear and a swept area in front. Big, shady trees were an important feature. Children playing in the shade waved and called out as we sped past in a cloud of dust. In several villages women were pounding maize, while their men folk sat in conversation. Several individuals had obviously given up the demands of life and lay asleep on the ground.

Fazili produced baguettes when we stopped out in the bush to eat lunch. The heat beat down on us but it was a relief to stretch our legs, free of the confines of the Toyota. Across the road there were some old paddy fields dotted with little thatched shelters raised on stilts.

"They're for bird scarers when the rice is ripe," Fazili explained. Causeways with bridges had been constructed through what must have been boggy or wet ground in the wet season. Now, all was bone dry and the road was ankle deep in sand in some places. Soon, we were making tracks in it again.

Just before 3 o'clock, we arrived at the gates of the Selous and in one kilometre, we were at the camp. What bliss it was to stand under a cool shower in the superb bathroom built onto the back of a comfortable tent. Then, with an even cooler drink to hand, we sat watching hippos enjoying their leisure hour before sundown on the Rufiji River below the camp site. Soon, it would be time for dinner!

To wake up under canvas at the river camp is to wake up to wraparound sound. How can you resist the urge to jump out of bed, open the tent flaps and step out into the picture that goes with the sound? So, it was that I found myself standing in my nighty looking down at the Rufiji as it meandered past the sand cliffs on which our line of tents was pitched.

Rising up out of the water were splashing noises made by lazing hippos simply readjusting their positions in the pools amongst the sand bars; a lumbering mother, then her tiny offspring and a widely yawning youngster. Hornbills floated across from the dark trees on the far side, some 20 or 30 birds, flying singly as if each had made up its own mind on the spur of the moment to leave the safety of the roost.

The air was thick with bird calls from the river to the forest. Now and then, there was a really dramatic splash as if something catastrophic had happened. It was just a hippo, one of dozens posing as rounded rocks in the flat creeks and bays along the Rufiji that had kicked up its heels and dived into deeper water for its morning swim.

There was a more discreet splash and another crocodile slipped down the low bank to become a malevolent log in the mirror-like water, just waiting for a carefree waterbuck or warthog to have a drink nearby. Raucous laughter from a hippo, a deep, rude guffaw, startled me then all was quiet except for the rasping background percussion of birds, mostly one-noters.

Mike had not felt well during the night, with worrying pains in his chest. After a dose of Alka Selzer and some TLC, he was still troubled but managed to be up for the walking safari at 8 o'clock. Louise was out of sorts too. She had been kept awake by Jim's snoring. Jim claimed he too had been denied sleep by the uncomfortable proximity of a hippo on its nocturnal perambulations, just outside the tent on his side. In fact, he claimed that only the canvas wall had separated him from the animal. He had remembered all the gory details he had read about this vicious water horse, which causes more deaths than any other animal, and was petrified to make a noise in case the beast heard him or smelt him. It wasn't clear whether the noisy snoring had occurred before or after the hippo incident but the net result was that Jim was banished to a distant tent for the following night.

The walking safari proceeded very slowly. Fortunately, the weather was overcast and it was not as unbearably hot as it had been the previous day. However, wearing the required long trousers and walking shoes made us feel very sweaty and irritable. The two cheerful scouts, one reassuringly armed with a rifle, picked their way carefully from tree to tree pointing out birds for us to peer at through our binoculars but, to be honest, it wasn't always easy to say with any certainty exactly what each species looked like. Nevertheless, we wrote down their names and looked them up afterwards. Our lists included such exotic sounding birds as a paradise flycatcher (cinnamon coloured), a red cheeked cordon bleu (on the ground), a drongo (black and long tailed), an emerald spotted wood dove, Batleur eagle, crested barbet, common scimitar bill, a broad billed roller and a grey headed bush shrike. Yellow seemed a popular colour, with yellow winged bats, yellow billed egrets and a yellow throated bee-eater to add to our collection.

Later, gathered round the open-air bar chatting to Jackie who had just served us cold beers, we began to feel at ease. The camp was run on a 'strictly informal' basis. "If no one's at the bar," Jackie said, "just help yourself and write it in the book. You can settle up when you leave." After all, it wasn't exactly a place that you could escape from without paying your bill.

Meals were eaten al fresco in the big dining/relaxation area overlooking a bend in the river. (It was only a short walk from our tents but as soon as darkness fell and animals were on the move, we needed an armed guard to accompany us.) During the day, you could read a book from the library, which was well stocked with natural history texts, have a drink or simply watch the wildlife whilst waiting for lunch. We admired the dugout canoes which formed part of the rustic decor and served as a camp fence. "They were confiscated from poachers," Jackie explained. "They won't be using them anymore!" We looked more closely and saw that each canoe had been holed.

The two afternoon game drives were something of an anti-climax and a disappointment after all the wondrous sights of the Northern game parks. The area round the camp was mostly wooded with only a few clearings, so during our two-hour long safaris, we caught but fleeting glimpses of an odd kudu lurking in the bushes or a sandy coloured duiker disappearing into the shadows. The whole area looked desiccated.

There had been a fire and the herds of antelope, zebra and wildebeest had gone elsewhere for grazing. However, late on the first afternoon, when we were driving beside the inlet of the river, we came upon a pride of six lions, a mother and five younger ones. Three were already drinking by the water's edge when the oldest female joined them. We could also see younger ones playing in nearby bushes, then, they too bounded across to join the elders.

As the scene unfolded a little boat came puttering up the inlet. It was the American couple from the camp. They must have taken a wonderful video of the lions that by now were all lying down gazing straight into the lens of the camera. We were suddenly uncertain of who was the observer and who the observed!

In contrast, the boat safari on the Rufiji was pure magic, a blend of beauty, intellectual stimulation and fear. Once out on the main waterway and away from the sandy shallows, we steered for the bank opposite the camp. This was kingfisher country. We saw the jewel bright malachite and the brown-hooded kingfishers, the pied and grey-headed.

The knowledgeable boatman explained that the pied kingfisher is the only one of the species that seeks out its prey by hovering above the water rather than by sitting at a lookout point on the bank. Further along, we came upon a giant kingfisher struggling to swallow a fish stuck in its beak, and then later, we spotted a more composed member of the same species and had time to admire its mahogany-coloured waistcoat, dark shoulders, black and white speckled shirt front and serious black eyes. Its spiky, gelled 'hair' hinted at a more flamboyant nature.

We gave a wide berth to the many families of hippo which watched us from afar, all rounded ears, flared nostrils and protruding brows. It's amazing to think that they have a life span of 45 to 50 years. For a hippo of the Rufiji, one could imagine it being a life of luxury and excess, especially on such a beautiful morning.

The river was full of other hazards. In the end of a submerged palm trunk, an Egyptian goose had made a nest big enough to accommodate her twelve large eggs. Some would hatch into handsome birds distinguished by their brown eye patches, golden eyes and bacon-pink legs.

The top of a tangle of dead trees nearer the bank was the favoured perch of a gang of white-fronted bee-eaters which continually darted out to pick off any unsuspecting insect on its way downstream. In much the same way, I felt, we might be snapped up by one of the many hippos or crocodiles lurking beneath our boat, should the boatman make a mistake. But I didn't like to dwell on that possibility.

A great variety of trees provided a backdrop for the river's meanderings. The most noticeable were the towering Borassus palms, their tall, single trunks—which at a distance looked as if they were made of concrete—sometimes without their topknots of feathery leaves. There were other palms too, lower and more thickset, as well as hardwoods and a sea of smaller trees.

A hamerkop had made its nest, a massive structure which we could see even without our binoculars, in a mahogany. In another tree, a fish eagle was calling with its young one beside it, whilst a dead tree provided a perch for a harrier hawk devouring a meal of snake.

Our interest next centred on a stretch of bank, as the current pushed us towards the outer edge of a curve. A colony of black-headed weaver birds was making nests on a bush overhanging the river. Some nests were still green, although in the hot sun, the grass would soon dry out, whilst others were mere skeletons of nests. We could see the bright bodies of the yellow birds at work inside.

The boatman slowed the engine so that we could watch a pale green monitor lizard, patterned to its finger tips, making its way down into the water, maybe into its secret hideaway.

Zigzagging our way back, we zoomed along, swinging from side to side following the high banks and the deep water. Thus, on a course cut by strong currents, we avoided dangerous sand banks and shallows. With the wind in our faces and blowing back our hair, we sat in silence, relying on the skill of our boatman to steer our flat-bottomed, aluminium craft safely back to camp through the vagaries of the mighty Rufiji.

A surprise decision had been reached the previous evening. We would not be travelling back to Dar es Salaam by car. Mike, Louise and Jim just couldn't face the idea of another six hours of African roads with their wearisome corrugations, dust and heat, especially at what was to be the beginning of a very long day, our last in Tanzania. The torture would have had to start well before dawn. It had been Mike's idea to approach the pilot of the light aircraft that had flown in some new guests, and over drinks at the bar, arrangements had been made to put on a flight to take us back to the capital in time for us to catch our plane to Nairobi. I was astounded at Louise's change of heart and could only conclude that her objections to the road trip must have been deep seated!

Whilst we were at breakfast, Jackie came to say goodbye before going on safari with a lone Japanese visitor. The other six guests had left earlier, on the boat trip, so we had the place to ourselves with plenty of time to watch the tiny monkeys playing round our tents. Each mother had a minute baby peeping out from where it was slung under her belly. We said our farewells to Fazili, with jokes and warm handshakes and a token of our thanks in cash. He had become an important part of our Tanzanian experience and now, he would be returning to Dar with a new passenger, Brian, the commercial and advertising manager of the River Camp.

Our plane was due to leave at noon so, after we had packed, Louise downed a very large whisky to stave off any last-minute panic attacks. At 11.30, our bags were collected, we had a last look around, and were off to the landing strip. It was exciting hearing the little plane's approach then seeing it sweep round, dip down and race up the runway, to turn and taxi towards us. Whilst the bags were being loaded into the tiny luggage compartment, a Land Rover approached at speed and came to a stop close by. Out jumped a man holding Mike's specs. He'd left them in the tent. It was a marvel that the staple used to secure the earpiece to the frames was still holding.

Very quickly, we were all seated and the side door was locked. Somehow, Louise had got herself isolated in the back and Mike was sitting next to the pilot, leaving me to sit beside Jim in the middle; something to do with the distribution of weight we were told. It was too late to change places. However, Louise was fine. She spent the 45 minutes of the flight counting backwards from 500 with her eyes closed.

The rest of the journey went to plan, thanks to our man from Kearsley's, and even Jim's fantastic walking stick passed through security without a hitch. On the way up to Nairobi, despite heavy cloud, we were treated to a farewell glimpse of Kilimanjaro's two peaks, craggy Mwezi and Kibo a big, black hole.

My yearning to return to Lushoto and revisit old haunts in Tanzania had been satisfied, but the holiday made us all determined to explore further afield in Africa and to visit other countries in that amazing continent.